SECURITY AND PRIVACY IN USER MODELING

HUMAN-COMPUTER INTERACTION SERIES

VOLUME 2

Security and Privacy
in User Modeling

by

Jörg Schreck
*Formerly of GMD-Forschungszentrum Informationstechnik,
Germany*

KLUWER ACADEMIC PUBLISHERS
DORDRECHT / BOSTON / LONDON

A C.I.P. Catalogue record for this book is available from the Library of Congress

ISBN 1-4020-1130-X

Published by Kluwer Academic Publishers,
P.O. Box 17, 3300 AA Dordrecht, The Netherlands.

Sold and distributed in North, Central and South America
by Kluwer Academic Publishers,
101 Philip Drive, Norwell, MA 02061, U.S.A.

In all other countries, sold and distributed
by Kluwer Academic Publishers,
P.O. Box 322, 3300 AH Dordrecht, The Netherlands.

Printed on acid-free paper

Printed in the Netherlands.

Contents

Acknowledgments

I would like to thank all persons who have contributed to this book or have given support to the underlying research. Beside many others who have shown me to see things from a different perspective, provided me with basic thoughts from different subjects, and confirmed that it is not always the straight path that leads to the destination, these persons include: Josef Fink, Jörg Höhle, Rüdiger Hüttenhain, Judy Kay, Achim Nick, Andreas Nill, Gaby Nordbrock, Reinhard Oppermann, Ana Paiva, Wolfgang Pohl, Holger Schauer, and Marcus Specht.

I would also like to mention the GMD – Forschungszentrum Informationstechnik (now part of the Fraunhofer-Gesellschaft) which has supplied an adequate infrastructure for this kind of research. Especially worth mentioning are Erich Vorwerk, Alfred Kobsa, and Günther Pernul who accompanied the development with advice and patience and rendered it possible to summarize the findings in a PhD thesis.

Foreword

User-adaptive (or "personalized") systems take individual characteristics of their current users into account and adapt their behavior ac-
cordingly. Several empirical studies demonstrate their benefits in areas
like education and training, online help for complex software, dynamic
information delivery, provision of computer access to people with disabilities, and to some extent information retrieval. Recently, personalized systems have also started to appear on the World Wide Web where
they are primarily used for customer relationship management. The aim
hereby is to provide value to customers by serving them as individuals
and by offering them a unique personal relationship with the business.
Studies show that web visitors indeed spend considerably more time at
personalized than at regular portals and view considerably more web
pages. Personalized sites in general also draw more visitors and turn
more visitors into buyers.

Personalization therefore would look like a win-win technology for
both consumers and online businesses. However, it has a major down-
side: in order to be able to exhibit personalized behavior, user-adaptive
systems have to collect considerable amounts of personal data and "lay
them in stock" for possible future usage. Moreover, the collection of
information about the user is often performed in a relatively inconspic-
uous manner (such as by monitoring users' web navigation behavior), in
order not to distract users from their tasks.

Numerous recent surveys have consistently shown that computer users
are very concerned about their privacy on the Internet. A large majority of them are hesitant to divulge personal information on the web and
are concerned about being tracked online. In order to alleviate these
concerns, two different approaches are possible with respect to personalized systems. In one approach, users would receive guarantees that their
personal data will be used for certain purposes only. Such guarantees

can e.g. be given in individual negotiations, in publicly displayed privacy commitments (so-called "privacy policies"), or they can be codified in privacy laws.

The other approach is to allow users to remain anonymous with regard to the personalized system and the whole network infrastructure, whilst enabling the system to still recognize the same user in different sessions so that it can cater to her individually. Anonymous interaction seems to be desired by users (however, only a single user poll addressed this question explicitly so far). One can expect that anonymity will encourage users to be more open when interacting with a personalized system, thus facilitating and improving the adaptation to this user. The fact that privacy laws do not apply any more when the interaction is anonymous also relieves the providers of personalized systems from restrictions and duties imposed by such laws. Finally, anonymous interaction is even legally mandated in some countries if it can be realized with reasonable efforts.

Jörg Schreck's pioneering book explores the feasibility of this second approach. It discusses existing security methods that would allow users of personalized systems to be unidentifiable for everyone, allow the interaction between users and a system to be unobservable for everyone except the user-adaptive system, and allow different sessions of the same user to be unlinkable for everyone except the system. Moreover, users' data need to be secure during transport and may be accessed by authorized requesters only. A special difficulty is the fact that personalized systems are storing user data increasingly in central servers whose location must also be hidden to guarantee users' anonymity. On the basis of his theoretical discussions, the author develops a reference model for pseudonymous interaction between users and web-based applications in which full personalization can nevertheless take place.

Schreck's book offers a wealth of information on the topic of security for privacy in user-adaptive systems, as well as an application-independent technical solution that allows users of personalized systems to remain anonymous whilst still benefiting from full personalization. A number of obstacles may complicate its deployment in practice though. Hardly any readily-available distributed anonymization infrastructures that he requires have as yet been put in place. Anonymous interaction is currently difficult to maintain when payments, physical goods and non-electronic services are being exchanged. Anonymity on the Internet may harbor the risk of misuse, and currently even seems to have an air of disreputability. Finally, web retailers also have a considerable interest in identified customer data as a business asset. While pseudonymous data would be equally helpful for an analysis of shopping behavior and for customer segmentation, they cannot be used for "cross-channel" personalization (sending a web customer a targeted brochure by mail, recognizing him in a brick and mortar store and serving her individually). This becomes increasingly important since the number of web-only businesses continues to decline. The factual deployment of personalized anonymous interaction will thus strongly hinge on social factors, such as regulatory provisions that mandate anonymous and pseudonymous access to electronic services, and articulated consumer demand which gives businesses that offer personalized anonymous interaction a competitive advantage that outweighs its commercial downsides.

Alfred Kobsa
University of California, Irvine

Abstract

User adaptive software systems facilitate interaction for the user, for instance, by highlighting important functionality, omitting unnecessary information or executing frequent actions automatically. They do this on the basis of information about the user which is collected, processed, and extended through inferences by the user model and which is supplied to user adaptive software systems as a basis for adaptation.

The information processed in a user model is often assigned unequivocally to a specific user and is therefore personal data. Personal data is subject to special regulations and its processing must fulfill requirements such as controllability, confidentiality, and integrity. The restriction of data collection to the minimum required from the perspective of data protection is in contrast to the tendency of adaptive systems to derive optimum adaption from a maximum of available assumptions about the user. In general, the necessary compromise can only be reached by involving the user who is able to weigh the extent to which the information processed in a user model is worth being protected against the benefit of this information to the adaptive system. For this reason, the user is included in the definition of the security requirements in this book.

The complex problem *security in user modeling* can be broken down into the three components: confidentiality, integrity, and availability of processed information. As availability involves no specific requirements with regard to user modeling it is not discussed in depth.

The integrity of user modeling information is discussed with regard to internal integrity of data within the user modeling system and the specific representation techniques as well as with regard to external integrity of the user modeling system from the perspective of the user and the adaptive system.

Confidentiality of processed information is guaranteed in several respects. A role-based access control model enables the user to control the shared maintenance of a user model through different adaptive application systems by filtering the permitted information flow. The description of access rights based on roles makes it possible for the user to provide adaptive application systems with information in accordance with its intended role (e.g. information filtering). This method also enables users to assume different roles when presenting themselves to application systems.

Confidentiality of user model information is a requirement that comes into play when different adaptive application systems jointly access parts of the user model. Furthermore, the secrecy of processed information can also be required. This is achieved by processing user model information anonymously or pseudonymously. User model information is thus no longer personal data, though it remains usable for adaptive application systems. In addition to a discussion of different types of anonymity and pseudonymity, an implementation is described which enables the user to determine how reliable the disclosure avoidance process must be.

For maintaining secrecy and authenticity of the user model contents exchanged during their transportation through an electronic network, the transportation mechanism has been extended to include methods for encryption and for the verification of the authenticity of the messages exchanged.

The methods presented here for increasing security in user modeling systems are used as a basis for the formulation and automatic enforcement of concrete policies on the use of user information through adaptive application systems. They are intended to enable users to make individual adaptations to given policies or to define their own policies. This also enables users to weigh their individual privacy requirements against the added value of the adaptive system.

List of Figures

List of Tables

List of Abbreviations

ACE	Adaptive Courseware Environment
API	application programmer interface
DAC	discretionary access control
AVANTI	Adaptive and Adaptable Interactions for Multimedia Telecommunications Applications
BGP-MS	Belief, Goal, and Plan Maintenance System
CONT-DIV	divided content
CONT-INCL	included content
CONT-SEP	separated content
CONT-SHAR	shared content
GUMAC	General User Model Acquisiton Component
GUMS	General User Modeling Shell
JatLite	Java Agent Template Lite
KAPI	KQML Application Programmer Interface
KQML	Knowledge Query and Manipulation Language
KQMLmix	Chaum mix for KQML messages
LPWA	Lucent Personalized Web Assistant
MAC	mandatory access control
OA(N)	Order-N anonymity, complexity of anonymity
OTTER	organized techniques for theorem-proving and effective research
P3P	Platform for Privacy Preferences Project
PROTUM	Prolog based Tool for User Modeling
RBAC	role-based access control
RIPEMD	RACE (Research and Development in Advanced Communication Technologies in Europe) integrity primitives evaluation message digest
RPI	return path information
RSA	Rivest, Shamir, and Adleman (encryption algorithm)
SKAPI	secure KAPI
SKQML	secure KQML
SSL	Secure Sockets Layer
TAGUS	Theory and Applications for General User/Learner-modeling Systems
UMFE	User Modelling Front-End Subsystem
UMT	User Modeling Tool

0

Introduction

Human-computer interaction is characterized by a vast number of frequently occurring actions. This is partly due to an increase in the amount of information being presented. A certain segment of information being presented is usually needed by only a small number of users. A small segment is usually needed by almost all users and parts of the remaining segment are of use to some users but not to all[1]. The average user might face the following problems in using general-purpose software (i.e., software produced for many users):

- unneeded information is presented (information overload)

- desired information is missing (subjective information need)

- needed information is missing (objective information need).

User modeling might solve some of these problems by adapting the software system to the current user based on the following types of data: [Kobsa et al., 2000, Chap. 3]:

- user data: demographic data, user knowledge, skills, capabilities, interests, preferences, goals, and plans

- usage data: observable usage (e.g., selective actions and ratings) and usage regularities (e.g., usage frequency and action sequences)

- environment data (e.g., software and hardware environment or the user's current location).

These factors establish the foundation for the adaptation to a specific user and must therefore be acquired for each specific user individually. The resulting set of factors, the so-called *user model*, consists of user related data which can, in most cases, be linked to an identifiable person.

The fact that *user related data* (i.e., *personal data*) which is processed in a user model should be treated in a more restricted manner than general data has so far only rarely been discussed in the user modeling literature (see [Kobsa, 1990], [Pohl, 1998, p. 234], [Schreck, 2001], [Kobsa, 2001b], and [Kobsa, 2002]) and from the perspective of data protection (see [Herrmann, 1990] and [Peters, 1999]). A focused discussion of security and privacy issues in user modeling was initiated by [Schreck, 1997a] at the *Doctoral Consortium* of the 1997 International Conference on User Modeling.

---

[1] Beside the adaptation of the amount and structure of information which is to be presented (see [Brusilovsky, 1998]) also the functionality of the software system used can be adapted. See [Linton et al., 1999] for discussion of the usage and adaptations of a general text processing software.

This book focuses on the security of user modeling systems and of the data processed within such systems as well as on the privacy of the user being modeled. The security of the user modeling system is a prerequisite for the definition and enforcement of policies regulating the usage of the user model data in order to protect the user's privacy. The scope of this work covers security issues involved when acquiring, processing, and using personal data for the purpose of user modeling.

To date, issues relating to the user's privacy in user adaptive systems have not been treated in depth. Discussions of such systems and their applications mention privacy concerns only on a very general level, if at all. The sensitivity of the processed data is widely recognized but the risks involved in collecting and processing such data are either not discussed or are justified in a general way in comparison to the added value of the user adaptive system. The conflict between the amount of user related data necessary for reasonable and well founded adaptations and the user's privacy has not been discussed to a satisfactory extent in the literature so far. The current trend towards user models with standardized user model entries accessible through an electronic network (see [Fink and Kobsa, 2001]) is increasing the risk for the processed data. A focused discussion of security and privacy issues of user adaptive systems and in particular of user modeling systems is therefore indispensable.

Another aspect which has so far been neglected in discussions of privacy in user modeling is the fact that privacy is contingent on certain fundamental conditions which must be present in user modeling. For the purpose of this book, the fundamental conditions supporting privacy are considered to be a *policy* and *security measures* guaranteeing that this policy will be followed. A policy specifies the procedure for processing user model information, for instance, *who* (i.e., which user adaptive application system) is allowed to access *which* user model entry for *what* purpose. The security measures for the user modeling system assure the user that the established policy will be complied with by all clients of the user model. In general information systems which deal with personal data (e.g., in clinical information systems), the kind and the amount of data which is to be processed is known in advance (for instance, determined by the area of expertise of the clinic). Usually, security measures for these systems are adjusted[2] to the maximum sensitivity of the processed data (without regard to a particular user) and cannot be changed

---

[2]For instance, the use of several pseudonyms per patient which cannot be interlinked can be applied for different areas of treatment [Borking, 1998]. Further limitations for the processing of the data can be achieved through application of the *least privilege* and *separation of duties* principles (see p. 118).

according to a particular user's estimation about the sensitivity of his[3] data. Thus, the processing of the data is limited by predefined usage policies and cannot be extended in order to enrich the functionality of the information system.

For user adaptive systems (and therefore for user modeling), the security measures should be tailorable by the user (to cater, e.g., to different privacy policies of a web site). The user's confidence in the system's security (and therefore its privacy) can promote the acceptance of user adaptive systems. The user's increased confidence in the security of the system may also lead to an increase in the quality of the data processed. In the case of anonymous use of a user adaptive system, it is likely that users will be more frank in revealing personal information, thereby facilitating better adaptations of the system. In this way, the sensitivity of the processed data increases with the user's confidence in the system's security (for instance, anonymity).

Therefore, it seems to be more advantageous to put security features first and let the user determine the sensitivity and the amount of data processed, rather than providing security features in dependence on already available data. For this reason, we include the user in the definition of security features and their performance in order to encourage sufficient confidence in the security features of the user adaptive system. The necessary security features might be different in grade and number for each user dependent on the user's privacy demands.

This book is divided into five parts. *Part I, User Modeling, Security, and Privacy*, gives a brief introduction to the field of user modeling and its utility for user adaptive systems. It describes the general principles of user modeling and highlights selected user modeling mechanisms and the user modeling agents (or user modeling shell systems) applying these mechanisms. An example system illustrates the benefit of adaptations in information provision that are based on information about the user gathered through his previous interaction with the system. The relation between security and privacy in user modeling is also described, and the necessity for privacy is justified theoretically and pragmatically. This part concludes with a substantiation for security in user modeling based on laws, guidelines, ethics, and user demands.

In *Part II, Requirements for Security and Privacy in User Modeling*, we provide an analysis of the security requirements in user modeling. The first chapter of this section, *Chapter 4*, deals with the sensitivity of user model information which is personal data of a uniquely identifiable

---

[3]To avoid the construction *he/she* (*his/her*) when concerning the user, the masculine or plural pronouns will be used.

person. Based on the definition of *information* as *data in context*, the *context* is defined here as the relationship between the data and the user being modeled. By removing this context (i.e., through anonymization), the information about the user is reduced to person-independent data which is subject to fewer privacy constraints. Several kinds of anonymity are discussed, with an emphasis on the special case of pseudonymity which masks the relationship between users and their data, thus allowing for adaptations with reduced privacy risks. We propose also several types of pseudonyms and their applicability in user adaptive systems.

Chapter 5, concentrates on the security of a user model, the user modeling agent, and the data processed therein. Adhering to its most prevalent definition, *security* is divided into the components *secrecy*, *integrity*, and *availability*.

We assume that the amount of user modeling which takes place in a user adaptive system should be flexible in order to adapt to a particular user's privacy requirements. For this reason, user adaptive systems cannot rely that user modeling functionality is always present and must be able to cope with reduced or even missing user modeling functionality. An assessment of *availability* is therefore only carried out regarding the system integrity of the user modeling system.

In contrast to this, we discuss the requirements regarding *secrecy* in user modeling extensively. It is obvious that the sensitivity of the data processed in a user model is based on the relationship between the data and the user. Therefore, two requirements are defined where the first focuses on the secrecy of the relationship between the data and the user (i.e. anonymization) and the second on the secrecy of the data itself (i.e., encryption). Furthermore, confidentiality, as a less stringent form of secrecy, is also discussed. Confidentiality is described as access permission for particular user model clients (e.g., user adaptive application systems) to user model information which is kept secret from the remaining clients. Through confidentiality, responsibility for the maintenance of specified parts of the user model can be transferred to particular user model clients which share the information within these parts. As the third constituent of security, the *integrity* of a user model is discussed from the perspective of user model clients as *external integrity* and from the perspective of developers of user modeling agents as *internal integrity*.

Part III, Solutions and their Applicability for User Modeling Purposes, parallels *Part II* and, where possible, points out solutions for the requirements given in the corresponding chapters of that part. Requirements which cannot be satisfied by user modeling alone (e.g., the *completeness* of the user model information) are discussed and mutually exclusive requirements (e.g., the requirements for confidentiality and integrity in access control models) are contrasted.

Chapter 6, covers solutions for the requirements regarding the different types of anonymity, namely *environmental, content-based,* and *procedural anonymity.* It is shown that *procedural anonymity* can be provided for a wide range of user adaptive systems by the *mix technique* introduced by Chaum. Therefore, we have implemented a mix mechanism which allows for procedural anonymity of messages in the KQML language used for the exchange of information between components of the user adaptive system. In particular, this implementation allows for sender and receiver anonymity and can thus be used to establish an information exchange between the user model and its clients with mutual anonymity. It also allows for the inclusion of the components of the user adaptive system and the user in the anonymization process, thus increasing the user's confidence in the system's anonymity.

In *Chapter 7,* we describe solutions for the requirements regarding security and integrity of user modeling systems and the information processed within such systems. Solutions for secrecy through denial of access and secrecy through selective access (i.e. confidentiality) are proposed. Secrecy through denial of access to the information processed (i.e., exchanged between components) in a user adaptive system is achieved by encryption. An existing software library for information exchange with the KQML language has been adapted to include the *Secure Sockets Layer* making encrypted and authenticated communication in electronic networks possible. This extended software library can be used with minor modifications to the components of the user adaptive system and is therefore applicable to a wide range of systems.

Secrecy through selective access to user model information is defined as the ability to specify which components should be able to operate on particular user model entries by dedicated actions (e.g., *read, delete*), thus assuring confidentiality of the particular entries between these components. Some well-known models from the security literature for access control and information flow control are described and supplemented with examples of user modeling. For the sake of wider applicability, we have chosen an access control model which acts as a filter (i.e., a reference monitor) between the user model and its clients for implementation because of the lower demands it imposes upon the user model and the user modeling agent (in comparison to information flow control models) by which it is hosted. We propose the usage of a role-based access control model for user modeling purposes. Our implementation offers a high degree of flexibility and comprehensibility to the user. It can be used for the authorization of the user model clients as well as for the representation of the users being modeled in different roles they assume while interacting with user adaptive systems.

Because of the various representation and inference techniques and methods applied in user modeling and the general scope of this work which does not focus on a particular user modeling agent, it is not possible to supply solutions to all requirements listed in *Part II, Requirements for Security and Privacy in User Modeling*. Instead, we summarize noteworthy solutions for the requirements implemented in different user modeling systems in *Chapter 7.2*. The inherent partial contradiction between confidentiality and integrity is also discussed.

The final part of this book *Part IV, Discussion*, covers implementations in the field of user modeling, their security features, and the potentials which can be achieved through inclusion of further security features. In *Chapter 8*, descriptions of the security features of user modeling agents, for instance, those of the *Doppelgänger* and *BGP-MS* systems, which we discuss in several preceding chapters, are being reviewed.

A new user modeling component called *User Model Reference Monitor* combines the three implementations for encryption, anonymization, and access control and demonstrates their integration into a user adaptive system. The combination of this three implementations – together with auxiliary components (e.g., certification authorities) – can serve as a default security architecture for user adaptive systems. Also only parts of the *User Model Reference Monitor* can be provided either as software packages (e.g., for encryption) or as services (e.g., authorization of information requests). As an example of a user adaptive system, we discuss the AVANTI system which processes user information considered sensitive. The application of the *User Model Reference Monitor* is described and its superiority over previously available security mechanisms are explored. We also sketch the current developments in the *Platform for Privacy Preferences Project* (P3P) as an example of the usage policies of user information based on the security features of the underlying system.

The last chapter provides an overview of the main concepts of anonymity and security in user modeling and their implementation. Findings gained through this work are reviewed and proposals for further research on security and privacy in user modeling are made.

I

User Modeling, Security, and Privacy

Chapter 1

USER MODELING

A *user model* contains the previously described set of user data (i.e., *primary assumptions*), rules to extend the given set of data (i.e., *inference rules*), and further assumptions (i.e., *secondary assumptions*) which are derived from the previous two sets, either in explicit or implicit form. This definition summarizes the constructive definitions of user models which describe user models as data sets containing particular items:

> "A user model is that knowledge about the user, either explicitly or implicitly encoded, which is used by the system to improve the interaction." [Finin, 1989, p. 412]

> "A *user model* is a knowledge source in a natural-language dialog system which contains explicit assumptions on all aspects of the user that may be relevant to the dialog behavior of the system. These assumptions must be separable *by the system* from the rest of the system's knowledge." [Wahlster and Kobsa, 1989, p. 6]

or [Pohl, 1998, p. 1]:

> "[...] a user model is a source of information, which contains assumptions about those aspects of a user that might be relevant for behavior of information adaptation."

A definition which emphasizes the differentiation of individuals in addition to the representation and inference mechanisms is that of Allen:

> "[...] a user model is the knowledge and inference mechanism which differentiates the interaction across individuals." [Allen, 1990, p. 513]

Differentiation of users is useful for adapting software systems which offer different functionality to different user groups. A coarse approach to the differentiation of users is achieved by the employment of stereotypes which assign users to groups according to certain criteria:

"Stereotypes are simply collections of facet-value combinations that describe groups of system users.

A system that is going to use stereotypes must also know about a set of *triggers* – those events whose occurrence signals the appropriateness of particular stereotypes." [Rich, 1979b, p. 333]

Stereotypes arrange users into predefined groups. An a priori definition of user groups before applying the adaptive system is not possible for all domains. Therefore, other methods have been considered which group users without explicitly defining the groups. For instance, the user modeling system *Doppelgänger* groups users with similar characteristics through analogical user modeling[1] by means of clustering algorithms:

"DOPPELGÄNGER compensates for missing or inaccurate information about a user by using default inferences from *communities*, which resemble traditional user modeling stereotypes with two major differences: membership is not all-or-nothing, but a matter of degree; and the community models are computed as weighted combinations of their member user models, and thus change dynamically as the user models are augmented." [Orwant, 1995, p. 109]

In the last 15 years several user modeling (shell) systems have been developed, each focusing on different representation and inference methods. Table 1.1 gives an overview of major generic user modeling systems (both research prototypes and commercial systems), and some of the methods they employ (see [Fink and Kobsa, 2001, Kobsa, 2001a] for a more detailed discussion).

Table 1.1 focuses on academic[2] user modeling shell systems for several reasons. Shell systems have been developed with an emphasis on several characteristics (for instance, *generality*, *expressiveness*, and *strong inferential capabilities*, see [Kobsa, 2001a]) that are considered to be important for *general user modeling* for a wide range of domains. The systems have been described in detail in the literature (see the references in Table 1.1), especially with respect to their knowledge representation mechanisms and inference procedures. Where systems have implemented security features, these have been described[3]; where they lack security features this has been pointed out sometimes. Most of these systems concentrate on only one representation mechanism and inference procedure, which simplifies the discussion of their security features.

With the recognition of the increased value of web personalization, especially in the area of electronic commerce, many commercial user

---

[1] Analogical user modeling aims at grouping user models on the basis of similarities, for instance, derived from analogous reasoning about user characteristics (see [Kobsa et al., 2000], [McCalla et al., 1996], and [Konstan et al., 1997]).

[2] See [Kobsa, 2001a] for an overview and descriptions of these systems.

[3] See *Chapter 7.2* and *Chapter 8*, for examples.

Table 1.1. Generic user modeling systems (research prototypes and commercial systems)

System name	References	Characteristics
GRUNDY	[Rich, 1979b], [Rich, 1979a], [Rich, 1983]	stereotypes, default assumptions
UMFE	[Sleeman, 1985]	propositional logic, conceptual hierarchies, numerical gradation of attributes
GUMS	[Finin, 1989]	Prolog, stereotypes
GUMAC	[Kass, 1991]	assumptions, rules, stereotypes
PROTUM	[Eydner and Vergara, 1993]	Prolog, stereotypes, truth maintenance system
UMT	[Brajnik and Tasso, 1994]	propositional logic, stereotypes, truth maintenance system
um	[Kay, 1995]	frames, propositional logic, inspection and modification
BGP-MS	[Kobsa and Pohl, 1995], [Pohl, 1998]	propositional, first-order, and modal logic, stereotypes, partitions, shared user models
Doppelgänger	[Orwant, 1995]	shared user models, propositional logic, statistics, machine learning, inspection and modification
TAGUS	[Paiva and Self, 1995]	Prolog, inspection
GroupLens	[Net Perceptions, 2002]	collaborative filtering
Personalization Server	[Art Technology Group, 2001]	production rules
FrontMind	[Manna, 2001]	production rules, Bayesian networks
DPS	[Fink, 2002]	content-based filtering, collaborative filtering, production rules

modeling tools have been developed (e.g., *GroupLens, Personalization Server, FrontMind* and *DPS*, see Table 1.1) which are discussed in [Kobsa et al., 2000] and [Fink and Kobsa, 2001]. These systems often employ a mix of several techniques described previously in the academic systems. For the sake of clarity, it therefore seems appropriate to focus on the academic systems for the description of security features specific to user modeling. Where current commercial user modeling tools offer comparable solutions for security (e.g., for encryption), they can replace the solutions proposed in this work. As solutions for confidentiality or anonymity are only partially provided by current commercial user modeling tools such solutions are discussed without respect to those systems.

User modeling servers form the basis for user adaptive systems. For the scope of this book, the term *user adaptive system* denotes the *user model*, the *user modeling server* (often called *user model agent* or *user modeling (shell) system*), the *user adaptive application system* (often called *user model client*, in the following shortened as *application system* or *user adaptive application*), and the particular user being modeled which uses the application system (e.g., through a web browser):

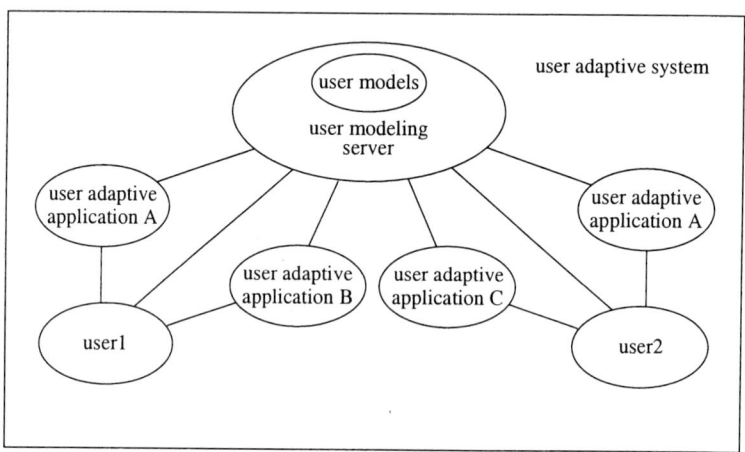

Figure 1.1.   Components of a user adaptive system

Usually, considerations about user modeling agents focus on representation and inference issues. There are only a few examples which include the user in the maintenance of their models and the supervision of the user adaptive system (for instance, [Cook and Kay, 1994], [Jones, 1989], or [Paiva and Self, 1995]). For the scope of this book, the supervision of the user adaptive system (i.e., defining security mechanisms and ensuring they are complied with) always takes the user into account.

Based on the interaction of the user with the system, user adaptive application systems generate assumptions which are stored and processed in the user model. On the basis of these assumptions, the further interaction is adapted to the current user. As an example, the adaptations of the *Adaptive Courseware Environment (ACE, see [Specht and Oppermann, 1998])* are discussed. As in many tutoring systems, these adaptations are based on the learner's knowledge which the learner often considers to be sensitive. ACE is a WWW-based tutoring framework which adapts its lessons according to the respective learner's preferences, interests, and knowledge. In the following figure, a presentation of a concept to learn (in this case the "Contract of Maastricht") is shown:

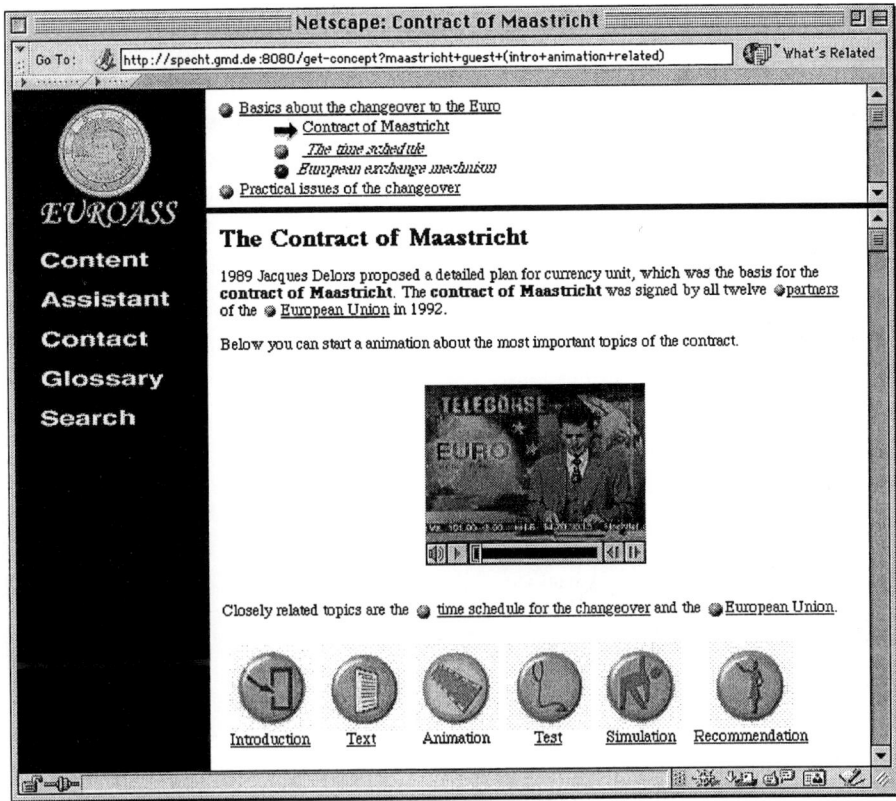

Figure 1.2. An example of a user adaptive system

The presentation is supplemented with elements of *adaptive navigation support* which modify the structure of the hypermedia document either by hints through color-coded elements or by the inclusion and hiding of links. ACE annotations to concepts guide the learner through lessons where the elements have the following semantics: concepts which are not recommended to the learner (due to missing prerequisites at the current stage, for instance, missing knowledge) are annotated with a red[4] ball, recommended concepts are annotated with a green[5] ball, and links for which the necessary prerequisites are given, but which are not recommended, are annotated with an orange[6] ball (see the top of Figure 1.2). The most appropriate concept with which to proceed is annotated with an arrow. In this way, the learner is guided through the tutoring

---

[4]For example, *European exchange mechanism* in Figure 1.2.
[5]For example, *Basics about the changeover to the Euro* in Figure 1.2.
[6]For example, *The time schedule* in Figure 1.2.

system on the basis of what he already knows; he is neither overtaxed by learning material that is too demanding, nor bored with concepts he has already mastered.

Due to the huge number and diversity of user adaptive systems, a concise description or classification of all systems would exceed the scope of this brief introduction. For a more thorough treatment of user adaptive systems and the underlying user modeling techniques, the reader should refer to [Blank, 1996], [Brusilovsky, 1998], [Kobsa et al., 2000], [Kobsa and Wahlster, 1989], or [Pohl, 1998].

Chapter 2

PRIVACY

Security in user modeling is not a goal in itself, but an auxiliary means for realizing privacy. Security measures are usually described and designed to be applied by experts. They have to be adapted to a particular use in order to provide the protection demanded by users. This can be done for elementary demands (e.g., confidentiality, authenticity, accountability, anonymity) and provided to the user as components. Furthermore, these components might be grouped and described in terms that are intelligible to the user, for example, as policies which specify *who* can do *what* with *which* data item *when* for *what* purpose. Users can modify these policies to meet their own personal demands for privacy.

Personal demands for privacy in user modeling can be influenced by such factors as:

- personal preferences for privacy in information technology (for instance, whether anonymous or identifiable use of information systems is preferred)

- personal attitudes towards monitoring and classification through software systems (for instance, whether the inference of further assumptions based on the information provided by the user is accepted)

- personal expectations for user adaptive systems and their adaptations (for instance, whether the added value an adaptive system offers is worth disclosing personal information)

- personal needs to keep different sets of characteristics of different user adaptive systems apart from each other (for instance, whether different adaptive systems may share only a small part of the set of personal information or can share a large part of it)

- personal roles which a user assumes while using a user adaptive system (for instance, the adaptive system should not only adapt to the users, but also to their different roles in their interaction with the system).

Traditional definitions of privacy, which are often influenced by the "right of the individual to be let alone" (Warren and Brandeis 1890, [Warren and Brandeis, 1890]), separate a person or their actions from a group of persons [Egger, 1993, p. 135]:

> "Privacy in our common sense is strongly connected with the idea that there are some things another person should not be able to see or know."

Privacy may also be defined as the right to determine the amount of personal information which should be available to others [Westin, 1970, p. 7]:

> "Privacy is the claim of individuals, groups, or institutions to determine for themselves when, how, and to what extent information about them is communicated to others. "

More recent discussions of privacy include economic aspects on a macro-economic level [Lunheim and Sindre, 1994, p. 30]:

> "Successful and sustained generation of knowledge, which is vital to the growth and maintenance of a modern industrial economy, is, among other factors, contingent upon the following two aspects of privacy:
>
> - Knowledge and power are mutually generative entities, tending to reinforce each other. Hence, in order to maintain vital knowledge-generating processes within a society, protected regions of life must be available, where human consciousness is partly shielded from the political consequences of knowledge [...].
> - Generation of knowledge presupposes mechanisms for evaluation of ideas: Unevaluated knowledge is non-knowledge [...]."

as well as on a micro-economic level [Posner, 1984, p. 336]:

> "The fact that disclosure of personal information is resisted by (is costly to) the person to whom the information pertains, yet is valuable to others, may seem to argue for giving people property rights in information about themselves and letting them sell those rights freely. The process of voluntary exchange would then ensure that the information was put to its most valuable use. The attractiveness of this solution depends, however on (1) the nature and source of the information and (2) transaction costs."

Therefore, privacy seems to be both an intrinsic value ("right of the individual to be let alone") as well as an instrumental value serving other goals (e.g., generation of knowledge, profit). Besides these theoretical considerations, privacy also serves pragmatic purposes when it is included in the design of software systems, e.g., resulting in higher acceptance by users (see *Chapter 2.3* for a detailed discussion).

Privacy is usually discussed as a social matter, i.e., in negotiation within a community regarding the information processing of personal information. The more widely communities are distributed, the more they need artefacts (e.g., the Internet) to communicate this information and to negotiate its use. This also applies to user adaptive systems, since developers of such systems try to anticipate special characteristics of potential users (e.g., personal information relating to knowledge or interests) in order to adapt the information the system will provide. Unfortunately, developers and users so far usually cannot negotiate how personal information will be processed. Therefore, the system should be designed in such a way that it can be adjusted to varying demands.

Hence negotiation on privacy is not only a matter between people but also between users and systems that have been enabled to perform negotiations. An initial approach to negotiation can be to offer several policies from which the user can choose. A *policy* is a set of specifications which regulates the processing of the data in the user adaptive system. The accepted policy should be modifiable by users in order to satisfy their demands regarding the privacy of the user adaptive systems (see *Chapter 8.5*).

A flexible definition of the policy serves two purposes. First, it enables users to adjust their preferences regarding privacy and to make an informed decision about the use of a user adaptive system. Second, developers of user adaptive systems are able to gain experience with user demands regarding privacy and to develop systems that are more user-oriented. Until recently, the only choice users had was to accept the system or get along without it.

The scope of this work does not include proposals for policies in user modeling. Security issues are rather the basis for the definition and enforcement of policies within user adaptive systems and therefore a prerequisite of privacy in user modeling.

There are several factors which call for privacy protecting measures in user modeling systems. The most prominent factor is the fact that much of the data processed is related to an identifiable person (i.e., *personal data*). Therefore, the processing has to be carried out on the basis of acknowledged rules (e.g., laws). Moreover, user adaptive systems especially consider human factors in information systems. To this end, additional factors have to be taken into account in order to help the user understand and control the system, and to improve their confidence and satisfaction when using the system. These factors (e.g., anonymity, confidentiality of information, inspection and modification of the user model, and supervision of the system) are contingent upon the security of the underlying system. In the following, we will show the need for privacy and security in user modeling on the basis of laws, ethics, and user demands.

1.   Laws

Laws regulating the processing of personal data vary among countries [Kobsa, 2002]. As an example, some of the regulations applicable in Germany will be discussed. The most prominent law is the *Bundesdatenschutzgesetz* [BDSG90, 1990] which has regulated the processing of personal data by organizations since 1979. The corresponding data protection laws of the individual German states implement the federal law for each state.

The 1995 *EU Data Protection Directive* [ECDIR95,], which has been converted into national law, defines *personal data* as follows:

> "For the purposes of this Directive:
> a) 'personal data' shall mean any information relating to an identified or identifiable natural person ('data subject'); an identifiable person is one who can be identified, directly or indirectly, in particular by reference to an identification number or to one or more factors specific to his physical, physiological, mental, economic, cultural or social identity; "

Most applicable is the *Informations- und Kommunikationsdienste-Gesetz* (see [IuKDG97, 1997] and [IuKDG97a, 1997]) which was introduced in 1997 in order to regulate online services (e.g., a user adaptive system provided via the Internet) and the processing of personal data within such systems. Article 1 (*Teleservices Act, Teledienstegesetz TDG*) of this law specifies the scope of the law which covers also user adaptive information systems provided over the Internet. Therefore, Article 2 (*Teleservices Data Protection Act, Teledienstedatenschutzgesetz TDDSG*) which specifies the protection of personal data used in teleservices also applies to such systems. This article[1] specifies among other things the circumstances under which usage profiles are permitted and guarantees the user access to information about stored personal data:

> §4: Obligations of the provider
> "(4) User profiles are permissible under the condition that pseudonyms are used. Profiles retrievable under pseudonyms shall not be combined with data relating to the bearer of the pseudonym."
>
> §7: User's right to information
> "The user shall be entitled at any time to inspect, free of charge, stored data

---

[1]See also the changes introduced by the modification of the law [IuKDG2001, 2001].

concerning his person or his pseudonym at the provider's. The information
shall be given electronically if so requested by the user. [...]"

User profiles are permissible where pseudonyms are applied [Bizer and
Bleumer, 1997]. This cross between personal data and anonymous data
is not clearly defined and it is conceivable that borderline cases will
appear in user modeling in which it is not clear whether data is personal
or not. Types and advantages of pseudonyms will be discussed in detail
in a later chapter.

The *Teleservices Data Protection Act TDDSG* declares also the general applicability of the *Bundesdatenschutzgesetz* [BDSG90, 1990] where
no specific regulation is given in the TDDSG (see TDDSG Article §1(2)
and [Schwarz, 2000, p. 11-2.1/18]).

Technically problematic from the perspective of user modeling is the
observance of *user's right to information*. User modeling techniques also
frequently include knowledge based systems which use certain rules to
extend an initial set of facts (so-called *primary assumptions*) to cover a
larger set of facts (so-called *secondary assumptions*). Neither the rules
nor the assumptions derived are self-explanatory and both are unsuitable
for modification by the user himself. The information in a user model
has often been represented in a form that cannot be easily communicated
to users (like semantic networks or neural networks).

Even though the user has a right to *his* personal data, it is not clear
whether the user's right extends also to the rules and assumptions based
on these rules, and if so, how they should be explained (see for instance,
[Kobsa, 1991], [Cook and Kay, 1994], and [Paiva et al., 1995]).

2.   Ethics

Laws are mandatory for everyone they affect. Guidelines (see *Chapter
3.1*) are less restrictive and summarize principles which are generally
recommended and which should be applied to some extent. Ethics offer
different coherent sets of attitudes towards actions and values. Usually
the decision as to which attitude is appropriate depends on the domain
in which the user adaptive system is applied. Hence, it would be too
restrictive to promote one ethical direction in user modeling. But it is
beneficial to describe the basic conditions for arriving at a consensus
on ethical issues. Because of the general nature of ethics, the group of
parties concerned is also broad [Summers, 1997, p. 49]:

"Who must apply ethical principles and ethical analysis to computer security issues? First, computer professionals. Second, leaders of businesses and
other organizations who make decisions and set the ethical tone for their organizations. Third, computer users. Finally, all of us as citizens in deciding

which laws and government policies are right and as consumers, employees, and stockholders in "voting" for ethical companies."

The process of developing ethics is independent of the domain in which the user adaptive system operates. A short description of the development cycle in ethics is given by Winograd [Winograd, 1995, p. 35]:

"There are three key components in "doing" ethics and social responsibility:
1. Identifying social/ethical issues.
2. Entering into serious discourse about the possibilities, with yourself and with others.
3. Taking actions."

For a serious discussion and an informed decision about operating a user adaptive system, it is necessary to specify factors influencing "social/ethical issues" (e.g., for confidentiality or anonymity). These factors are often contingent on the underlying security mechanisms of the system. This work focuses on the security mechanisms and security risks in user adaptive systems in order to provide a reliable technical basis for the specification of *policies* which can help to prevent ethical conflicts.

Some examples for ethical guidelines in computer science are listed below:

- ACM Code of Ethics and Professional Conduct (see [ACM92, 1992] and [Gotterbarn et al., 1999])

- Ethical Guidelines issued by the Gesellschaft für Informatik (GI) [Gesellschaft für Informatik, 1995]

- British Computer Society Code of Conduct [BCS, 2002]

- Australian Computer Society Code of Ethics [ACS, 2002]

- IEEE Code of Ethics (see [IEEE, 2002] and [Gotterbarn et al., 1999]).

In addition to these general guidelines there may also exist guidelines for the particular domain of the user adaptive system (e.g., company policies).

3.   User Demands

The previous sections covered requirements which must, should, or can be met. Strong and decisive demands against which user modeling systems should be measured are also given by the respective users. Because few empirical evaluations of user models [Chin, 2000] are available and none of them focus on the security and privacy aspects, user's demands for processing personal information will be discussed on the basis of the *10th WWW User Survey* of the GVU Center [GVU's WWW Surveying Team, 1998].

The questions, ratings, and percentages relevant for these considerations are summarized in the following table:

Table 2.1. Selected GVU survey results

Question/Statement	Ratings	Percentage
1. I would give demographic information to a Web site	if a statement was provided regarding what information was being collected.	56.5%
	if a statement was provided regarding how the information was going to be used.	73.1%
	if the data would only be used in aggregate form (i.e., not on an individual basis).	56.1%
	in exchange for some value-added service (e.g., notification of events, etc.).	31.0%
	I would not give the site any demographic information.	8.8%
2. What conditions cause you to refrain from filling out online registration forms at sites?	Requires me to give my name	35.8%
	Requires me to give an email address	32.3%
	Requires me to give my mailing address	51.3%
	Information is not provided on how the data is going to be used	75.2%
	I do not trust the entity collecting the data	67.3%
3. I value being able to visit sites on the Internet in an anonymous manner.	Agree Strongly	66.3%
	Agree Somewhat	21.8%
4. In general, which is more important to you: convenience or privacy?	Privacy	77.5%
5. There should be new laws to protect privacy on the Internet.	Agree Strongly	40.6%
	Agree Somewhat	30.8%
6. Ought to be able to Assume Different Aliases/Roles on the Internet	Agree Strongly	31.9%
	Agree Somewhat	26.9%
7. I ought to be able to communicate over the Internet without people being able to read the content.	Agree Strongly	81.6%
	Agree Somewhat	11.6%

(1.) Demographic information would be provided by most of the participants, as long as it is clear which information is collected and for what purpose. Of special interest is the desire for anonymity expressed in the willingness to provide information if data is used in aggregate form. The exchange of personal information for value-added services seems to be attractive for only 31%. Only a minority of 8.8% would refuse to share any information.

(2.) Another indication of the desire for anonymity is the withholding of identifying information by a third of the participants. Nearly three quarters of the respondents would not register online unless they can make an informed decision about the data processing and two thirds would not register if they don't trust the collection entity.

(3.) If asked directly, 88.1% prefer to use the Internet anonymously.

(4.) Three quarters of the participants rate privacy over convenience. This is enough evidence to justify including (sometimes inconvenient) security mechanisms in value-added functions such as user modeling in order to maintain privacy.

(5.) 71.4% apparently think that current laws do not sufficiently protect privacy.

(6.) More than 50% of the participants would like to act in different roles when using the Internet. Just as the information we pass on to others in real life is selected on the basis of our respective roles, it should also be possible to disseminate personal information selectively in virtual environments.

(7.) 93.2% of the respondents want secrecy when communicating via the Internet.

Similar results have been found in different studies in the e-commerce domain which are summarized in Table 2.2.

These results illustrate the users' privacy concerns and their preference for confidentiality, anonymity, and selective dissemination of personal information. Current user modeling agents provide only few possibilities to adapt to various privacy preferences and usage policies of the user's information. To support the user with reliable privacy policies user modeling agents need to include security measures.

Table 2.2.   User concerns regarding privacy on the Internet

Respondents asserted to	% agreement ("strong"/"very" and "somewhat")
being (very) concerned about threats to their privacy when using the Internet	81% [Westin and Maurici, 1998], 87% [Cramer, 1999]
being extremely/very concerned about divulging personal information online	67% [Forrester Research, 1999], 74% [DePallo, 2000], 70% [Culnan and Milne, 2001]
being (extremely) concerned about being tracked online	54% [Fox, 2000] 77% [DePallo, 2000]
having left web sites that required registration information	41% [Boston Consulting Group, 1997]
having entered fake registration information	40% [GVU's WWW Surveying Team, 1998], 27% [Boston Consulting Group, 1997], 32% [Forrester Research, 1999], 24% [Fox, 2000], 34% [Culnan and Milne, 2001]
having refrained from shopping online due to privacy concerns, or bought less	32 - 61% [IBM, 1999], 32% [Forrester Research, 1999], 24% [DePallo, 2000] , 64% [Culnan and Milne, 2001]
being willing to give out personal data when they get something valuable in return	31% [GVU's WWW Surveying Team, 1998], 30% [Forrester Research, 1999], 51% [Personalization Consortium, 2000]

Chapter 3

SECURITY

Security in information technology is a very broad term composed of related topics which have been discussed for nearly as long as computers have been in use. The roots of the problem can be traced back to at least two millenia to a time when people recognized the value of information and the value of keeping it secret [Kahn, 1967].

With the growing dissemination of computers in various areas of everyday life, the meaning of security has become ambiguous. Usually what is considered to be of sufficient value to be protected depends on the domain. Therefore, it is not astonishing that there is no consensus on a single definition of *security*.

In *Part II, Requirements for Security and Privacy in User Modeling*, an analysis of the relevant concepts involved in the complex problem *security* will be given from the perspective of user modeling. The scope of this book can neither cover all concepts nor can it elaborate the selected concepts to their full extent. The objective is to point out which security risks have to be taken into account when developing or using user adaptive systems. Some of the risks can be reduced by employing the methods and techniques we propose here.

The most apparent feature encountered when analyzing security in user modeling is the fact that information processed is mostly related to an often identifiable person. For this reason it is impossible to assess objectively the value of the information and the potential damage its misuse might cause. Almost as relevant as experts' opinions about the security of a system is the user's confidence that using the system will not endanger his privacy. The risks and requirements in user modeling can therefore not be estimated without regard to the person to be modeled.

This means that measures taken to ensure security must be adaptable to the personal demands of the respective user.

Without regard to personal preferences concerning the security and privacy of a user adaptive information system, several *guidelines* for the security of general information systems have been established which can likewise serve as a basis for considerations about security in user modeling.

1.   Guidelines

A previous section covered laws which are mandatory for all organizations that process personal data. In addition to the mandatory laws, guidelines exist which summarize the essential security factors of information systems. These guidelines can be seen as recommendations with different focuses from which the designer of an information system can choose the one that seems most appropriate. They have been published by numerous organizations. The following criteria and guidelines are among the most important recommendations:

- Trusted Computer System Evaluation Criteria (TCSEC, see [TCSEC85, 1985]),

- Information Technology Security Evaluation Criteria (ITSEC, see [Commission of the European Communities,]),

- Common Criteria for Information Technology Security Evaluation (CCITSE, see [CC99, 1999]),

- OECD Guidelines for the Security of Information Systems (see [OECD92, 1992]).

In the following, we will focus on the *OECD Guidelines for the Security of Information Systems* because of their general nature and will discuss them from the perspective of user modeling. The most important factors of these guidelines are the following [Summers, 1997, p. 7]:

1 Accountability
"All parties concerned with the security of information systems (owners, providers, users, and others) should have explicit responsibilities and accountability."

2 Awareness
"All parties should be able to readily gain knowledge of security measures, practices, and procedures. A motivation for this principle is to foster confidence in information systems."

3 Ethics
"Information systems and their security should be provided and used in ways that respect the rights and legitimate interests of others."

4 Multidisciplinary principle
"Security measures should take into account all relevant viewpoints, including technical, administrative, organizational, operational, commercial, educational, and legal."

5 Proportionality
"Security measures should be appropriate and proportionate to the value of and degree or reliance on the information systems and to the risks of harm."

6 Integration
"Security measures should be coordinated and integrated with each other and with other measures, practices, and procedures of the organization so as to create a coherent system of security."

7 Timeliness
"Parties should act in a timely and coordinated way to prevent and to respond to security breaches."

8 Reassessment
"Security should be reassessed periodically as information systems and their security needs change."

9 Democracy
"The security of information systems should be compatible with the legitimate use and flow of information in a democratic society."

Despite their general nature, these guidelines have implications for user modeling systems, some of which are discussed in this section (see *Chapter 5* for an extensive discussion of security in user modeling systems):

Accountability (see 1.) is based on security mechanisms within the system. In electronic networks, this includes the proof of identity of the components involved in the system and the authenticity of the information processed. In user models which are shared between various application systems, it is essential to know which application system originated a particular user model entry. This is a prerequisite if the user wants to assess the quality of an individual application system. On the other hand, student-adaptive systems which rate the proficiency of users on a scale of attainment and issue transcripts require certainty regarding the identity of the current user.

The *awareness* principle (see 2.) enables all participants to gain knowledge of security measures, practices, and procedures involved in the information processing. Moreover, it affords insight into the security measures, practices, and procedures applied in the information system to an extent which usually can only be achieved through some effort (for instance, by reading the documentation).

User *awareness* in user modeling is usually handled in a different way. User modeling is not the main task of the system used, it only supports the user. Consequently, the construction and maintenance of the user model should not distract the user from his main tasks. This is achieved when the user model is maintained in the background without direct interaction with the user, as demanded by [Rich, 1979a, p. 720]:

> "The model must be built dynamically, as the system is interacting with the user and performing its task. Because the model is to be built implicitly and because users do not want to be forced to answer a long list of questions before they can begin to use the system, it is necessary that the system be able to exploit a partially constructed user model and that it be able to tell, as it is performing its major task, when it is appropriate to update the user model and how to do so."

This assumes that decreased user awareness of the modeling process is advantageous for the main task of the system. In addition, the adjustment of the security mechanisms related to the user model should not distract the user from his main task. For this reason, the security mechanisms of the user model must not hinder users either in the maintenance of their user model or in performing their main task. Therefore, the security mechanisms of the user model should be optimized to satisfy the user's need for privacy as far as is necessary without being overly complicated (for instance, via selection of predefined and adjustable categories). Obviously, there will still be a discrepancy between the demand for awareness of security measures and the implicit maintenance of the user model.

The *multidisciplinary principle* (see 4.) emphasizes not only the technical perspective, but also human factors (e.g., administrative, organizational, educational, and legal). These factors are particularly important in user modeling, where not only "technicians" but also users themselves should be responsible for the maintenance of the security mechanisms for their user model. Technical factors (e.g., encryption of communication), administrative factors (e.g., allowing access to the user model), organizational factors (e.g., pseudonymous user models), and legal factors (as outlined in a previous section) should be summed up and expressed in policies for the utilization of a user model, which are intelligible and manageable by the user. The effort involved in learning to use and modify security measures should be kept to a minimum in order not to distract the user or keep him from applying the necessary security mechanisms.

The *proportionality* (see 5.) of the security measures in regard to the use of the processed information (e.g., whether the access control model is commensurate with the user model or the type of anonymity) can be judged by the user only to the extent that he is able to estimate the value of the processed information. In contrast, the proportionality of the strength of the security measures (for instance, the minimum key length for a cryptographic algorithm) can best be ascertained by the developers of the (secure) user adaptive system. The latter proportionality can be established by recommendations provided by experts from which the user can choose. As the former proportionality will vary for each user because of the different user demands for privacy and the resulting different extent of security measures, the user should be included when this proportionality is established. This can be done either by choosing between previously selected combinations of security measures (for instance, represented by *policies*) or by combining certain security measures on the user's behalf.

Advancing from these guidelines for general information systems, we will provide in the following part requirements for the security of user modeling systems.

II

Requirements for Security and Privacy in User Modeling

In this part, requirements for *security in user modeling* will be analyzed.

The first chapter focuses on the relationship between the user model data and the user being modeled because most of the sensitivity of the user model information ensues from this relationship. Fortunately, this relationship can be weakened without restricting substantially the performance of user adaptive systems. For this reason, several levels, complexities, and types of anonymity (and thereby pseudonymity) which can be required in user modeling are discussed.

The second chapter concentrates on the security of user models, user modeling agents, and the data they process. Particular emphasis is placed on requirements for the *secrecy* and *integrity* of the information processed. Secrecy of information is regarded as secrecy of the relationship between the user model data and the user and as secrecy of the data itself. In addition to these kinds of secrecy, a weaker form of secrecy (namely *confidentiality*) is required as a prerequisite for the joint processing of confidential data by particular components of a user adaptive system. The integrity of a user model is discussed from the perspective of user model clients as external integrity and from the perspective of developers of user modeling agents as internal integrity.

Chapter 4

REQUIREMENTS FOR ANONYMITY AND PSEUDONYMITY

The sensitivity of user modeling information is mainly caused by the relationship between uniquely identifiable persons and their data. This relationship means that the data processed in user adaptive systems (and especially in user modeling) is actually *personal data*. When distinguishing data which can be assigned to a user (i.e., personal data) from data which cannot, we define *information* as *data in context*, where *context* refers to the relationship between the users and their data.

The processing of user modeling information (personal data) faces restrictions due to legal regulations as well as to users' concerns *Chapter 2*. By removing the context (i.e. anonymization), the information about the user is reduced to mere data which is subject to fewer constraints. The action of most user adaptive systems does not depend on knowing the identity of their current user, since the main task of such systems is to produce a sequence of adaptations (see Figure 1.2 on p. 15) on the basis of a sequence of user interactions.

What is needed is a means for relating consecutive user interactions with the user adaptive system (e.g., interactions in different sessions) to a sequence of interactions which also interlinks sessions. The user's identity *can* be used to construct a sequence of user interactions which belong together. However, the user's identity is neither the only means for this purpose, nor is it always appropriate. In the following sections, several ways of replacing the user's identity (e.g., with pseudonyms) and of doing entirely without the user's identity (e.g., through anonymity) are discussed from the perspective of user modeling. The relinquishment on the user's identity has the following advantages beyond meeting user demands (see Table 2.1 on p. 23). The processing of personal data gives reasons for the applicability of some of the laws and guidelines discussed above. The crucial point in deciding which laws apply is the question whether the processed data can be traced to an identifiable person and how this assignment of data to the user is or can be established. The weaker this assignment of data to the user becomes, the lower the requirements for the processing will be. For this purpose, it is also useful to analyze the varying levels of the assignment of the processed data (e.g., through pseudonyms).

1.   Aspects of Anonymity

In this section, a variety of aspects of anonymity which are important for user modeling purposes are introduced. First, different levels of anonymity ranging from identification of the users (and the user model) by means outside of the adaptive system to anonymity of all components are described. Next, a measure for the complexity of anonymity is discussed which permits the rating of user adaptive systems with regard to the anonymity they supply. Finally, three types of anonymity are distinguished, all of which must be provided by the user adaptive system in order to preserve the user's anonymity.

1.1   Levels of Anonymity

Depending on the type (e.g., tutorial systems) or the domain (e.g., electronic commerce) of the user adaptive system, different levels of the user's anonymity can be required within a user adaptive system. The following itemization provides a vocabulary, descriptions, and examples for different levels of anonymity applicable to user adaptive systems. A particular level of anonymity may be required not only for the user but also for components of the user adaptive system (e.g., the clients of the user model or the user model itself). Due to the diversity of user adaptive systems, no single level is suitable for all user adaptive systems.

Flinn and Maurer [Flinn and Maurer, 1995] identify six levels, ranging from the unequivocal assignment of data to a person to the complete disengagement of data from the person. The different levels are as follows:

Super-identification: With super-identification, the user's identity is authenticated by means based on the environment of the user adaptive system. This guarantees that no component of the user adaptive system can counterfeit the identity of the respective user or the identity of components of the user modeling system (e.g., clients of the user model). The assignment of the data needed for authentication to the user or to the components is delegated to an administrative entity outside the system architecture. Examples of this kind of identification and authentication are the X.509 standard [International Organization for Standardization, 1995] and the German law for digital signatures (see [IuKDG97, 1997, Artikel 3] and [SIGV97, 1997]).

Identification: The user identifies himself and demonstrates knowledge of a secret (e.g., a password) which is then compared by the system to a stored value. The system is responsible for the confirmation of the user's identity. As an example, this mechanism is often implemented in current operating systems (e.g. Unix).

Latent identification (controlled pseudonyms): The user identifies himself to the system and adopts one of the defined pseudonyms. Subsequently, he[1] is able to act without revealing his identity to particular components of the system while acting under a pseudonym. The pseudonym can be revealed under defined circumstances in order to ascertain the identity of the user. For example, this procedure is widely used in box number advertisements.

Pseudonymous identification (uncontrolled pseudonyms): When using the system for the first time, the user decides on a unique pseudonym and a secret (e.g., a password) which he will also use for following sessions. The system is unable to ascertain the identity of the user, therefore it is also unable to link the pseudonym to the user's identity. This method is used in most Web-based services. It is also used in anonymous remailers which allow email exchange by means of uncontrolled unique pseudonyms.

Anonymous identification: The user gains access to the system by providing a secret (e.g., a password) without disclosing his identity. The system is unable to distinguish between users which have knowledge about the same secret. The users of the same secret constitute an *anonymity set*[2]. For instance, a bank account might be managed as a numbered account where clients only have to provide a password to get access.

Anonymity: The user neither identifies nor authenticates himself to the system. The system is unable to distinguish among the users or to differentiate between users. Anonymity is given in most real life situations (e.g., museum visits) but not in the World-wide Web (e.g., visits of virtual museums), where electronic trails on several layers

---

[1]To avoid the construction *he/she* (*his/her*) when concerning the user, the masculine or plural pronouns will be used.
[2]An *anonymity set* consists of all users which cannot be differentiated.

make it possible to link the current user and his system interactions with additional information to the point of revealing his identity.

Several levels of anonymity with respect to user modeling should be considered. From the perspective of user modeling, not all levels are of equal relevance. *Anonymity* and *anonymous identification*, for example, are only suitable either for user groups or for short-term modeling. When groups of users must be modeled, the user model entries refer to the *average user* of the whole user population. This is particularly relevant for applications which attempt to balance characteristics across all users, e.g., notification services which keep a user population up to date, where the members of the user population have only slightly different fields of interest. In the case of short-term modeling (e.g., at information kiosks which can be used by only one person at a time), user modeling can be applied within anonymity sets, possibly of size 1, but only within the same session.

Pseudonymous identification is the most valuable compromise between privacy demands and the requirements of user modeling. Through identification by a pseudonym, successive sessions can be linked, making long-term modeling possible. This type of identification also differentiates users based on the different pseudonyms which they themselves have chosen and it authenticates them. Users are not required to reveal their identity. Moreover, they may acquire more than one pseudonym in order to act in different roles (see *Chapter 2.3*). *Latent identification* offers the same potential with the added feature that the system can determine the identities behind the pseudonyms. This might be desirable in cases of potential misuse or when interaction that requires identification of the user (e.g., in electronic commerce scenarios) becomes necessary.

In the case of *identification* by the system, all components are aware of the identity of the respective user. If there is a possibility that a user's identity could be counterfeited by a component of the (possibly distributed and open) system, *super-identification* should be introduced. Responsibility for the assignment of data to the user is hereby delegated to a component outside the system which all participants consider to be trustworthy. This is especially useful for assessment systems which attribute to the user a specific quality (e.g., successful passing of tests) where the identity of the respective user, the identity of the attributing component of the system, and the authenticity of the data must be provable to some other entity.

1.2   Complexity of Anonymity

The establishment of anonymity[3] usually requires a further component within the user adaptive system which carries out the procedure for anonymization. The user has to trust this single entity which is able to defeat the user's anonymity. From the user's perspective, a single entity may not be enough to inspire confidence. It can therefore be beneficial to include more than one entity in the anonymization process, distributing trust in the process among several entities in which the user trusts collectively (e.g., trust centers or other users).

To assess the anonymization process, Garvish and Gerdes [Gavish and Gerdes Jr., 1998, p. 301] define the *complexity of anonymity* according to the number of components which must collude in the anonymization process to defeat anonymity:

> "Define the system's *anonymity complexity* as the maximum number of colluding entities which cannot defeat the anonymity of the system. *Order-N anonymity*, represented as OA(N), indicates that N+1 entities must collude to defeat the anonymity."

By means of this measure, systems providing anonymity can be assessed. Some particular values are worthy of consideration:

OA(0): In systems with anonymity complexity 0, a single entity can defeat the anonymity. This is the case for *identification* (see *Chapter 4.1.1*) by the system, where each component is aware of the identity of the user and therefore a single entity can misuse this knowledge.

OA(1): In systems using *pseudonyms*, two entities must act jointly to defeat the anonymity: a component of the user adaptive system and the component managing the assignment of identity and pseudonym (i.e., a registrar for pseudonyms).

OA(N): is the case when N out of N+1 entities are unable to defeat the anonymity of the user. To assure his anonymity, the user has to include *one* trustworthy entity to the set of N components which might jointly defeat his anonymity. This procedure can adapt to individual requirements for anonymity and pseudonymity by including as many entities as are demanded.

With the complexity of anonymity, individual user requirements regarding the number of entities involved in the anonymization process can be expressed. A user adaptive system which supports complexity OA(N)

---

[3]If not differentiated explicitly, *anonymity* also covers *pseudonymity*.

is most beneficial for users, because it can adapt to the number of entities required by the particular user, thereby satisfying different user requirements for trust in the anonymization process.

1.3   Types of Anonymity

To be effective, anonymity must be introduced on different levels. For instance, a well designed system providing anonymity or pseudonymity in a secure and provable manner might be futile if it is used only by one person whose identity is known by means outside the system (e.g., when all terminals from which the system can be accessed are being videotaped).

Garvish and Gerdes [Gavish and Gerdes Jr., 1998, p. 306] mention three types of anonymity which must be considered:

Environmental anonymity is determined by factors outside the scope of the user adaptive system used. These factors include: the number of participants, their diversity, and previous knowledge about the participants. These factors cannot be altered by the design of the system and have to be observed while the system is operating.

For instance, a user model server which hosts the user models of several users can be required to check whether the number of user models is large enough and their diversity is low enough (i.e., the models have to be similar to some extent), which is a prerequisite for anonymity of users (and their models). In most cases, the user model server cannot rectify situations in which these conditions do not hold but it can inform the users that anonymity is at stake.

Content-based anonymity is present when no identification can be established by means of the exchanged data. The exchanged data might give clues for deanonymization, for instance, either by content (e.g., name, address, email address), structure (e.g., representation of data typical for particular users or software systems they use), or by sequence (e.g., repeating patterns which make it possible to link otherwise unconnected sessions).

As an example, a user adaptive system which serves electronic commerce purposes is usually dependent on the user's identity (e.g., name and address), either for charging for some services or for delivering goods. Obviously, if the user's identity is disclosed, anonymity cannot be present. Other clues to the user's identity can be the language used for queries, the style of writing, the topics involved, etc.

Procedural anonymity is determined by the communication protocol and the underlying communication layers. This type of anonymity can be provided by the system and should be considered in the design phase of the system. Related to this type of anonymity are the two independent directions of anonymity: *sender anonymity* and *receiver anonymity*. Sender anonymity is given if the sender of a message cannot be ascertained in the set of potential senders. Receiver anonymity means that the identity of the receiver is not known to the sender of a message. The latter is especially important for answering queries received under sender anonymity. Receiver anonymity is essential for user modeling purposes when *notifications*[4] about changes in the user model have to be transmitted to the application system which may not be connected to the user model at that time.

For instance, the address of the network node from which a user accesses a user adaptive system can reveal the user's identity if the node is unambiguously associated with the user. This should be prevented by means for ensuring procedural anonymity.

To protect the user's privacy through anonymity, these three types of anonymity must be present simultaneously within the user adaptive system.

1.4   Risks and Potentials of Anonymity

Anonymity in human communication harbors several risks, e.g. insults, copyright infringement, pretense of false identities, reduced social filtering, or missing credit for contributions (see [Anonymous, 1996], [Gavish and Gerdes Jr., 1998, p. 299]). Most of the arguments cited against anonymity are valid only within the context of group communication between persons. In the case of user modeling, a person interacts with a software system, and not with other people. Therefore, most of the arguments against anonymity do not hold in user modeling. Nevertheless, some of the known positive effects of anonymity [Gavish and Gerdes Jr., 1998, p. 299] may also apply to user modeling:

Anonymity reduces group thinking: The individual who is not biased by group pressure and who is acting on his own behalf may be more strongly differentiated from others, making the adaptation process of the user adaptive system more discriminating.

Anonymity has a deinhibiting effect: Entry barriers for users sceptical towards user modeling may be lowered (see Table 2.1 on p. 23).

---

[4]See *Chapter 7.2.1.4.*

Anonymity allows treatment of sensitive issues: The absence of personal stigmatization when treating sensitive issues anonymously within a user adaptive system (e.g., retrieving information about a disease) might encourage users to make more profitable use of the system.

To summarize the above effects, if users could interact anonymously with an adaptive system, they may be more willing to reveal personal (sensitive) information, providing a better foundation for adaptations. This can also lead to an increased sensitivity of the information about the users processed in the system which requires stronger or additional security measures.

The extent of interaction depends among other things on the user's belief in the privacy (in this particular case, anonymity) of the system. Remarkably, the user's belief in the anonymity is not only determined by expert assessment of the anonymization process but also by the user's own perception of his anonymity [Gavish and Gerdes Jr., 1998, p. 314]:

> "If anonymity is being used as a device to encourage a more open and frank exchange of information, a system's perceived level of anonymity may be more important than its actual anonymity."

These considerations lead to the following requirements for anonymity in user adaptive systems:

- Anonymous use of the user adaptive system should be provided to foster a franker and more extensive interaction with the system which leads to a stronger basis for adaptations.

- To increase the perceived level of a system's anonymity, it appears to be advantageous to include the user in the anonymization process (which leads to a complexity[5] of anonymity OA(N+1) for a system which previously showed a complexity of OA(N)).

2.   Pseudonymity

Chapter 4.1.1 covered levels of user identification ranging from *super-identification* to *anonymity*. From the perspective of user modeling, the range of pseudonymity (*latent identification* and *pseudonymous identification*) is of special interest. With the use of pseudonyms, it is possible to string sequences of consecutive user interactions with the user adaptive system (e.g., in different sessions), creating a sequence of interactions which also interlinks different sessions without revealing the identity of

---

[5] See *Chapter 4.1.2.*

the particular user. Pseudonyms also makes it possible to link a user model and the user being modeled without revealing the user's identity to components of the user adaptive system or to the user modeling system.

2.1 Types of Pseudonyms

Pseudonyms[6] can be further subdivided according to their bearers as well as to their uses [Pfitzmann et al., 1990]:

- person pseudonym

  - public person pseudonym
  - closed person pseudonym
  - anonymous person pseudonym

- role pseudonym

  - transaction pseudonym
  - application pseudonym.

Person pseudonyms are associated unequivocally with a person, whereby a person can bear more than one pseudonym. In the case of *public person pseudonyms*, the association of pseudonym and bearer is publicly known (e.g., a telephone number). A *closed person pseudonym* is publicly known, but the identity of the bearer is only known to the authority issuing the pseudonym (e.g., a box number). *Anonymous person pseudonyms* can be obtained without revealing the identity of the bearer which will be the only entity which is aware of the relationship between the identity and the pseudonym (e.g., a self-chosen nickname in a chat discussion).

Role pseudonyms are associated with actions persons perform and can be shared among persons performing the same actions. A *transaction pseudonym* is valid only for a single transaction. A transaction pseudonym might be generated for a user of a kiosk information system (see [Fink et al., 1998] and [Fink et al., 1997]) which is valid for the transaction of this particular user with the system and will be discarded with the following user. In contrast, *application pseudonyms* last for several sessions with the same application system and can be different for different application systems.

---

[6]In this section, no distinction will be made between controlled and uncontrolled pseudonyms (see *Chapter 4.1.1*).

Role pseudonyms enable users to act in different roles (see Table 2.1 on p. 23) or to act on behalf of others for a certain period of time. Whereas transaction pseudonyms only last for a short period and are therefore of limited benefit for user modeling, application pseudonyms have an extended scope and are appropriate for long-term modeling. Person pseudonyms interlink all actions of a person in all his sessions with a user adaptive system. Even though pseudonyms are intended to conceal the identity of a user, the stream of information collected about *one* person may provide sufficient clues for deanonymization[7].

3.   Using Anonymity and Pseudonymity in User Modeling

Anonymity and pseudonymity offer considerable advantages for user modeling. By limiting or disguising the relationship between persons and their data, they reduce the demands made by laws, guidelines, and ethics. In addition, by satisfying user demands for privacy (see *Chapter 2.3*), they can lead to better acceptance of user adaptive systems.

The enforcement of anonymity and pseudonymity in user adaptive systems means that the current architecture of user adaptive systems and user modeling systems must be considered and new means and procedures for establishing anonymity and pseudonymity must be developed. Proposals for meeting these requirements will be made in (see *Chapter 6*).

---

[7]An example of deanonymization is given in *Chapter 7.2.2.4*.

Chapter 5

REQUIREMENTS FOR SECURITY

This chapter compiles requirements for the security of a user model, the user modeling system, and the data that is processed within them. Security in general information systems is a collective term for several related and sometimes overlapping areas. In this chapter, security will be subdivided according to the prevailing definition of *security in information systems* into the following three factors (see [Summers, 1997, p. 3], [Bertino, 1998, p. 199], [Pfleeger, 1989, p. 4], and [Dierstein, 1990, p. 138]):

- secrecy

- integrity

- availability.

Because the amount of user modeling functionality within user adaptive systems should be adjustable according to the user's changing preferences, user adaptive systems cannot rely on a fixed amount of user modeling functionality and must as well cope with missing user modeling functionality. The *availability* of a user modeling system (i.e., the quality that user modeling systems and their functionality are always provided to user adaptive systems) is therefore not considered in detail in this work. Risks caused by special user modeling techniques which endanger the availability of user modeling systems are discussed with regard to the user modeling system's internal integrity (see *Chapter 7.2.2*).

The requirements for *secrecy* in general information systems have been, and continue to be, discussed extensively in the literature. This is also the case for certain information systems (e.g., information systems

47

for statistical data, see *Chapter 7.2.2.4*) but not for user modeling systems. It is obvious that the sensitivity of the data processed in a user
model is mostly based on the relationship between the data and the user.
Therefore, two requirements are defined where the first, *anonymization*,
focuses on the secrecy of the relationship between the data and the user
and the second, *encryption*, is intended to ensure the secrecy of the data
itself. Furthermore, *confidentiality*, as a weakened form of secrecy, is
also discussed here. Confidentiality is described as granting particular
user model clients access to user model information which is kept secret
from the remaining clients. Thereby, responsibility for the maintenance
of specified segments of the user model can be transferred to particular
user model clients who share the information within these segments. As
the second constituent of security, the *integrity* of a user model (i.e., the
quality that all processed data is accurate and consistent with regard to
the world it describes) is discussed from the perspective of user model
clients as *external integrity* and from the perspective of developers of
user modeling systems as *internal integrity*.

In addition to the "higher-level" factors *secrecy*, *integrity*, and *availability*, several "lower-level" factors which can determine the security of
an information system also exist. Unfortunately, in many cases no clear
correspondence between the "lower-level" factors and the "higher-level"
factors can be found. Also, there is some disagreement as to what should
be included among the important "lower-level" factors, as can be seen
from the following table:

Table 5.1. Further factors which affect the security of information systems

	[Longley and Shain, 1987]	[Dierstein, 1990]	[Summers, 1997]	[Pfleeger, 1989]	[Gollmann, 1999]	[Leveson, 1995]	[Russell and Gangemi Sr., 1991]
access control	x	x	x	x	x	x	x
accountability	x		x	x	x		x
audit	x		x	x	x	x	x
authentication	x	x	x	x	x		x
authorization	x	x	x		x		
confidentiality	x	x	x		x		x
controllability	x	x				x	
correctness	x	x		x			
functionality	x	x	x	x			
identification	x		x	x	x		x
plausibility		x					
recovery	x	x	x	x		x	
reliability	x	x		x	x	x	x
robustness		x				x	
safety			x		x		x
supervision	x	x			x		
trustworthiness	x		x	x	x		
etc.							

The "lower-level" factors we consider especially relevant for security in user modeling will be discussed in the following sections.

1. Requirements for Secrecy

The concept of *secrecy* has not been adequately defined in the literature. It is therefore appropriate to offer some reflections on the concept *secret* before defining the requirements. One of the few definitions of a *secret* is that of Nelson:

> "One 'common sense' definition of a secret is some information that is purposely being kept from some person or persons. It is interesting to investigate the behavior and characteristics of secrets; this can lead to doubts about secrets being easily defined objects." [Nelson, 1994, p. 74]

As Nelson also points out [Nelson, 1994, p. 75], the relationship between information and secrecy is opaque as well:

> "Another interesting question is what piece of information contains or communicates a secret. The relationship between information and secrecy is complicated, as the following examples suggest.
>
> 1. If we cut a secret in half, is it still a secret? [...]
> 2. If we move a secret out of context, is it still a secret? [...]
> 3. If we collect enough non-secret information and process it correctly, we may have a secret. [...]
> 4. Some observers may already know something about a secret or have a good guess on it; in that case, a large secret can be communicated with very little information flow. [...]
> 5. Secrets can be communicated by very condensed codes, [...]
> 6. In encrypted communications, we can communicate large amounts of data with no secrecy leak, because there is another secret protecting the flow. [...]
> 7. Sometimes the information content of binary data is easy to extract because the data representation is an easily guessed standard. [...]"

In terms of user modeling, Nelson's concerns may have the following implications:

cf. 1.: Limited to the field of user modeling, the question is whether a segment of a user model is still a secret and how small the segments must be before they cease to qualify as secrets (see *Chapter 5.1.2*).

cf. 2.: The removal of the information's context (i.e. concealing the relationship between the user and his data through anonymization) was dealt with in the previous chapter. Information processed in user adaptive systems usually is classified as being secret only because of its relationship to an identifiable person (i.e., because the data is personal data). The data (anonymized, no longer personal data) processed in user adaptive systems (e.g., "an arbitrary user is interested in advice on disease X") is usually neither secret nor worthy of being kept secret (for instance, because it is widely known that information centers on disease X exist and that users regularly access information from these centers).

In the case of user modeling, moving the secret out of its context (i.e., anonymizing the information processed) releases the system from some of the requirements for secrecy.

cf. 3.: Accumulation of unrelated (i.e. anonymous) data is problematic in user modeling. According to Allen (see p. 11) user models ought to differentiate interaction across individuals. Therefore, they need to accumulate enough information about users through entries in the respective user models. The number of necessary entries and their content depends on the application system and the domain of the user adaptive system. With increasing number and diversity of entries, the differentiation across individuals improves, but the probability that the combination of the entries in a user model is unique (and different from entries in all other user models) increases as well. With a unique combination of user model entries, deanonymization, or at least inference of further entries of the user model, becomes possible (see the example of *Chapter 7.2.2.4*).

cf. 4.: Related to the issue of accumulation of data is the inclusion of knowledge about the environment of the modeled user which can lead to deanonymization of a user model with a unique combination of entries.

cf. 5.: User model entries can be highly complex, very large, and numerous (see [Pohl, 1998]). If, instead of the user model entries, we consider their relationship to a concrete user to be the secret, the secret may be encoded in a very condensed form. For instance, the encoding of the relationship as a bit sequence will not be longer than $l = log_2(n)$ for n anonymous user models. It is therefore possible to hide an identifying sequence of length l (for instance, a pointer to another user model containing identifying information) in the data which, thought to be anonymous, would actually make it possible to relate anonymous data to identifying data.

cf. 6.: Encryption of communication is just as important in user modeling as it is for communication in information systems in general. A discussion of the requirements for encryption in user modeling is given in *Chapter 5.1.1.2*.

cf. 7.: In the past, user models have commonly been implemented as add-ons to individual user adaptive application systems. For that reason, the encoding of the user model entries was only known to the developer of these systems. However, with the trend toward open user models which are applicable to several application systems, the user model entries must be standardized and documented. The encoding of the entries therefore no longer ensures secrecy.

As the above discussion shows, it is not obvious what should be treated as a *secret* in user modeling. Because of the vagueness of the term *secret*, we offer no definition of the term *secrecy in user modeling* in this book. Instead, requirements for the different aspects of secrecy in user modeling which support the security of the user adaptive systems are discussed in the following sections.

Shannon [Shannon, 1949, p. 656] divides "secrecy systems" into "concealment systems" (i.e. steganographic systems[1]), "privacy systems" which require "special equipment" (e.g., the encoding mechanism of a particular application system for user model entries) to discover the information, and "true secrecy systems" (i.e. *cryptographic systems*) where knowledge of the information is entirely contingent on knowing a smaller secret, for instance a cryptographic key. Among these secrecy systems, cryptographic systems are most appropriate for user adaptive systems, because the secrecy of these secrecy systems depends entirely on the knowledge of a cryptographic key. This key can easily be distributed over networks (for which, if necessary, it can also be encrypted) and can also be verified by cryptographic systems.

Simmons' definition [Simmons, 1992, p. 180] of *secrecy* does not mention the mechanisms or systems used for the establishment of secrecy:

"Secrecy refers to denial of access to information by unauthorized individuals."

Rather, it is based on the division of individuals (who can also be seen as different user model clients) into the groups of authorized individuals that are granted access to information, and unauthorized individuals. This definition does not mention explicitly what is to be kept secret and how to do so, but it mentions the individuals who are intended to share and to keep a secret. From the perspective of user modeling, this definition means it must be possible to group user model clients through authorization into a group which is able to act jointly to maintain certain user model entries which are unknown to the other (unauthorized) group of user model clients. Several such authorizations should exist, so that each user model client can be in at least one group which has access to a particular user model entry.

Nelson [Nelson, 1994, p. 75] also avoids defining a *secret* and focuses instead on the conditions which protect a secret:

---

[1]See [Menezes et al., 1997, p. 46], [Schneier, 1996, p. 9], or [Chapman and Davida, 1997].

"Whatever the definition of a secret is, it seems clear that if no information is passed from the holder of a secret to the observer who desires the secret, then no secrets are passed either."

Prevention of an information flow (within the user model) between two user model clients also prevents the exchange of knowledge about secret user model entries between these two user model clients. This means that Simmons' demand for authorization must be extended to include the condition that no user model client is allowed to be in more than one authorized group. Otherwise, an information flow between two groups could be established through a user model client which belongs to both groups.

In the following sections, further requirements for secrecy in user modeling will be developed from the previous descriptions of secrecy in user modeling and the mechanisms for keeping user model entries secret or confidential. For the scope of this book, *secrecy in user modeling* is defined to be composed of *denial of access* to information (i.e., user model entries and their relationship to an individual) and of *selective access* to information (i.e., *confidentiality* of user model entries which are shared between user model clients).

1.1 Secrecy through Denial of Access

Secrecy in user modeling can be achieved through denial of access to the processed information. Denial of access to information can either be interpreted as denial of access to the relationship between the user and the processed data or as denial of access to the information (i.e., user model entries) of a particular user. These two cases are dealt with in the following sections.

1.1.1 Secrecy through Anonymization

Anonymization[2] of the information processed by a user model system dissolves the relationship between a particular user and the data. The processed user model entries are no longer assignable to a particular user. This uncertainty about the relationship between a user and the processed data ensures that the data of any given user will remain secret. Therefore, secrecy through anonymization of the user modeling information can be required as a basis for the secrecy of user adaptive systems.

---

[2]For the scope of this section, *anonymity* also covers *pseudonymity*.

1.1.2 Secrecy through Encryption

The previous section covered secrecy of the user's information (i.e., the relationship between the user's identity and the user model entries) through anonymization. In many cases, anonymization of the user model information cannot be implemented, due to the purpose of the user adaptive system (e.g., user adaptive systems employed in electronic commerce scenarios where physical contact has to be established for certain transactions).

To protect personal data from inspection when it is exchanged between the user model and its clients, the information must be encrypted. Through the option of an appropriate cryptographic system (e.g., a symmetric or an asymmetric cryptographic system[3]), the authorized users of the information can also be determined before the encryption process.

1.2 Secrecy through Selective Access

In the previous two sections, the focus was on denial of access within a user adaptive system. Denial of access was described as denial of access with regard to unauthorized components of a user adaptive system by anonymization of users' information. When anonymization of the user model information is impossible or would be detrimental to the user (e.g., the information kept in the user model of a tutorial system might be advantageous for the user if presented to some other entity) the information must be kept personalized.

The encryption of the user model information is most useful for protecting the exchange of information between the user model and its clients. If encrypted entries are stored in a user model which can only be decrypted by particular user model clients, the user modeling agent would be inhibited in its ability to process the entries. Their integrity, for example, could not be checked (see *Chapter 5.2*).

Secrecy through anonymization or encryption of user model information was intended to deny access to the information for unauthorized components (see Simmons quotation on p. 52) of a user adaptive system (e.g., user model clients). It is characteristic of both methods that some components of the user adaptive system are excluded from the processing of information by a condition with a negative statement.

Another possibility is to specify via a positive statement which user model clients should be able to jointly maintain particular user model entries. All clients not mentioned explicitly through the authorization process should be excluded implicitly from the processing of these en-

---

[3]See [Menezes et al., 1997, 544], [Schneier, 1996, p. 4], or [Diffie and Hellman, 1976].

tries. This method makes it possible to specify and enforce the *confidentiality* of specific user model entries between particular user model clients. The joint maintenance of particular user model entries benefits user adaptive systems in two ways. Firstly, explicit personal data must be provided only once by the user, and secondly, user model clients can profit from the extensions which other user model clients have added to the model.

Possible modes for cooperation between two user model clients are shown in the following diagram (*cont(A)* denotes user model entries maintained by user model client A):

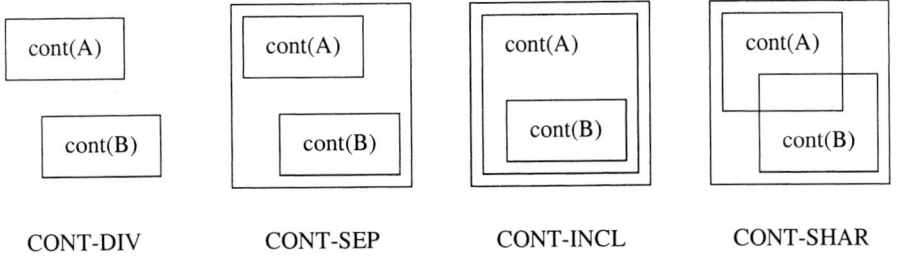

Figure 5.1. Modes of cooperation between application systems

The different modes are:

CONT-DIV depicts the mode where user model entries from client A and client B are completely unrelated, e.g., constituents of two different user adaptive systems. The user modeling agent is unable to correct inconsistencies between *cont(A)* and *cont(B)*.

CONT-SEP shows two clients maintaining entries in one user modeling agent without interfering. The entries are hosted by one user model without mutual reuse of entries by two clients and each user model client is itself responsible for the confidentiality of its entries. Nevertheless, the user modeling agent is able to make modifications in *cont(A)* in dependence on *cont(B)* and vice versa (for instance, if *cont(B)* contains an entry which is contradictory to an entry of *cont(A)*).

CONT-INCL denotes the mode where the user model entries of client B are a subset of the entries of client A. All entries made by B are also known by A and must also be kept confidential by A. The entries of *cont(A)* which are not in *cont(B)* are not accessible to B. Therefore, no requirements for the confidentiality of these entries must be set up with respect to B.

CONT-SHAR is the mode where the user model contains entries which are shared between (at least) two clients. The entries in the intersection of $cont(A)$ and $cont(B)$ are maintained jointly by the user model clients A and B and have to be kept confidential between them. Through these entries, an information flow exists between the two user model clients.

Which of these four modes is required depends on the particular user adaptive system, the type of cooperation between the components of this system, and the benefit of sharing user model entries between user model clients. Measures for supporting the confidentiality of user model entries are required to support at least one of these four modes. In addition to this basic requirement for confidentiality in user modeling, several other requirements, which focus on the effectiveness of the security features and their applicability for users when defining their individual requirements for the confidentiality of user model information, must be defined:

Confidentiality: The information (i.e., user model entries) which is provided by the user explicitly (e.g., through filling out forms) or implicitly (e.g., gained through the interaction with an adaptive application system) must be treated according to the user's individual requirements for the confidentiality of the information submitted. The user must be able to define which user model clients will be permitted to share particular information from his model (see the different modes in Figure 5.1).

Grade of confidentiality: Different grades of confidentiality might be required in order to reflect the different sensitivity of the processed information and the amount of trust placed in particular user modeling clients.

Flexibility: The confidentiality demanded of the processed information should be definable in a flexible manner to accommodate it to changing conditions (e.g., varying sensitivity of information, different user demands, temporary need for cooperation between clients, changing trust in application systems, etc.).

Scalability: The confidentiality of the system should be ensured in spite of the fact that clients are added to or removed from the user adaptive system. The mechanisms which ascertain confidentiality, in particular, should be independent of the number of clients.

User orientation: The process for defining demands for confidentiality should be intuitive and intelligible to the user who is intended to arrive at a definition based on his personal opinions.

Delegation of administration: To support the user in defining the confidentiality he demands, as much as possible of the administrative effort should be delegated to the system. The user should be asked only how he wishes to combine, refine, and extend existing definitions.

In *Part III, Solutions and their Applicability for User Modeling Purposes*, the compatibility and enforcement of the requirements for secrecy and confidentiality will be discussed. Possible ways of meeting particular requirements will be proposed and their applicability for user modeling will be described in detail (see *Chapter 7.1*).

2. Requirements for Integrity

The integrity of a user adaptive system is contingent on a multitude of factors which include the integrity of the user model, the clients of the user model, the user adaptive system which employs the user model, the domain of the user adaptive system, and the user model information. The number of factors involved and their diversity indicate that integrity (and therefore its requirements) cannot be defined in a concise manner. Even for more narrow fields, there are manifold definitions of *integrity*, as is evident from Campbell 's conclusion regarding the field of *database integrity*:

> "We've seen a list of 150 definitions of 'integrity'." [Campbell, 1995, p. 745]

Instead of adding another definition for *integrity in user modeling*, we will discuss the requirements for integrity for selected factors[4] (see Table 5.1 on p. 49) which we consider especially relevant for user modeling. Regarding the user model as the main component of a user adaptive system, integrity can be divided into *external integrity*, which is contingent on factors outside the user model, and *internal integrity*, which depends on the internal state and processes of the user model.

2.1 Requirements for External Integrity

The requirements for external integrity of a user model can be described from the perspective of the user model clients (i.e., the user adaptive application systems) which make use of the entries in the user model. The external integrity of the model is dependent on a complex of factors (see Table 5.1 on p. 49). Beyond the factors for integrity in general information systems, which are not mentioned in detail in this section, there are particular requirements which are of special relevance

---

[4]See [Summers, 1997], [Pfleeger, 1989], or [Castano et al., 1994] for a more extensive discussion of integrity in information systems.

for user modeling. The following is a compilation of these requirements for the external integrity of a user model:

Completeness: The entries in the user model must be complete with respect to the application system and domain in order to permit all adaptations the application system is able to perform. Obviously, this requirement is in contrast to the demand that a user model should be constructed implicitly in an incremental way (see Rich quotation on p. 30) to avoid distracting the users from their main task (e.g., information retrieval). Because the ability to cope with incomplete information about the user is contingent on the particular adaptive application system which employs the user model, this requirement is not considered further.

Consistency: The information in the user model must be consistent. At any given time a model must not contain an assertion about the user and its converse.

Correctness: Given a user model with the ability to generate new assertions from an initial set of assertions by applying rules which represent the domain (e.g., by means of a production system, see [Genesereth and Nilsson, 1987]), correctness requires that all assertions generated about the user are also valid in the domain of the adaptive application system.

Adequacy: On the analogy of a calculus in logic [Genesereth and Nilsson, 1987], adequacy of the user model is defined as given if completeness and correctness are present. Assuming completeness with regard to a specific domain can be achieved, for most user models it will be present only after an initial phase (of arbitrary length) in which the user model is constructed dynamically. During this phase adequacy is not given.

Timeliness: Extending the requirements for correctness and completeness is the demand for timeliness of the user model (entries). The application systems (and the user) must include user model entries which reflect the current characteristics of the user. The user model must be able to handle entries which change frequently and which can accept contradictory values in different states with respect to time.

Authorization: A user adaptive system in which several user model clients jointly maintain the user model should be able to confer different areas of responsibility within the user model onto different clients, possibly with some areas of responsibility shared between particular clients (see Figure 5.1 on p. 55). By authorization, the allocation of permissions to clients concerning different sets of user model entries can be formalized and enforced. In *Chapter 5.1.2*, authorization was introduced as a means for ensuring the confidentiality of user model entries. Authorization can be used equally well for the maintenance of the integrity of user model entries. For example, the permission to modify particular user model entries might only be granted to selected clients which are known to respect the integrity (or validity) of the entries.

Identification: Authorization makes it necessary to distinguish the different user model clients maintaining a shared part of a user model from each other. The identification of clients can be required on different levels (see *Chapter 4.1.1*).

Authentication: Authentication of the clients enables the user model to verify their identity. Furthermore, user model entries can also be authenticated, thereby enabling a retrieving client to verify the authenticity of an entry and/or the identity of the inserting client. This means that a client can verify that an entry was made by a particular client. For instance, an adaptive application system could verify that an entry which certifies a certain level of expertise was made by a competent entity and had not been changed (e.g., by the user).

Accountability: With different clients maintaining a shared user model, the accountability for modifications of a particular user model entry is essential for the accuracy of the user model. It must be possible to trace a specific user model entry to the client which is accountable for it or its modifications.

Supervision: The user should be able to control and supervise the user model and the user adaptive system in order to observe its functioning and evaluate its usefulness, check and correct the data processed within the user model, monitor the information flow, and interfere with the processing if necessary. Supervision therefore requires measures for inspecting and correcting the user model and its entries.

When these factors are taken into consideration, the external integrity of a user model can be substantially improved. Since a concise definition of *integrity in user modeling* could not be found, further factors should be added with respect to a given user adaptive system and its domain.

2.2 Requirements for Internal Integrity

The internal integrity of a user model depends mainly on the methods and mechanisms employed for the representation and processing of the data within the user modeling system which hosts the user model. Internal integrity is also influenced by constraints on the user model data caused by the adaptive application systems and the domains in which they operate.

The requirements for internal integrity of user models, and of the user modeling systems that host them, extend common integrity requirements[5] to include the following factors (see [Kay, 1995] and [Jones, 1989] for a discussion of several factors):

Data integrity: The integrity of the data must be considered while inserting, storing, modifying, deleting, processing, and retrieving data within a user model. A basic integrity condition is that all data inserted has to be retrievable (with unchanged value). As a further condition, the processing of the data is only allowed to produce new data consistent with the inserted data (e.g., in particular, the converse of an inserted data item must not be generated by a production system). After deletion or modification of the entries underlying a derivation, it must be possible to re-infer data which was derived on the basis of a particular model entry.

System integrity: The system implementing the user model (i.e., the user modeling system) has to ensure system integrity as a basis for the correct operation of the procedures it is executing (e.g., concurrency control).

Transition integrity: State transitions of the user model must either ensure integrity with respect to the complete execution of the intended state transition (e.g., prevention of deadlocks, compliance with information flow restrictions) or provide means to enable the user model to recover from imperfect state transitions (e.g., rollback mechanisms, backup and recovery procedures).

Inference integrity: User model clients which are authorized with well-defined access permissions for particular user model entries must not be able to obtain more information than intended, e.g., by means of inference or combination of access modes.

Constraint integrity: Constraints on the user model and its data (e.g., providing anonymous data) should be supported as far as possible (e.g., through prevention of deanonymization).

---

[5]For example, integrity requirements for databases, see [Ullman, 1988], [Maier, 1983], [Pernul and Luef, 1992], or [Cook and Kay, 1994].

Semantic integrity: Restrictions on values of user model entries (e.g., a set of integer values for the age of the user) as well as restrictions on combinations of values of particular user model entries (e.g., age and permissions) or evolution of entries (e.g., strictly monotonically growing values for the user's age) should be respected.

Alteration integrity: Certain user model entries should be protected from alteration regardless of the authorization of the client (e.g., an identifier for the user being modeled or particular entries made by other clients). If protection from alteration is not feasible, alteration should at least be observable.

In *Chapter 7.2*, these requirements will be discussed in detail. Solutions for requirements which have been implemented in different user modeling systems will be discussed and examples given. Possible solutions for requirements which have not been met so far are proposed and their applicability for user modeling is discussed. Requirements which are incompatible with other requirements for integrity or incompatible with requirements for secrecy will be examined and their pros and cons weighed against each other.

3. Requirements for Availability

User adaptive systems pose no additional requirements for availability in comparison to general information systems. Factors ensuring availability for general information systems have been described in the literature (see [Burns et al., 1992], [Leveson, 1995], [Pfleeger, 1989], [Gollmann, 1999], and [Summers, 1997]) and are not further considered in this work. Because user adaptive systems cannot rely that user modeling functions are always present – depending on the user's current preferences – the availability of user-selected user modeling agents and the functions they provide cannot be guaranteed due to the user. We discuss factors which peril the availability through certain user modeling techniques with regard to the user modeling system's internal integrity in *Chapter 7.2.2*.

III

Solutions and their Applicability for User Modeling Purposes

The structure of this part of the book corresponds to that of *Part II, Requirements for Security and Privacy in User Modeling*. Wherever possible, solutions for meeting the requirements outlined in the corresponding chapters of the previous part are proposed here. Requirements which cannot be satisfied by user modeling alone are pointed out (e.g., the requirement for *completeness* of the user model information), and mutually exclusive requirements, such as those for *confidentiality* and *integrity*, are contrasted.

In *Chapter 6*, solutions for the requirements regarding the different types of anonymity (i.e., environmental, content-based, and procedural anonymity), complexity of anonymity, and levels of anonymity are discussed. The value of the *mix technique* introduced by Chaum in providing *procedural anonymity* for a wide range of user adaptive systems is demonstrated. To make this mix technique available for user modeling, we implemented the mix technique which ensures the procedural anonymity of messages in the KQML language used for exchanging information between components of the user adaptive system. To accomplish this, the KQML language was extended to the *SKQML* language, which makes it possible to exchange encrypted and authenticated messages – a prerequisite for the *KQMLmix* implementation. The properties of sender anonymity and receiver anonymity provided by the implementation are discussed with respect to their importance for user modeling purposes. The implementation makes it possible to include the components of the user adaptive system and the user in the anonymization process. Not only does this enable the user to commit the user adaptive system to a particular complexity of anonymity, but it also permits the inclusion of the user in the anonymization, giving the user greater confidence in his anonymity.

Chapter 7, describes solutions for the requirements for secrecy and integrity of user modeling systems and of the information these systems process. Methods for maintaining secrecy through denial of access and through selective access (i.e. confidentiality) are proposed and their applicability for user modeling is discussed in detail.

Secrecy through *denial of access* to the information processed (i.e., exchanged between components) in a user adaptive system is achieved by encryption. An existing software library for exchanging information via the KQML language was extended by means of the *Secure Sockets Layer* making encrypted and authenticated communication in electronic networks possible. Since the use of this extended *SKAPI* software library requires only minor modifications of the components of the user adaptive system, it can be applied to a wide range of systems. It enables a flexible use of encryption and authentication algorithms which can be determined by the application system and the user model without being limited to the fixed infrastructure provided on the network layer for such purposes.

Secrecy through *selective access* to user model information means that the components which should be able to operate on particular user model entries by dedicated actions (e.g., *read, delete*) are specified, thereby ensuring confidentiality of the particular entries between these components. Some well-known models from the security literature for noninterference, access control, and information flow control are described and supplemented with examples of user modeling. For the sake of wider applicability, an access control model which acts as a filter between the user model and its clients was chosen for implementation, because this reduces the demands[6] on the user model and the user modeling system which hosts it. The role-based access control model offers a high degree of flexibility and comprehensibility. It can be used for authorizing the user model clients and for representing the users being modeled in the different roles they assume while interacting with user adaptive systems.

Considering the wide variety of representation and inference techniques as well as user modeling methods and the general scope of this work (which does not focus on a particular user modeling system), it has not been possible to meet all the requirements outlined in *Part II*. Instead, noteworthy solutions for the requirements implemented in different user modeling systems are summarized in *Chapter 7.2*. Also, the inherent partial contradiction between confidentiality and integrity is outlined.

---

[6]In comparison to information flow control models.

Chapter 6

SOLUTIONS FOR ANONYMITY AND PSEUDONYMITY

In this chapter, solutions for the requirements of anonymity and pseudonymity given in *Chapter 4* are presented. The solutions proposed here are independent of particular user modeling systems and user adaptive systems. Hence, requirements which depend on the type of adaptive system, its domain, or the user modeling system employed are discussed only in terms of features common to many such systems. Ways of using the implementation in providing *environmental anonymity* for a wide range of user adaptive systems are described. The *KQMLmix* implementation also makes it possible to include components of the user adaptive system and the user in the anonymization process, giving the user greater confidence in the anonymization process.

1. Anonymity

In the following sections, ways of achieving the different types of anonymity required in *Chapter 4.1.3* are discussed. Solutions which apply to the majority of user adaptive systems and the user models employed by them are discussed in detail, whereas solutions that depend on particular systems are only touched on briefly.

1.1 Environmental Anonymity

The technical means of user adaptive systems are inadequate to ensure environmental anonymity (see *Chapter 4.1.3*) since this type of anonymity is contingent on such administrative factors in the environment of user adaptive systems as: the number of users, the diversity of the users, the temporal sequence of interactions, the types of application systems involved, and the data processed.

In some cases, user adaptive systems can be enabled to detect conditions critical to anonymity (for instance, detect potential deanonymization and prevent it, see *Chapter 7.2.2.4*). However, mitigating such conditions usually lies beyond the means of the system and must be handled in the environment in which the user adaptive system operates.

1.2   Content-based Anonymity

Content-based anonymity can be further subdivided into *formal anonymity* and *contextual anonymity*. Formal anonymity involves removing all unique identifiers and identifiers which are unique in combination from the exchanged information. For instance, the name of a user might serve, perhaps in combination with the address, as a unique identifier for that user. All information exchanged between the application system and the user model must be purged of such identifiers in order to protect the user from being singled out within an anonymity set (see *Chapter 4.1.1*). When trustworthy application systems submit information without scrambling[1], this might be achieved through filters which sort out such information. For user models serving application systems which operate anonymously and application systems which depend on identifying information, a compartmentalized user model, where anonymous and identifying information is kept separate, is appropriate. This approach will be discussed in *Chapter 7.1.2*.

Contextual anonymity is present when no deanonymization by means of the exchanged message content is feasible. Deanonymization often follows the pattern of selecting (combinations of) attributes of single occurrence and assigning these attributes (e.g., user model entries) to entities (e.g., users) by integrating knowledge about the environment. An example of deanonymization which uses the content (i.e., user model entries) is given in *Chapter 7.2.2.4*. Because procedures for this type of anonymity must be developed in dependence of the respective user adaptive system and user model, no solutions common to all scenarios can be proposed.

1.3   Procedural Anonymity

To provide procedural anonymity, any information on the communication layer which might provide clues to the sender's or receiver's identity must be concealed. The necessity for this type of anonymity becomes evident when we consider the amount of research on procedural anonymity for the special case of Internet usage. In the following pages, several

---

[1]Scrambling might be performed, e.g, through encoding in an application dependent format.

implementations and their most important mechanisms for providing procedural anonymity for different applications are described:

Anonymizers for web access increase the complexity of anonymity OA(N) (see *Chapter 4.1.2*) by (only) 1 while serving as an intermediary between the web browser and the web server. Current systems[2] route requests through *one* proxy which intermits the relationship between client and server and establish a complexity of anonymity of OA(0) where there had previously been no anonymity whatever. All information exchanged between one client and several servers is routed through one node (i.e., the Anonymizer) which must be trusted to not reveal the identity of the client.

LPWA: The *Lucent Personalized Web Assistant* acts as an intermediary between the web browser and personalized Web services (see [Gabber et al., 1997] and [Gabber et al., 1999]). It extends the mechanism of an *Anonymizer* (see above) by generating a different pseudonym, a password, and also an email address for each personalized web service the user accesses through the LPWA and thereby conceals the identity of the user. Unfortunately, all personalized information is also routed through only one node (i.e., the LPWA server) which has to be trusted. The complexity of anonymity with this approach is also OA(0).

Anonymous Remailers allow users to send email messages without revealing their identity (i.e., email address) to the receiver (see [Chaum, 1981], [Gülcü and Tsudik, 1996], and [Mazières and Kaashoek, 1998]). In addition to the two solutions described above, an anonymous remailer can do more than act as an intermediary between sender and receiver. Several anonymous remailers may be combined to a sequence (of length n) through which messages are routed, thus establishing a complexity of anonymity OA($n - 1$). The messages are encrypted in a way that conceals the relationship between sender and receiver of a message but allows each remailer in the sequence to decrypt the information needed for routing the message. This means that remailers within the sequence are able to determine their direct neighbors in the sequence (i.e., their predecessor and their successor), but not all constituents of the sequence. The mechanism used with anonymous remailers will be covered in the following sections.

Onion Routing provides anonymity and secrecy on the network layer (see [Goldschlag et al., 1999] and [Syverson et al., 1997]). It is based

---

[2]See http://www.anonymizer.com , http://www.rewebber.de .

on a mechanism similar to that employed with anonymous remailers, with several restrictions. Between the numerous intermediaries which intermit the relationship between sender and receiver, symmetrical encryption is employed, because this reduces processing time, to keep the exchanged information secret from a network observer and the intermediaries. For this purpose, after an initial phase, the sequence of intermediaries is kept stable and provides complexity of anonymity $OA(n - 1)$ for a previously determined number n of intermediaries. With the number and the sequence of intermediaries, a proxy which can provide an *anonymous connection* between the sender and the receiver must be configured prior to its use. Using a pre-configured proxy is convenient for application systems because of its transparency. However, if the parameters of this connection (e.g., the complexity of anonymity or the receiver) are changed, a new proxy must be established with the new parameters. For a user model server which hosts x user models of which each wishes to communicate anonymously with y application systems, the number of necessary proxies is $x \cdot y$. These proxies operate on the network layer (see Figure 6.6 on p. 92) and must be established by means which are external to the application system.

Crowds allows a group of users to browse the web in an anonymous manner (see [Reiter, 1998] and [Reiter and Rubin, 1999]) within an anonymity set. The browser requests are routed through a network which hides the link between browser and web server by a mechanism similar to those described above. The number of intermediaries, as well as the set of intermediaries used, is determined randomly and changes with every connection made from the sender to the receiver. The application system (and consequently the user of the user adaptive system) is not able to determine the parameters of the anonymization process. Another drawback is the encryption method used with *Crowds*, which allows each intermediary to gain knowledge of the information exchanged and keeps this information secret only while in transit[3] between the intermediaries.

This listing gives an overview of the state of the art for anonymization on the Internet and its different application systems. Each of the previously described mechanisms focuses on different aspects (see [Berthold et al., 2000] for an analysis of the different protection goals). *Anonymizers* and the *LPWA* allow for anonymity while browsing the Web. They offer con-

---

[3]A better approach can be found in JAP (Java Anonymity Proxy, [Berthold et al., 2001]) which keeps information also secret from the intermediaries.

venience (for instance, by generating pseudonyms automatically) within the limited application of web browsing. They offer anonymity only to a very limited degree (i.e., complexity of anonymity (OA(0)) and do not keep the information secret while in transit. *Anonymous Remailers* introduce encryption mechanisms to protect the secrecy of the exchanged information. Information is not only kept secret while in transit, but is also kept secret from the intermediaries involved. In addition, the user is able to define the number and sequence of the intermediaries to be used for anonymization of email traffic. *Onion Routing* generalizes these mechanisms in a way that allows various application systems to use the Internet anonymously (through TCP, see Figure 6.6 on p. 92), regardless of the specific protocol the application system uses. This versatility has two drawbacks: First, it offers no means for configuring the anonymization process provided to the application system, and second, a proxy is dedicated to a connection between *one* sender and *one* receiver. *Crowds* implements a mechanism similar to that introduced with *Anonymous Remailers* for the specific case of web browsing via a proxy which routes the browser's requests through a network of other *Crowds* participants. The generation of an intermediary sequence cannot be influenced by the user and the information processed is not kept secret from the intermediaries.

This comparison shows that the implementations that have been discussed so far (in this work) are either designed for specific application systems (e.g., web browsing through LPWA) or for anonymous access to the Internet in general (e.g., through Onion Routing). All implementations include elements which are appropriate for user modeling (e.g., the automatic generation of pseudonyms or the independence of the proxy from the application system) but no implementation offers all aspects simultaneously. In the following sections, we describe the KQMLmix implementation. This implementation combines factors of the implementations described above which are considered to be important for user modeling purposes: sender anonymity, receiver anonymity, secrecy, authenticity, and the dynamic configuration of these factors.

2. Procedural Anonymity through Mixes

Anonymity is contingent on the ability to remain incognito within an anonymity set (see *Chapter 4.1.1*). This requires uniformity of the information exchanged between the communication partners. However, uniformity of the exchanged messages is not compatible with the generally different contents which should be exchanged between the communication partners. For this reason, a new component is included in the user adaptive system which makes it possible to handle messages uniformly and which conceals the relationship between sender and receiver.

Several techniques have been proposed with different focuses regarding sender anonymity or receiver anonymity in communication networks.

With *Implicit Addresses and Broadcasting* (see [Farber and Larson, 1975] and [Pfitzmann and Waidner, 1987]) all potential recipients receive the messages emitted by a sender. Since the message has been prepared cryptographically, only the intended recipient is able to perceive that it is the addressee and is able to decrypt the message. In this way, receiver anonymity is ensured with respect to an observer capable of inspecting all messages exchanged. The number of messages to be transported within the communication network with this technique is the product of *potential* recipients times the number of messages destined for any recipient. Therefore, this is feasible only in networks with either few communication partners or little traffic. Another drawback is the lack of sender anonymity (the recipient is able to determine the sender of a message).

DC-Networks (see [Chaum, 1988] and [Pfitzmann and Waidner, 1987]) superpose a message with previously exchanged secret keys from each participant of the network. This provides *information-theoretic* sender anonymity in exchange for a massive amount of key administration for a previously defined anonymity set.

The previously described techniques are appropriate for user modeling to a limited extent only. They provide sender anonymity or receiver anonymity, but not both simultaneously. Furthermore, since they apply to fixed sets of participants only, they are not suited for an open network where user adaptive application systems can be removed from or added to the user adaptive system. The mix technique, which is described in the following sections, is more applicable.

2.1   The Mix Technique

The mix technique was introduced by Chaum as a technique:

> "[...] that allows an electronic mail system to hide who a participant com-
> municates with as well as the content of the information – in spite of an
> unsecured underlying telecommunication system. [...] One correspondent can
> remain anonymous to a second, while allowing the second to respond via an
> untraceable return address." [Chaum, 1981, p. 84]

This technique provides sender anonymity as well as receiver anonymity by means of asymmetric cryptography (i.e., public key cryptography, [Menezes et al., 1997, p. 544], [Schneier, 1996, p. 4], [Diffie and Hellman, 1976]). The main task of a so-called *mix* is to serve communication partners with an intermediary which collects messages from different senders and forwards those messages to the respective receivers after re-shuffling the sequence of the messages. The main actions of a mix include [Chaum, 1981]:

1 receipt of n messages from different senders

2 decryption of the messages

3 change of the sequence of the messages

4 dispatch of the messages to the respective receivers.

In the following, the main actions are described in more detail:

Receipt of n messages: The mix waits for n messages from m different senders, where n ≥ m. The number n of buffered messages and the number m of different senders depend on the number of participants, the traffic, the latency, and the probability of anonymity which should be achieved (see [Kesdogan, 2000], [Gülcü and Tsudik, 1996], [Kesdogan et al., 1998], [Abe, 1998] for calculations).

Decryption of messages: The use of an intermediary can conceal the sender identity from the receiver and vice versa. For an observer capable of inspecting the messages routed through the network (e.g., the messages which are handled by the mix), the relationship between sender and receiver is obvious. To prevent this linking of sender and receiver by means of the message's content, encryption is used to forestall inspection while the message is in transit through the network. The algorithm for encryption and decryption is described in *Chapter 6.2.3*. When layered public key encryption is used, the mix gains no knowledge of the processed message's content.

Change of sequence: Despite encryption, an observer of the mix component is able to relate incoming and outgoing messages (and therefore sender and receiver) by their sequence. The change of the message sequence in a random manner impedes this relation. Since similar clues might be acquired on the basis of the message length, messages should be padded to uniform length (see below).

Message dispatch: The decrypted messages are forwarded to the respective receiver. To prevent undue latency while waiting for n messages (see 1.) dummy messages might be generated and sent to arbitrary receivers which must ignore such messages [Franz et al., 1998]. Even with n-1 dummy messages, receiver anonymity (concerning an observer of the network) is given.

The following figure shows the process scheme of the mix component.
Messages from different senders are received, decrypted (illustrated by
removing the box frame in Figure 6.1), mixed, and dispatched to the
receivers:

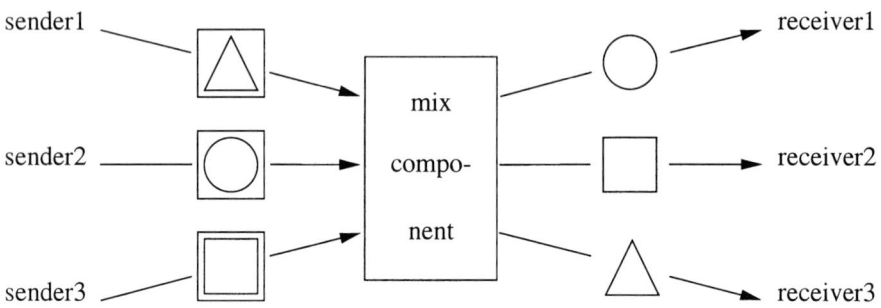

Figure 6.1. Mix scheme

The process shown in Figure 6.1 contains one mix and provides a
complexity of anonymity of OA(0) (see *Chapter 4.1.2*), because one mix
can defeat anonymity since the relationship between sender and receiver
can be established by means of the message routed through this mix.
To increase the complexity of anonymity, several mixes can be used in
a sequence. This enables the user to adjust the system to his expectations regarding complexity of anonymity. The following figure shows an
example of OA(3) with four mixes:

Figure 6.2. Mix sequence

Three out of these four mixes are unable to defeat anonymity. Each mix
only has knowledge about its direct neighbors, i.e., its predecessor (which
can be the sender) and its successor (which can be the receiver). To relate
the sender to the receiver of a message, knowledge of all four mixes is
required. With that knowledge, the partial sequences of predecessor,
mix, and successor can be joined to a sequence which relates the sender
to the receiver. It is therefore possible to defeat anonymity under certain
conditions (for instance, when *all* mixes agree to dissolve the anonymity
of the relationship between sender and receiver for a particular message).

For an observer which can only inspect the messages exchanged between mixes (i.e., while being transported via the network), deanonymization is not possible. In the following sections, the mix component we developed especially for user modeling purposes is described.

2.2 The Secure Knowledge Query and Manipulation Language (SKQML)

2.2.1 The Knowledge Query and Manipulation Language (KQML)

The *Knowledge Query and Manipulation Language (KQML)* (see [Finin and Weber, 1993], [Labrou and Finin, 1997], and [Covington, 1998]) was proposed as an interface language for user modeling agents at the *User Modeling Standardization Workshop*[4] at the Fifth International Conference on User Modeling [UM96, 1996]. KQML has found application as an interface language between application systems and user modeling agents (e.g., [Paiva and Self, 1995], [Pohl, 1998, p. 206]). An example of a KQML message used in the BGP-MS user modeling shell system is given in [Pohl, 1998, p. 207]:

```
(ask-if :sender    tcp://diva:8094
        :receiver  tcp://asterix:8091
        :language  VI
        :content   (SBUB "dangerous(shark56)")
        :reply-with query23)
```

A KQML message is a LISP-like [Steele, 1990] structure which starts with a so-called *performative* (e.g. *ask-if*) and is followed by an arbitrary number of *keyword value pairs* (e.g., *:reply-with* and *query23*). The performative defines how the value of the *:content* value has to be processed, whereas the *:language* value defines the language in which the *:content* value is expressed. With the *:reply-with* value, the receiver of the message is asked to include an equal *:reply-to* value in the reply in order to allow the original sender to synchronize related messages. From the example it is obvious that the sender (e.g., `tcp://diva:8094`) as well as the receiver (e.g., `tcp://asterix:8091`) of the KQML message are specified by their network nodes (`diva` and `asterix`) and their port numbers (`8094` and `8091`). These values can give clues to the identity of the user of the adaptive system. The following sections cover measures

---

[4]See the *Results of the Workshop "Standardization of User Modeling Shell Systems"* (`www.ics.uci.edu/~kobsa/papers/1996-kobsa-pohl-fink-rfc.pdf`) on `http://www.um.org/conferences.html` .

which support procedural anonymity through hiding these values though messages can still be exchanged between user modeling components.

Because KQML is deemed to be a standard[5] for user modeling agents and because of its flexibility it was chosen as a language for communicating with the mix component[6]. This enables components of a user adaptive system (e.g., application systems, user modeling agents) to use the mix without modifying the ways in which communication takes place. The extensions made to KQML to specify the parameters required by the mix are described in the following section.

2.2.2 Extensions to KQML

The KQML specification allows for extension of the set of performatives as well as the set of keywords. The mix makes use of the following additional performative and keywords which this work introduces (with the exception of the *:content* and *:language* keywords). The performative and keywords are briefly described in the following table and are covered in detail in the following sections of this chapter:

---

[5]KQML is currently used in the user modeling shell systems BGP-MS (see *Chapter 8.2*) and TAGUS (see Table 1.1 on p. 13).
[6]Despite the limitation of the mix component to KQML, it is denoted *mix* for short.

Table 6.1. SKQML, extensions made to KQML

mix-it	The performative *mix-it* instructs the mix to process the message either in the way described in *Chapter 6.2.1* or if the keywords *:mix-list* or *:rpi-list* are present, to prepare the message sent as the *:content* value for routing through other mixes.
:language MIX	The value advises the mix to apply Base64 decoding to the value of *:content*, and then to decrypt it with its secret key (Base64 encoding keeps the message parsable despite encryption).
:content	The value of the *:content* keyword contains either a message to be prepared for routing through further mixes or an encrypted message for the current mix which is intended to be decrypted and dispatched.
:mix-list	An application that is not aware of cryptographic functions is able to send a message to a mix, assigning it to prepare the message for routing through several mixes. The value of the *:mix-list* keyword consists of a sequence of mixes which ought to be used.
:rpi-list	With a sequence of mixes as the value of the *:rpi-list* keyword, the application can specify the mixes through which the response to this message ought to be routed.
:signature	The value of the *:signature* keyword is a Base64 encoded signature of the *:content* value which enables the receiving mix to prove the authenticity of the message.
:RPI	The value of the *:RPI* keyword contains the Base64 encoded *return path information* necessary for receiver anonymity.

Details on these keyword value pairs will be given in the following section. Two examples of messages for a mix are given below. The first is a request from an application system which is unaware of the cryptographic functionality required for preparing a message to be routed through a sequence of mixes. The second is an example of a message which has already been prepared for routing through mixes:

```
(mix-it :sender    application34
        :receiver mix1
        :language MIX
        :content  RTE1MzdO...GiZQ==
        :mix-list (mix1 mix34 mix2)
        :rpi-list (mix34 mix3 mix5))


(mix-it :sender    mix5
        :receiver  mix3
        :language  MIX
        :content   QWNQeHAO...oOOl4=
        :signature BBICDH+8...4D+Yw=
        :RPI       1S8md5lo...LUJTw=)
```

Similar extensions of KQML which focus on the authenticity of messages and aspects of key exchange but not on encryption have been proposed in [Finin et al., 1995]. In the following, the acronym *SKQML (secure KQML)* subsumes the extensions to KQML through the abovementioned keywords and the algorithms described below.

2.3   KQMLmix

KQMLmix[7] is a software package which implements the mix functionality described above. It is designed to support standalone components of a user adaptive system (e.g., mixes and intermediaries between mixes and application systems) and to be included in existing application systems. It is written in Java[8] in order to be usable with many operating systems. KQMLmix takes advantage of the *Java Agent Template Lite (JatLite)*[9] which was developed at Stanford University's Center for Design Research (see [Petrie, 1996] and [Jeon et al., 2000]). JatLite enables Java programs to exchange KQML messages and provides several features that are particularly convenient for user adaptive systems (e.g., message router, name server, asynchronous communication). As a provider for cryptography, the Cryptix[10] package for Java is applied.

In the following sections, the structure and the values of the *keyword value pairs* of SKQML messages which are processed by a mix will be described.

2.3.1   Message Forwarding

One of the main functions of a mix is the forwarding (dispatch) of received messages which have been encrypted in order to protect them from inspection while being transported (see p. 73). Each mix in a sequence removes one of the layers of encryption in which the message was wrapped (see Figure 6.2 on p. 74). By decrypting the processed message, the mix learns what mix precedes it in the sequence and which follows it, but knows neither the content of the message nor the originating sender (e.g., sender1) or the ultimate receiver (e.g., receiver2) – as long as the current mix is not marginal in the sequence. Neither can it determine its order in the sequence (despite the first and the last mix in the sequence) or the sequence's length.

---

[7]See http://www.KQMLmix.net .
[8]See http://java.sun.com .
[9]See http://java.stanford.edu .
[10]See http://www.cryptix.org .

The process of wrapping a message in encryption layers so that it can be routed through a sequence of mixes and the successive decryption by the mixes are described in the following paragraphs.

Message Encryption

The encryption of a message for a single mix involves a single step (see Figure 6.1 on p. 74).

A message m is encrypted in a hybrid cryptographic system[11] which encrypts the message m with the (symmetrical) Blowfish[12] algorithm and a key k_{BF}, denoted by: $m_{enc} = e_{BF}(m, k_{BF})$ with e_{BF} as the Blowfish encryption function. The key k_{BF} used for the Blowfish algorithm is encrypted with the (asymmetrical) ElGamal[13] algorithm and the public key $k_{EG,p,A}$ for an agent A, denoted by: $k_{BF,A}(k_{BF}) = e_{EG}(k_{BF}, k_{EG,p,A})$ with e_{EG} as the ElGamal encryption function. The key lengths are variable and are currently set to 128 bits for the Blowfish algorithm and 1024 bits for the ElGamal algorithm.

The ciphertext $ct(m, k_{BF}, k_{EG,p,A})$ of the message m, the symmetrical key k_{BF}, and the public key $k_{EG,p,A}$ is calculated by $ct(m, A) = e_{EG}(k_{BF}, k_{EG,p,A}) \circ e_{BF}(m, k_{BF})$ for a randomly chosen k_{BF}.

KQML messages, in particular the *:content* value of a KQML message, must be constructed with characters of a defined alphabet (see [Finin and Weber, 1993] and [Labrou and Finin, 1997]) and must not contain special characters. Therefore, the encrypted content of a KQML message is transformed while being transported. For the transformation, the Base64[14] algorithm is applied ($b64_{enc}(b)$ denotes the Base64 encoding of a binary array b and $b64_{dec}(s)$ the decoding of a string s). A *:content* value c ready for sending to an agent A within a KQML message is computed by $b64_{enc}(ct(c, A))$. The decryption of the value is achieved through the function pt: $c = pt(b64_{dec}(b64_{enc}(ct(c, A))), A)$.

Message Signature

To guarantee the authenticity (see *Chapter 5.2.1*) of the messages exchanged with mixes, the keyword *:signature* is introduced (see Table 6.1 on p. 77). The value consists of a hash value of the content value which is calculated by the RIPE-MD[15] algorithm.

---

[11]See [Schneier, 1996, p. 32].

[12]See [Schneier, 1996, p. 336] or [Menezes et al., 1997, p. 281].

[13]See [Schneier, 1996, p. 532] or [Menezes et al., 1997, p. 294]. Both algorithms were chosen because they are available without license restrictions.

[14]See Request for Comments (RFC) 2045: Multipurpose Internet Mail Extensions (MIME) Part One: Format of Internet Message Bodies.

[15]RACE (Research and Development in Advanced Communication Technologies in Europe) integrity primitives evaluation message digest, see [Schneier, 1996, p. 445], [Menezes et al.,

The signature value s of a message m (i.e., the *:content* value) and an agent A is calculated by $s = sign(m, A)$ (which can only be accomplished by agent A) and is verified by $verify(s, m, A)$ (which can be accomplished by each agent) by integration of the hash function and asymmetrical encryption (i.e., RIPEMD160 and ElGamal). The signature value is also transformed with the Base64 algorithm to meet the requirements of the KQML syntax.

After Base64 encoding, the signature value s which contains the signature for the *:content* value m can be added, together with the keyword *:signature*, to the KQML message. This value enables the receiver to check the authenticity of the message's content and also the sender's identity (see *super-identification, Chapter 4.1.1*).

Message Padding

The message sequence of received and dispatched messages is changed in a random manner in order to make it impossible to link incoming and outgoing messages (and thereby sender and receiver) of a mix on the basis of their sequences. However, although the sequences of incoming and outgoing messages are changed, these messages can be correlated based on the lengths of the messages. Therefore, outgoing messages are padded in order to make them similar. After padding, the *:content* values of the message to be dispatched are of uniform length and cannot be related to the *:content* values of received messages.

The padding algorithm is usually dependent on the encryption algorithm. To eliminate this dependence, the following algorithm is used for a given content value c for an agent A, the padding length l, and a random string s:

$$
\begin{aligned}
paddingLength \quad &:= \quad l - length(c) \\
paddedString \quad &:= \quad c \circ " \; " \circ firstNChars(s, paddingLength - 1) \qquad (6.1) \\
c' \quad &:= \quad b64_{enc}(ct(paddedString, A))
\end{aligned}
$$

After exchanging the *:content* of the respective message with the modified value c', the *:content* values of all messages are of equal length and cannot be used to relate incoming and outgoing messages.

Mix Sequence

The user must choose a set of mixes which he trusts to process the message in the defined manner without trying to defeat anonymity (e.g.,

---

1997, p. 350], and the Cryptix object
Signature.getInstance("RIPEMD160/ElGamal/PKCS#1").

$mix1, mix2, mix3, mix4$). He is able to choose n mixes, thus achieving a complexity of anonymity $OA(n - 1)$ (see *Chapter 4.1.2*). By giving the set of chosen mixes a certain order, the user creates the sequence ms. For a receiver which is aware of cryptographic functionality, ms should be extended by the receiver. This means that the message will be wrapped in an additional encryption layer which can only be dissolved by the receiver (in contrast to Figures 6.1 and 6.2 where the content is transported over the network without encryption in the final step). This keeps an observer from inspecting the message content sent from the last mix in the sequence to the respective receiver.

Sequence Encryption
Messages are usually routed through several mixes and must be encrypted for each distinct mix. For each mix, a layer of encryption which can only be dissolved by the respective mix is wrapped around the message. For the example in Figure 6.2 with the sequence of mixes $ms = (mix1, mix2, mix3, mix4)$, the encryption layers for a message m are depicted in Figure 6.3.

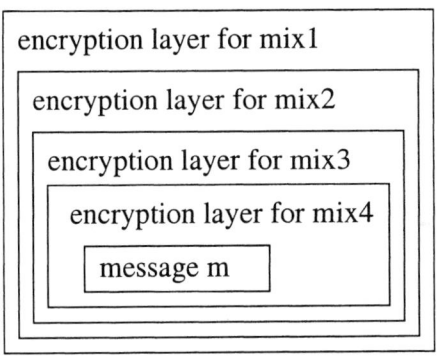

Figure 6.3. Encryption layers for a mix sequence

For user modeling components which are unaware of cryptographic functions, a mix can be advised to prepare a message for routing through a mix sequence. For instance, the message m which is to be routed through the mixes $mix2$, $mix3$, and $mix4$ can be generated by the following performative (see Figure 6.2 on p. 74 and the following section for the *:rpi-list* keyword):

$$
\begin{aligned}
\text{(mix-it} \quad &\text{:sender sender1} \quad &&\text{:receiver mix1} \\
&\text{:content } b64_{enc}(m) \quad &&\text{:language MIX} \\
&\text{:mix-list (mix2 mix3 mix4)} \quad &&\text{:rpi-list (mix4 mix3 mix2))}
\end{aligned} \qquad (6.2)
$$

Thereby, $mix1$ is advised to prepare the message m for routing through the mix sequence $(mix2, mix3, mix4)$. KQMLmix can thus be used by application systems which cannot be modified to include cryptographic algorithms.

The algorithm for the successive message encryption for a message m of a sender s for a sequence of mixes ms is:

$$
\begin{aligned}
i &:= 0 \\
m_0 &:= m \\
mixArray &:= makeArray(reverse(ms)) \\
mixArray[length(ms)] &:= s \\
while \quad i \quad < \quad & length(ms) \\
\{ \quad mix \quad &:= \quad mixArray[i] \\
sender \quad &:= \quad mixArray[i+1] \\
m_i \quad &:= \quad b64_{enc}(ct(m_i, mix)) \\
m_i \quad &:= \quad (\text{"mix-it :sender " } \circ sender \circ \text{" :content " } \circ m_i \\
& \qquad \circ \text{" :receiver " } \circ mix \circ \text{" :language MIX)"} \\
i \quad &:= \quad i+1 \\
\} & \\
m_{mix} \quad &:= \quad m_i
\end{aligned}
\tag{6.3}
$$

The message m_{mix} is ready to be sent to the first mix of ms (e.g., $mix2$) and is subsequently routed through the rest of the sequence ms to the last mix in ms (e.g., $mix4$).

To summarize the procedure for forwarding messages through a mix sequence – when messages which contain the $mix\text{-}it$ performative and which are formulated in the *MIX* language (see p. 77) are received by a mix, they are processed in the following manner:

1 (unpadding of the *:content* value)

2 decoding of the *:content* value with Base64 algorithm

3 signature verification

4 decryption of the *:content* value

5 change of the sequence of the messages

6 (padding of the *:content* value of the decrypted message)

7 message dispatch of the decrypted messages.

With the procedures described above, it is possible to route a message through a sequence of mixes. The message is always encrypted (as long as the mix is not at the beginning or at the end of the sequence) and cannot be inspected while being transported in the network. The mix technique veils the relationship between sender and receiver. To unveil the relationship, *all* mixes through which a message has been routed must collude.

2.3.2   Message Backwarding

As the above paragraphs demonstrate, (sender) anonymity can conceal the identity of a message's sender from the receiver or a network observer by using encryption and mixes. In the case of user modeling, many messages require a response which must be transmitted from the current receiver back to the sender (see *ask-if* and *reply* performatives, [Pohl, 1998, p. 207]). Therefore the current receiver needs to reply to a message without knowing the sender's identity.

Chaum [Chaum, 1981] proposes a procedure for anonymous return addresses where the sender (e.g. appl12) of a message has to maintain some values which the receiver also needs (e.g. um42) in order to prepare a reply to a query which was received from the anonymous sender (appl12). Gülcü and Tsudik [Gülcü and Tsudik, 1996] improved this procedure by including these values in the forwarded message, thereby relieving the originating sender (appl12) from the responsibility for maintaining these values (i.e., the sender becomes stateless with respect to these values).

With message forwarding, the sender uses asymmetrical encryption to encrypt the messages for all mixes in the sequence. The message contains all layers of encryption before entering the mix sequence. With message backwarding, the message is not wrapped in encryption layers, but is encrypted successively by means of symmetrical encryption. The mixes in the sequence encrypt the message instead of decrypting it as is done on the forward path. The (symmetrical) keys, different for each mix, for the encryption with the Blowfish algorithm are provided by the sender (appl12) of the message for which an anonymous reply is expected and are sent with that message. The generation and preparation of the different keys for a given key seed *ks* and a symmetrical key k_{BF} known only by the sender *s* (appl12) with respect to a mix sequence *rpi-list* (see performative 6.2 on p. 82 and the *:rpi-list* keyword) is expressed in the following algorithm [Gülcü and Tsudik, 1996]:

$$
\begin{aligned}
&i \ := \ 0 \\
&while \ \ i \ < \ \ length(\textit{rpi-list}) \\
&\{ \ \ i && := \ \ i+1 \\
&\quad symKeySeed && := \ \ i \circ keySeed \\
&\quad symKey && := \ \ e_{BF}(symKeySeed, k_{BF}) \\
&\quad symKeyArray[i-1] && := \ \ b64_{enc}(symKey) \\
&\}
\end{aligned}
\tag{6.4}
$$

The array $symKeyArray$ contains different symmetrical keys, each of which is to be used by a different mix of the sequence. The encoding and encryption of the keys is depicted by the following algorithm:

$$
\begin{aligned}
symKeySeed \quad &:= \quad length(rpi\text{-}list) \circ keySeed \\
rpi \qquad\quad &:= \quad b64_{enc}(ct(symKeySeed, last(rpi\text{-}list))) \\
i \qquad\qquad &:= \quad 1 \\
while \quad i \quad &< \quad length(rpi\text{-}list) \\
\{ \quad mix \qquad &:= \quad elementAt(length(rpi\text{-}list) - i, rpi\text{-}list) \\
mix_{next} \quad &:= \quad elementAt(length(rpi\text{-}list) - 1 - i, rpi\text{-}list) \\
rpi \qquad\quad &:= \quad symKeyArray[length(rpi\text{-}list) - 1 - i] \circ mix \circ rpi \\
rpi \qquad\quad &:= \quad b64_{enc}(ct(rpi, mix_{next})) \\
i \qquad\qquad &:= \quad i + i \\
\} & \\
rpi \qquad &:= \quad elementAt(0, rpi\text{-}list) \circ rpi
\end{aligned}
\tag{6.5}
$$

The variable rpi contains the *return path information* (see Table 6.1 on p. 77 and the example on p. 75) which is needed by each mix in the sequence in order to encrypt the message symmetrically and dispatch it to the next mix. The message to which an anonymous reply is expected (e.g., m in Algorithm 6.3 on p. 82) must be enhanced with the keyword value pair ":RPI " $\circ$ rpi in order to enable the receiver (e.g. um42) to send a reply to the anonymous sender (see the sample message on p. 75).

While the message m is being processed at the receiver (e.g. um42), the ":RPI" keyword indicates that an anonymous reply should be generated. The anonymous reply to the sender (e.g. appl12) with a given rpi is processed by the receiver using the following algorithm (where rpi as calculated in Algorithm 6.5, *message* the reply to be sent back, $x = deconc(x \circ y)$):

$$
\begin{aligned}
receiver \quad &:= \quad deconc(rpi) \\
rpi \qquad\;\; &:= \quad deconc(deconc(rpi)) \\
message \quad &:= \quad "(\text{mix-it :sender } " \circ getMyName() \circ " \text{ :receiver } " \circ receiver \\
&\qquad \circ ":\text{content } " \circ b64_{enc}(message) \circ ":\text{RPI } " \circ rpi \circ ")"
\end{aligned}
\tag{6.6}
$$

Mixes which are not at the beginning or at the end of the sequence *rpi-list* encrypt the message content symmetrically with one of the keys prepared in Algorithm 6.4 and encoded in Algorithm 6.5. The encryption follows the algorithm given below (with rpi and *content* as values of the according keywords of the received message):

$$
\begin{aligned}
rpi &:= pt(rpi, getMyName()) \\
symKey &:= b64_{dec}(deconc(rpi)) \\
receiver &:= deconc(deconc(rpi)) \\
rpi_{next} &:= deconc(deconc(deconc(rpi))) \\
content &:= b64_{enc}(e_{BF}(content, symKey)) \\
message &:= \text{"(mix-it :sender " } \circ getMyName() \circ \text{ " :receiver " } \circ receiver \\
&\quad \circ \text{":content " } \circ content \circ \text{ ":RPI " } \circ rpi_{next} \circ \text{ ")"}
\end{aligned}
$$

$$(6.7)$$

After being signed[16] by the current mix, the resulting *message* can be dispatched to the receiver mix and thus successively routed backward to the sender (e.g. appl12) along the given sequence of mixes *mix-list* which might be different from the sequence used on the forward path. With each mix in the sequence the message is again[17] encrypted symmetrically. Thus, no mix within the sequence (except the mixes at the beginning and the end) is able to gain knowledge of the content of the input message of Algorithm 6.6. Before an anonymous reply is delivered to the receiver (i.e., the sender of the reply request, e.g., appl12), the message has to be decrypted successively with the keys used for symmetrical encryption along the mix sequence. In contrast to the method proposed by Chaum [Chaum, 1981] where the keys must be stored until the message arrives, the keys in Gülcü and Tsudik's method [Gülcü and Tsudik, 1996] are calculated by means contained in the message, leaving the receiver stateless (see Algorithm 6.4):

$$
\begin{aligned}
rpi &:= pt(rpi, getMyName()) \\
n &:= deconc(rpi) \\
keySeed &:= deconc(deconc(rpi)) \\
i &:= 0 \\
while \quad &i \ < \ n \\
\{ \quad i &:= i+1 \\
symKeySeed &:= i \circ keySeed \\
symKeyArray[i-1] &:= e_{BF}(symKeySeed, k_{BF}) \\
\} \\
i &:= n-2 \\
while \quad &i \ >= \ 0 \\
\{ \quad content &:= e_{BF}(content, symKeyArray[i]) \\
i &:= i-1 \\
\}
\end{aligned}
$$

$$(6.8)$$

---

[16]See *Chapter 6.2.3.1.*

[17]Successive symmetrical encryption offers no better secrecy than single encryption. Through renewed encryption at each mix in the sequence, the outgoing message looks different than the incoming. This prevents an observer from relating these two messages.

With the algorithm described above, the message is symmetrically decrypted in a sequence which exactly reverses the sequence in which it was encrypted while passing through the mix sequence. Therefore it is equivalent to the input message of Algorithm 6.6. The fact that the mixes at the end of the sequence gain knowledge of this message is a design feature which enables components of user adaptive systems which are unaware of cryptographic functions to use the mix component. To close this gap (of encryption), several additions might be implemented independently:

- The communication between the user modeling component and the mix component can also be encrypted.

- The mix component and the user modeling component can be placed in a trusted environment.

- The mix component can be included in the user modeling component.

2.3.3   Known Attacks to Mixes

Several attacks to mixes are known. They attempt to establish a relationship between incoming and outgoing messages. Some of the attacks and ways of defeating them are listed below:

n-1 Attack

The mix does not start its process cycle until n messages have arrived (see *Chapter 6.2.1*), where n must be fixed with regard to the frequency of messages and maximum latency. An attacker might send $n - 1$ messages which are dispatched to receivers cooperating with the attacker. The process cycle starts when the next message arrives. Since the receivers of $n - 1$ messages are known to the attacker, the one message with a previously unknown receiver is the message which was not sent by the attacker.

This attack can be prevented when the process cycle of the mix is not only determined by the receipt of n messages but also by the condition that these messages are from up to n different senders. The identity of the senders can be proven by the transport medium (i.e., the value of the KQML keyword *:sender*). The KQMLmix implementation uses means of *super-identification* (see *Chapter 4.1.1*) when checking the signature of the sender for the content value contained in the *:signature* value.

Message Replay

An attacker can observe all input and output messages of a mix processed in one cycle. If a particular input message is fed into the mix by the attacker in more than one process cycle, it will always be dispatched to the same receiver (see Algorithm 6.3 on p. 82). Therefore, after a number of replay attacks enough evidence about the receiver of the message is gained to enable the attacker to identify the receiver (e.g., certainty about the receiver is present if only one and the same receiver in each process cycle receives only one message).

To prevent messages from being replayed, the mix has to keep track of previously sent messages. It is sufficient to retain a summary of the message rather than the whole message, for instance, as a hash value. It is also possible to retain the key used for symmetrical encryption of the message (i.e. k_{BF}, *Chapter 6.2.3.1*) or its asymmetrical encryption key (i.e. $e_{EG}(k_{BF}, k_{EG,p,A})$). The mix must compare this value of the current message with all values of previous messages (perhaps limited to a specific number of previous messages) and discard any message which has already been processed.

Length correlation

Another attack attempts to retrace the message sequence changes carried out by the mix. Inspection of the lengths of incoming and outgoing messages might give clues to the change of message sequence; message length decreases uniformly by removing one encryption layer of the message. The procedure for keeping the lengths of the messages uniform is described on p. 80.

This overview of known attacks to mixes shows that their vulnerability is dependent on the attacker model (e.g., a network observer or an active attacker). Since a detailed discussion of all possible attacks would not provide any specific results for user modeling purposes, we will not go into more detail here (see [Jerichow, 1999], [Kesdogan, 2000], [Gülcü and Tsudik, 1996], [Abe, 1998], [Franz et al., 1997], [Jakobsson, 1998], [Kesdogan et al., 1998], [Franz et al., 1998], and [Jakobsson, 1999] for a detailed discussion).

2.4   Sender Anonymity

When messages are sent through a sequence of mixes in order to conceal the relationship between sender and receiver of the message, sender anonymity (see *Chapter 4.1.3*) with complexity $OA(n - 1)$ can be achieved with n as the length of the mix sequence (see *Chapter 4.1.2*). Hence, the user of a user adaptive system is enabled to adjust the system to his personal requirements regarding anonymity by defining a mix sequence of sufficient length which is composed of components in which he trusts.

2.5   Receiver Anonymity

Components of user adaptive systems often send messages which require a reply [Pohl, 1998, p. 207]. These replies have to be delivered in the same anonymous manner as the request for the reply (see the *:RPI* keyword, *Chapter 6.2.2.2*). The same applies for *notifications* sent from the user model to an application system which is currently not connected to the user model (see *Chapter 8.4*).

With the *message backwarding* described above (see *Chapter 6.2.3.2*), the same complexity of anonymity can be achieved as with *message forwarding* (see *Chapter 6.2.3.1*). In addition, the sender is able to send a message (e.g., a *reply*) without knowing the receiver's identity (i.e., receiver anonymity, *Chapter 4.1.3*). Furthermore, different mix sequences can be chosen, making it possible to handle sender and receiver anonymity separately.

2.6   Mix Network

The mix component and its internal mechanism for the processing of messages were covered above. To be most effective, mixes must be arranged in a sequence (see Figure 6.2 on p. 74). The following paragraphs describe how mixes within a user adaptive system can be arranged into sequences.

2.6.1   Structure of a Mix Network

As described above, mixes must be arranged in a sequence of sufficient length to provide the complexity of anonymity demanded. Figure 6.2 shows a mix sequence which contains each mix only once and which is common to all senders and receivers. In general, mix sequences can:

- be different in length,

- be different for each sender,

- be different for message forwarding and message backwarding,

- vary with each message,

- contain each mix more than once,

- contain limited loops (e.g., the receiver of a dispatched message is the mix itself), and

- not be altered by a mix in the sequence.

Because mixes are not committed to a particular user or component of a user adaptive system, they may be arranged independently prior to being required by a particular user or component. The arrangement in which each mix can be a neighbor to a chosen mix in a potential sequence provides optimum flexibility within sequence generation. Furthermore, each mix should be accessible from each component (depicted in Figure 6.4 for UM1, UM2 and appl1 – appl5). Figure 6.4 shows a mix network with user modeling components sharing the network (dashed lines symbolize encrypted communication whereas solid lines symbolize communication which may or may not be encrypted, see (see *Chapter 6.2.3.1)).*

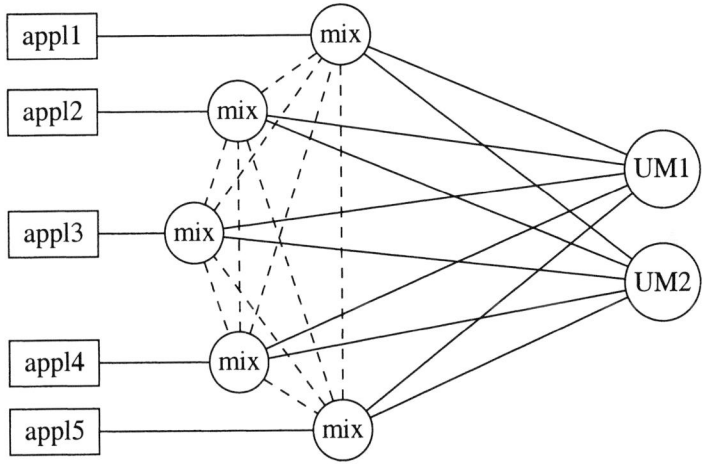

Figure 6.4. Mix network

With the structure depicted in Figure 6.4, it is possible to provide sender anonymity as well as receiver anonymity (see the previous sections) to both the user model or user modeling server (e.g. UM1) and the user adaptive application system (e.g., appl1, an adaptive information system). From these four possibilities, two are especially relevant for user modeling purposes:

1 sender anonymity for messages sent from UM1 to appl1

2 receiver anonymity for messages sent from appl1 to UM1.

(1.) Since the user model or user modeling agent may reside on the user's network node (instead in a remote user modeling server), the location (i.e., the network address) of UM1 must be concealed from appl1 when sending a message to appl1 (see *Chapter 6.2.4* and *Chapter 6.2.3.1*).

(2.) To send messages to UM1 appl1 must have some means to contact UM1 without knowing the network address of UM1. With the *return path information* (i.e., the *:RPI* value of an received message from UM1, see Table 6.1 and *Chapter 6.2.3.2*) appl1 is able to respond to messages sent from an anonymous user model(ing agent) (e.g. UM1). If appl1 is not only to respond to messages but also to start a message exchange, an *:RPI* value (which can be obtained from UM1) has to be provided to appl1 initially by the user.

A thorough discussion of generalized structures for mix networks is given in [Jerichow, 1999].

2.6.2   Mix Network including User Modeling Components

Mix Network including User Modeling Components The figure above shows an architecture where user modeling components which are unaware of cryptographic functions make use of a mix network (see Performative 6.2 on p. 82 and the solid lines in Figure 6.4). To prevent an observer from inspecting the messages exchanged between a user modeling component and the mix network, at least one of the methods described on p. 86 should be applied. Most effective is the incorporation of the mix component into the user modeling component. This makes unencrypted communication with an external component superfluous, and therefore not observable. Furthermore, the components of a user adaptive system can also serve as a mix in the mix network which produces messages autonomously. For an observer, it is not possible to decide which of the messages dispatched by a component are produced by that component[18] and which are only routed at the request of other components. The following figure shows a mixed approach where user modeling components (e.g., user adaptive application systems and user modeling agents) also implement mixes:

---

[18]This also includes dummy messages which are produced to prevent undue latency (see p. 73).

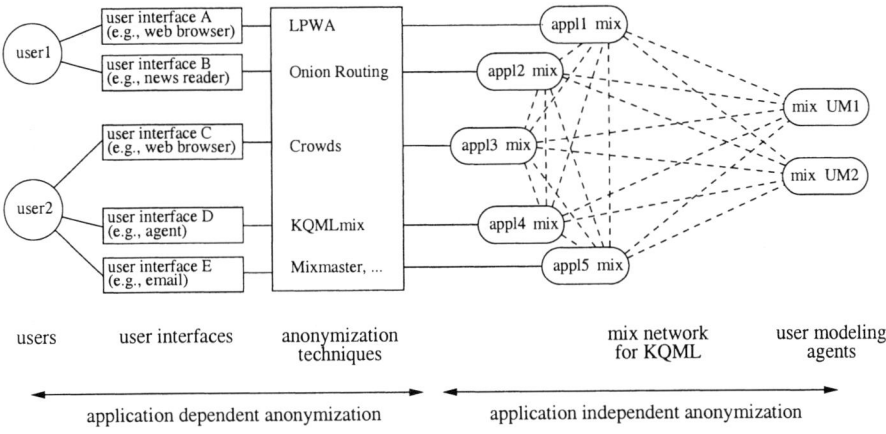

Figure 6.5. Mix network with included user modeling components

In contrast to Figure 6.4, the user modeling components (i.e., the user adaptive application systems appl1 – appl5 and the user modeling agents UM1 and UM2) take not only advantage of a mix network between them but also implement the mix network through inclusion of the mix components into the user modeling components. This inclusion yields several improvements:

- The content of messages exchanged between the user modeling component and the first or last mix in a mix sequence cannot be observed (see p. 86).

- Messages exchanged between the user modeling component and the mix network can be authenticated (see *Chapter 6.2.3.1*).

- Messages which originate from a user modeling component cannot be distinguished by a network observer from *dummy messages* (see p. 73) or messages which are routed through the mix network on behalf of another user modeling component (see *Chapter 6.2.3.1*).

So far only the application independent anonymization (see the right-hand side of Figure 6.5) of KQML messages exchanged between the user adaptive application system (e.g., a web server) and the user modeling agent have been discussed. To keep not only the user modeling agent anonymous from the user adaptive application system but also the user, similar techniques have to be applied between the application system and the user. In *Chapter 6.1.3* several application dependent anonymization techniques (see the lefthand side of Figure 6.5) have been discussed which are suitable to keep the user anonymous from an application system. Since these techniques are dependent on the application and its

particular protocol (e.g., HTTP[19], Email), they have to be chosen for
each application system.

3.   Pseudonymity

In the previous sections we explained how anonymity (see *Chapter
4.1.1*) within a user adaptive system might be achieved. In contrast to
other approaches providing anonymity (see *Onion Routing* and *Crowds*
in *Chapter 6.1.3*), the implementation of anonymity takes place on a
high layer in the communication model (i.e., on the *presentation layer*,
see the OSI reference model, [Pfleeger, 1989, p. 367]):

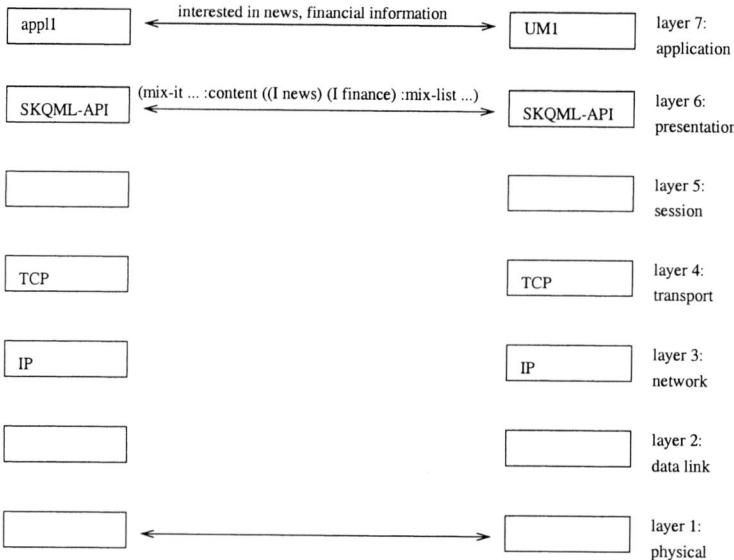

Figure 6.6.   Anonymity through SKQML within the OSI reference model

The implementation of the anonymization mechanisms on a high layer
enables the user modeling components to vary[20] these mechanisms in
cooperation with the communication system (i.e., the SKQML-API[21],
which forms the core of the KQMLmix implementation).   With the

---

[19]In addition to the anonymization techniques for web usage discussed in *Chapter 6.1.3* also
the KQMLmix implementation can be used to supply procedural anonymity for HTTP. We
developed a proxy which is able to route HTTP requests and the corresponding replies from
web servers through a mix network.
[20]In contrast to the solutions described in *Chapter 6.1.3* the parameters for the anonymization
process (e.g., the length of the mix sequence and the affected mixes) may change with each
KQML message.
[21]SKQML application programmer interface

methods described in the previous sections, both sender anonymity and receiver anonymity are feasible. Nevertheless, other levels of anonymity (see *Chapter 4.1.1*) can also be established. If a registrar for pseudonyms is included in the user adaptive system, it will be able to provide the system with controlled as well as uncontrolled pseudonyms (i.e., *latent* and *pseudonymous identification*). In addition to these levels of anonymity, *super-identification* is made possible by applying the *:signature* keyword (see p. 79) to messages exchanged between user modeling components. As we have seen, *super-identification* is also used in authenticating mixes (see *Chapter 6.2.3.1*, and p. 82).

4.   Summary

The solution proposed here for ensuring procedural anonymity (see *Chapter 6.2.3*) is more flexible than the solutions for anonymity summarized in *Chapter 6.1.3* which often permit only one level of anonymity. Mixes can be arranged into a mix sequence (see p. 80 and *Chapter 6.2.6.1*) based on the user's requirements for privacy. The components of the mix sequence can be chosen on the basis of the user's trust that they will carry out the mix procedure as defined and will not try to defeat anonymity. The length of the mix sequence can also be increased in order to convince the user that the anonymization process is effective.

In addition to the anonymization of the data processed, pseudonymization can also be provided, which is especially relevant for user modeling. With pseudonymous information, user adaptive systems can be used without revealing that (sensitive) information stems from a user which can be unambiguously identified.

The *KQMLmix* implementation can be used as an intermediary between components of a user adaptive system – making it usable for a wide range of components (e.g., including components which are not aware of cryptographic functions). The *KQMLmix* software package can also be incorporated within components, adding the mix functionality to these components and making the structure of the mix network more efficient.

Since the parameters of the anonymization process can be determined by the user modeling components via the SKQML language (on the *presentation layer*, see Figure 6.6 on p. 92) and changed dynamically, the KQMLmix implementation we have described here offers more flexibility than previously available solutions (see *Chapter 6.1.3*) which must be configured prior to their use. The user modeling components are also able to determine the parameters used with KQMLmix on the basis of a previous negotiation[22] process regarding the user's privacy demands. In particular, KQML messages may be exchanged between user modeling components under the following conditions:

- sender anonymity and/or receiver anonymity

- flexible complexity of anonymity

- different levels of anonymity (ranging from super-identification to anonymity)

- encryption of message content

- authenticity of message and sender

which we consider to be especially important for user modeling purposes.

---

[22]For instance, see the summary of *P3P, Chapter 8.5.*

Chapter 7

SOLUTIONS FOR SECURITY

In this chapter, the solutions developed so far will be juxtaposed with the requirements listed in *Chapter 5*. In cases where no appropriate solutions for meeting the requirements were found, the risks involved in employing a user adaptive system are described.

Corresponding to our division of *requirements for security* into *requirements for secrecy* and *requirements for integrity*, solutions will also be examined from the perspectives of *secrecy* and *integrity*.

1. Solutions for Secrecy

In *Chapter 5.1*, we demonstrated that *secrecy*, especially in user modeling, is difficult, if not impossible, to define. Nevertheless, requirements for the secrecy of the user model information (i.e., personal information) can be met either through denial of access to that information or through selective access to parts of that information.

1.1 Secrecy through Denial of Access

1.1.1 Secrecy through Anonymization

Secrecy through denial of access by means of anonymization was covered thoroughly in the last chapter. Anonymization (or pseudonymization) of the user model information conceals the relationship between a particular user and his user model information. Though the user model information is accessible to user model clients, the corresponding user cannot be determined for a given user model (entry). The user model (information) of a particular user is therefore *secret*, because it cannot be determined (i.e., singled out from among all user models).

1.1.2   Secrecy through Encryption

Secrecy through encrypted communication is an appropriate way for user adaptive systems to protect the communicated data while it is in transit between user modeling components. This is essential for user models which are not part of an application system and which can be accessed by several components (i.e., user model clients) via a network. The following sections describe a software package for user adaptive systems which allows for encrypted exchange of user model information within a network (e.g., the Internet).

KQML Application Programmer Interface (KAPI).

The *KQML*[1] *Application Programmer Interface (KAPI)*[2] provides means for exchanging KQML messages within a network over the TCP/IP layers (see Figure 7.1 on p. 104). As an example, the BGP-MS user modeling shell system takes advantage of this software package in order to communicate with application systems [Pohl, 1998, p. 205].

The KAPI software package, available as a library written in the programming language C, is incorporated into BGP-MS via the foreign function interface of LISP [Steele, 1990], in which BGP-MS is written. For BGP-MS, the following functions are available for communication with its clients (only the functions relevant to this section are listed):

- (defun Lisp-KInit () ...)
  With this function, the communication package is initialized.

- (defun Lisp-KListen (url) ...)
  To communicate over TCP [Hunt, 1992], a socket has to be established on which connections are accepted. The string url contains the node name and socket which should be used (e.g., tcp://asterix:8091, see p. 75).

- (defun Lisp-KSendString (message) ...)
  A KQML message (see [Pohl, 1998, p. 207] for examples) can be sent to the receiver through the function Lisp-KSendString which uses a string as an argument for the message to be sent.

- (defun Lisp-KGetString () ...)
  To receive a message from *any* sender, BGP-MS calls Lisp-KGetString which returns the oldest message received up to that point.

---

[1] See *Chapter 6.2.2.1.*
[2] See http://www.csee.umbc.edu/kqml/software/ .

For these basic communication functions, extensions have been implemented which make it possible to encrypt the user model information and to authenticate[3] the sender or the receiver, and the message exchanged. These extensions are described in more detail in the following sections.

Inclusion of the Secure Sockets Layer in KAPI (SKAPI).

The functions described above enable BGP-MS to communicate with application systems via the network. The data sent through TCP is transmitted as provided by the sender, meaning it can be observed by network components. The *Secure Sockets Layer (SSL)* makes it possible to encrypt communication by means of sockets (see [Hirsch, 1997] and [Freier et al., 1996]). The functions are located just above the transport layer (i.e., the TCP layer, see Figure 7.1 on p. 104) and require only a few arguments to establish an encrypted channel between two components (i.e., end-to-end encryption). With SSL, the following encryption algorithms can be used (see [Schneier, 1996] and [Menezes et al., 1997] for a description of the algorithms):

- no encryption algorithm

- stream ciphers: RC4 with 40 bit or 128 bit key length

- CBC block ciphers: RC2, DES40, DES, 3DES, 3DES_EDE, IDEA, Fortezza.

For the encryption of the communication, the IDEA algorithm was chosen (see `SSL_IDEA_128_CBC_WITH_MD5` in the SSL documentation). All of the above-mentioned algorithms encrypt symmetrically (see *Chapter 6.2*). To exchange the session keys which are used for symmetrical encryption, the *RSA*[4] *key exchange method* is used. With the RSA method, *certificates* which conform to the X.509 standard[5] can be used when establishing the communication [Menezes et al., 1997, p. 653]. An example of an X.509 certificate is given in the following table:

---

[3]See *Chapter 5.2.1.*
[4]Rivest, Shamir, and Adleman
[5]See Request for Comments (RFC) 2459: Internet X.509 Public Key Infrastructure Certificate and CRL Profile.

Table 7.1.   X.509 certificate

```
(01) Certificate:
(02)      Data:
(03)            Version: 3  (0x2)
(04)            Serial Number: 290 (0x122)
(05)            Signature Algorithm: md5WithRSAEncryption
(06)            Issuer: C=DE, ST=Staat1, L=Stadt1, O=Organisation1, OU=Unit1,
(07)                   CN=CA-Organisation/Email=ca@irgendwo
(08)            Validity
(09)                Not Before: Nov 18 13:22:38 1998 GMT
(10)                Not After : Nov  7 13:22:38 2000 GMT
(11)            Subject: C=DE, ST=Staat1, O=Organisation1, OU=Unit1,
(12)                   CN=Applikation1/Email=appl1@irgendwo
(13)            Subject Public Key Info:
(14)                Public Key Algorithm: rsaEncryption
(15)                RSA Public Key: (1024 bit)
(16)                    Modulus (1024 bit):
(17)                        00:d6:3a:cf:16:38:5b:f1:4b:3b:ba:7d:90:10:54:
....                          ...
(25)                        55:6f:66:de:81:88:d5:84:e1
(26)                    Exponent: 65537 (0x10001)
(27)            X509v3 extensions:
(28)                Netscape CA Revocation Url:
(29)                    .#http://www.cryptsoft.com/ca-crl.pem
        ....                  ...
(34)        Signature Algorithm: md5WithRSAEncryption
(35)            9f:19:e3:9c:82:8b:e1:3c:db:94:88:58:32:cf:91:6f:e6:b9:
....                ...
(42)            8c:9a
```

The fields[6] of the certificate give information about the holder, the issuer, the validity, and the cryptographic keys. Some of the important fields are (see the line numbers above):

(03) version of the X.509 standard

(04) the serial number of the certificate

(06) the issuer of the certificate

(08) the interval of validity of the certificate

(11) information about the holder of the certificate

(14) the cryptographic algorithm for the key certified

(17) the (public) key certified

(27) extensions, e.g., for key revocation

(34) the algorithm used by the issuer for the signature of the certificate

(35) the signature of the issuer.

---

[6]See Request for Comments (RFC) 2459: Internet X.509 Public Key Infrastructure Certificate and CRL Profile.

With an X.509 certificate, a cryptographic key (e.g., a public RSA key) can be related to a communicator (see lines (11) and (17)) by means of *super-identification* (see *Chapter 4.1.1*). This relation is affirmed by a trustworthy party (i.e., the certificate's issuer, see line (06), perhaps a trust center) through the signature (see line (35)) which is verifiable[7] by all communicators. While a communication link is being established[8] via SSL, the certified public key can be used to authenticate both communicators and to exchange a symmetrical session key to be used for further exchanges of encrypted information (for instance, through the IDEA algorithm mentioned above). After this phase, the encrypted information which is exchanged between the two communicators is not observable while being transported within the network.

The *SSLeay*[9] library [Hirsch, 1997] was chosen as an implementation for SSL, because: it is internationally available, it is in the public domain (licensing presents no problems), and the source code is readily available. By incorporating the functions of SSLeay into the KAPI library, we established the *SKAPI (secure KAPI)* library. The following example shows how a message is dispatched when SSL is included in KAPI:

---

[7]See [Schneier, 1996, Chap. 8] or [Menezes et al., 1997, Chap. 13] for key management techniques.
[8]See [Hirsch, 1997] for a detailed discussion of the SSL handshake phase.
[9]See http://www2.psy.uq.edu.au/~ftp/Crypto/ and *OpenSSL* (http://www.openssl.org/).

Table 7.2.   SKAPI function for message dispatch (example)

```
(01)   tcpSend(ParsedURL *purl, char *buffer, X509 **prover)
(02)   { SSL    *con;
(03)     int    i;
(04)     char   buf[256];
(05)     X509   *cert;
(06)
(07)     TCPInfo *info = (TCPInfo *) purl->transinfo;
(08)     if (purl->state != OPEN_CON)
(09)     { purl->fd = TCPconnect(info->host, info->port);
(10)       if (purl->fd == -1)   return -1;
(11)       SSL_CTX_set_verify(SSL_ctx, SSL_VERIFY_PEER, verify_callback);
(12)       con = SSL_new(SSL_ctx);
(13)       SSL_set_fd(con, purl->fd);
(14)       SSL_use_RSAPrivateKey_file(con, SSL_key_file, SSL_FILETYPE_PEM);
(15)       SSL_use_certificate_file(con, SSL_cert_file, SSL_FILETYPE_PEM);
(16)       prover_certificate(*prover);
(17)       i = SSL_connect(con);
(18)       if (i > 0)
(19)       { purl->SSL_accepted = 1;
(20)         purl->SSL_context = con;
(21)         purl->state = OPEN_CON;
(22)       }
(23)     }
(24)     if (purl->SSL_accepted)
(25)     { cert = SSL_get_peer_certificate(purl->SSL_context);
(26)       if (verify_cert(cert) && (!*prover || match7_certs(cert, *prover)))
(27)       { if (TCPsend(buffer, purl->SSL_context) < 0) { return (-1); }
(28)         *prover = cert;
(29)         return(1);
(30)       } else { return(-1); }
(31)     } else { return(-1); }
(32)   }
```

The extensions to the KAPI code are explained below:

(01) tcpSend is a function of KAPI which previously required the arguments purl (the address of the receiver) and buffer (the message). In SKAPI the argument list has been extended by prover which is a reference to a structure for the information contained in the X.509 certificate for which the receiver of the current message is expected to be the holder.

(08) If the receiver is contacted for the first time, an encrypted connection is established. The connection is stored for further use.

(09) The connection via a socket is established as in KAPI.

(11) The function for verifying the communication partner's certificate is defined.

(12) A new SSL context is created which proceeds from the current context. It contains parameters necessary for the encryption (e.g., the preferred encryption algorithms).

(13) The SSL context is assigned to the socket.

(14) The private and public keys of the sender are assigned to the SSL context.

(16) The certificate against which the receiver's certificate must be checked is defined.

(17) The establishing phase (i.e., the SSL handshake phase[10]) is started.

(18) When an agreement about the keys and algorithms to be used has been reached, the communication link is stored.

(24) With a previously stored encrypted connection (see (08)), the message dispatch is initialized.

(25) The current certificate of the communication partner is requested.

(26) The certificate's validity (e.g., issuer's signature) is verified and if a test certificate is defined (see (16)) with this message dispatch request, the certificate is checked against it.

(27) The message is dispatched by the KAPI function TCPSend which uses the SSL function SSL_write instead of the send function usually used with sockets. SSL_write encrypts the message and sends it to the socket.

(28) If no test certificate has been defined (see (16)), the sender obtains a reference to the receiver's certificate information and is able to identify the receiver of the message by means of super-identification (see *Chapter 4.1.1*).

This example shows that the dispatched message is encrypted using functions of the SKAPI library which are transparent to the application using that library. The application must only define the cryptographic keys

---

[10]See [Hirsch, 1997] for a detailed discussion of the SSL handshake phase (and encryption process).

that should be used (e.g., by a certificate). Therefore, the SKAPI interface is only slightly different from that of KAPI (see p. 96):

- `(defun Lisp-KInit (private-key-file certificate-file) ...)`
  The parameters `private-key-file` and `certificate-file` denote the files containing the private key and the certificate file (both encoded in PEM[11] format) which are the basis for the SSL handshake phase.

  The application system can accept several identities (e.g., *pseudonyms*, see *Chapter 4.1.1*), defined by certificates, in communicating with its partners. Associated with a certificate is the public key (see p. 98) used in the SSL handshake phase to establish an encrypted communication link. The corresponding private key for decryption at the handshake must also be defined.

- `(defun Lisp-KSendString (message certificate-file) ...)`
  In addition to the `message`, the certificate of the message's receiver can be defined in order to authenticate the receiver by means of super-identification.

  If the receiver's current certificate does not match the demanded certificate, the message will not be sent to the questionable receiver.

  If no certificate is defined (by the parameter `certificate-file`), the sender only obtains information about the certificate presented by the receiver and the message is sent without regard to the receiver's identity.

- `(defun Lisp-KGetString (certificate-file) ...)`
  The additional specification of the sender of the next message to be received assures the receiver of the sender's identity.

  If the certificate presented by the sender does not match the one specified by `certificate-file`, the message will be discarded.

  If no certificate is defined, the receiver obtains only information about the certificate presented by the sender and the message is received without regard to the receiver's identity.

These selected functions show how SKAPI can be included in a user modeling component (in this case, the BGP-MS user modeling shell system). The modifications which have to be made to a user modeling component in order to use the SKAPI instead of the KAPI are minor (for instance, a new parameter in the function call must be added).

---

[11] See Request for Comments (RFC) 1422: Privacy Enhancement for Internet Electronic Mail: Part II: Certificate-Based Key Management.

The SKAPI Library for Encrypted KQML Message Exchange.

The SKAPI library we have developed enables user modeling components to exchange KQML messages via an encrypted communication link. By encryption of the messages, secrecy of the information exchanged between two user modeling components (e.g., between an application system and the user modeling agent) is given. Furthermore, by means of asymmetric cryptography the expected identity of the communication partner can either be specified prior to exchanging messages or learned afterwards through certificates (i.e., the communication partner and the exchanged messages can be authenticated).

SKQML (see *Chapter 6.2.2*) also permits encryption of the message content to be communicated. The content must be encrypted before the communication software can send it (see *Chapter 6.2.2.2* and Algorithm 6.3 on p. 82). Since the encryption must be accomplished by the user modeling component, modifications within the component are required. Either the component has to prepare a message which instructs an intermediary mix to encrypt the message, or the component has to encrypt the message itself, which requires cryptographic capabilities (see the example messages on p. 75).

When the SKAPI library is used instead of the KAPI library, the user modeling component is able to communicate in encrypted form without modifications[12]. The encryption of the content to be exchanged takes place just above the transport layer, giving the user modeling component transparent access to encryption functions (see Figure 7.1 in contrast to Figure 6.6 on p. 92 where encryption takes place at the presentation layer).

---

[12]The additional parameters explained in the previous section (for instance, the certificate file) may be predefined within SKAPI for an invariable communication partner and need not be provided by the user modeling component using SKAPI. Thus, the additional parameters may be omitted.

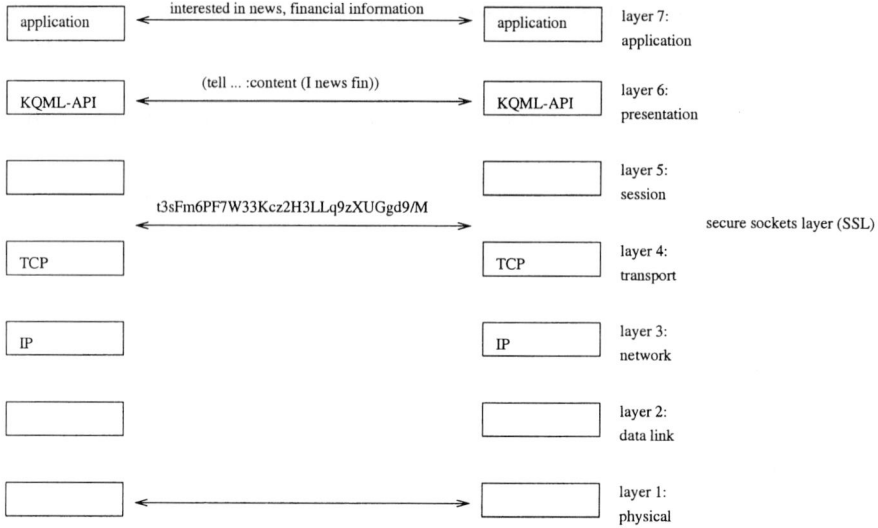

Figure 7.1.   Encryption through SKAPI

Two features of the SKAPI library are particularly noteworthy. First, SKAPI enables the BGP-MS user modeling shell system to maintain the secrecy of data while it is in transit through the network. And second, the authenticity of the user model clients and the authenticity of the exchanged KQML messages can be verified by means of X.509 certificates.

1.2   Secrecy through Selective Access

In *Chapter 7.1.1* we saw how user model information can be kept secret between the sender and the receiver of a message, either through anonymization or through encryption. For user model information which is useful to more than one user model client, the secrecy of this information between the user model and only one client is not appropriate. Several clients should share this information and keep it confidential among them.

The requirements for *confidentiality* in *Chapter 5.1.2* were formulated from the user's perspective. Therefore, these formulations can neither be used to analyze the mutual consistency of requirements nor are they directly convertible into automatic procedures which could be executed in a user adaptive system.

To reduce the gap between requirements and formal specifications, security research has developed so-called *security models* which are mainly concerned with the confidentiality and the integrity of information systems. In contrast to logical models [Chang and Keisler, 1990] which act as concretization[13], security models act as abstractions, neglecting irrelevant factors and concentrating on essential factors instead.

A definition of a *security model* is given in [Longley and Shain, 1987, p. 308]:

> "In computer security, a model that defines the system-enforced security rules. It specifies the access controls on the use of information and how information will be allowed to flow through the system. It also provides the mechanism for specifying how to change access controls and interfaces dynamically without compromising the system."

Security models are important in the design phase of an information system as well as in the duty phase and serve the following purposes:

Definition of Terms: The definition of terms is a prerequisite of security models. It specifies entities of the system which are relevant for confidentiality, clarifies what these entities mean and disambiguates the terms so that they can be processed automatically.

Description: The security model describes the form of confidentiality, for example, the circumstances under which a system component can acquire knowledge of information. It describes, either in an procedural or a declarative manner, the actions within the system relevant for the fulfillment of requirements regarding security.

Analysis: The description of the actions possible in the model enables the system to determine whether these actions are consistent and adequate for the system. The model also makes it possible to recognize what actions might lead to undesirable access to information and to prevent such access before the system is actually used.

Verification: Potential violations of the confidentiality requirements can be determined and forestalled in advance, e.g., by automatic procedures. In the modeling process, issues considered irrelevant for confidentiality are neglected by abstraction. Therefore, the model can only be interpreted within the limits set by the abstraction and cannot guarantee confidentiality beyond its formalism. Nevertheless, within these limitations, the model can be verified in a formal manner which assures the user that all information intended for access can

---

[13] A model of a given set of axioms exists only for a set of axioms which are free of conflict. An existing model represents only one of potentially many assignments for the syntactical elements of the set of axioms assigned by an interpretation function. The model thereby is a concretization (see [Chang and Keisler, 1990]).

be accessed, but information which was not intended to be accessed will not be.

Enforcement: By arranging unambiguous terms through actions, it is possible to generate automatic procedures from the model which can enforce the confidentiality requirements within the system.

Confidentiality requirements are often given as interdictions (e.g., particular application systems are never permitted to acquire knowledge of personal interests maintained in a user model). From its structure, an interdiction is a negated existence clause (e.g., $\neg\exists X : A(X)$, where X denotes a potential state of the system and $A(X)$ the access to information), which is equal to an all-quantified clause of the negation of the interdiction (e.g., $\forall X : \neg A(X)$). Empirical all-quantified clauses usually cannot be proven because not all states are known or can be tested (whereas they might easily be falsified, see [Amann and Kessler, 1993]). With formal security models, all permissible actions and states are described and can usually be enumerated. Through enumeration of all states, the compatibility of the system with the requirements can be proven or at least be tested. By means of positive conditions (defined by *permissions* in contradiction to interdictions) in a security model and the restriction that only actions which are allowed by the model can be performed, confidentiality requirements can be formulated and treated algorithmically.

In the following sections some well-known security models are described, examples of their uses are given, and their applicability for user modeling is evaluated.

1.2.1   Noninterference Models

Data which can be assigned to categories[14] and is only confidential if two categories are combined can be protected by *noninterference* [Summers, 1997, p. 137]:

> "A precise definition of information flow restriction is found in the concept of *noninterference*. One group of users is noninterfering with another group if the actions of the first group using certain commands have no effect on what the second group can see."

With noninterference, several user model clients can maintain the same user model, though being separated with respect to defined categories of the user model data. Figure 5.1 on p. 55 depicts several modes of

---

[14]For instance, in a user model, anonymous data about sensitive characteristics can constitute one category and identifying information about the user a second category.

cooperation between application systems: CONT-DIV and CONT-SEP show modes for which complete noninterference between the application systems A and B is given (either by application of two user models or by separation of $cont(A)$ and $cont(B)$ within one user model). In the mode CONT-SHAR, the area $cont(A) \setminus cont(B)$ is not interfering with $cont(B) \setminus cont(A)$.

The following sections describe two well-known noninterference models which ensure confidentiality by giving access to information to all entities which are not excluded from access by previously accessed information.

The Chinese Wall Security Policy.

The *Chinese Wall* security policy proposed by Brewer and Nash (see [Brewer and Nash, 1989] and [Kessler, 1992]) makes it possible to separate access to conflicting classes of information [Brewer and Nash, 1989, p. 207]:

> "The basis of the Chinese Wall policy is that people are only allowed access to information which is not held to conflict with any other information that they already possess."

Initially, the requester of information is allowed to access any information he requests (e.g., information of class A which contains anonymous data). Subsequent information requests (e.g., information requests referring to class B which contains personal information) are allowed if there is no conflict relation between the current information class and all information classes previously referred to. When class A and B are defined as *conflicting*, the latter information request cannot be satisfied. The conflict relation establishes a *Chinese Wall* between information classes (for instance, some *partitions* in user models [Kobsa and Pohl, 1995] may be defined as conflicting) where the requester is able to choose the side of the wall he wants to be on. CONT-SEP (see Figure 5.1 on p. 55) depicts the *Chinese Wall policy* within one user model, CONT-DIV (see Figure 5.1) establishes a *Chinese Wall* between two user modeling agents where consistency procedures (see *Chapter 7.2.1.1* and *Chapter 7.2.2.1*) must also be non-interfering.

Noninterference Model (Goguen-Meseguer).

Goguen and Meseguer (see [Goguen and Meseguer, 1982] and [Goguen and Meseguer, 1984]) describe their noninterference model in terms of automata theory. Beginning from a state $s_0 \in S$, state transitions can be conducted by the function:

$$do : S \times U \times C \to S$$

with U as the set of users[15] and C the set of *state changing commands*. The *output* (for instance, the display of a variable's value) a user is able to get in a state is defined by the function $out : S \times U \to O$, with O as the set of possible outputs.

The history of the system is denoted as the sequence of all pairs of users' commands $(u_i, c_i) \in (U \times C)$:

$$w \in (U \times C)^*, \quad w = (u_1, c_1) \circ \ldots \circ (u_n, c_n)$$

The state which is reached by applying the sequence w starting from the initial state s_0 is denoted by $[[w]]$. The output available for a user u in that state is given by:

$$[[w]]_u = out([[w]], u)$$

For given groups of users $G, G' \subseteq U$ and a set of commands $C_- \subseteq C$ the function p_{G,C_-} *purges* all pairs of w which contain elements of those subsets:

$$p_{G,C_-}(w) = \{w \ominus (u, c) \mid u \in G \wedge c \in C_-\}$$

The user group G *does not interfere with* G':

$$G :| G' \quad \Leftrightarrow \quad \forall w \in (U \times C)^*, \forall u \in G' : \quad [[w]]_u = [[p_{G,C}(w)]]_u$$

Also, for a given set of commands C_- *does not interfere with* G':

$$C_- :| G' \quad \Leftrightarrow \quad \forall w \in (U \times C)^*, \forall u \in G' : \quad [[w]]_u = [[p_{U,C_-}(w)]]_u$$

When combined, a group of users G and a set of commands C_- *do not interfere* with users in G':

$$C_-, G :| G' \quad \Leftrightarrow \quad \forall w \in (U \times C)^*, \forall u \in G' : \quad [[w]]_u = [[p_{G,C_-}(w)]]_u$$

---

[15] For Goguen and Meseguer (see [Goguen and Meseguer, 1982] and [Goguen and Meseguer, 1984]), the term *user* corresponds to a user model client which accesses information from a user model and not to the user being modeled.

Within Goguen and Meseguer's noninterference model, a *security policy is a set of noninterference assertions* [Goguen and Meseguer, 1982, p. 16]. With the assertions of noninterfering classes, a policy can be defined which assures the user that a group of user model clients cannot gain knowledge about user model entries maintained by a *conflicting* group of user model clients. For example, a group of user model clients which should only maintain anonymous data may *conflict* with a group of user model clients which should only maintain personal information.

The noninterference model makes it possible to specify *conflicting* groups of user model clients (or actions, see above). It neither specifies which user model client is able to access a particular user model entry nor does it mention particular access modes (e.g., *read*, *delete*). Therefore, it can be used for separating application systems of a user adaptive system while maintaining the user model, but it is not suitable when access to concrete user model entries has to be defined for particular application systems.

In order to compute the *output* presented to a user u (i.e., a user model client), the history w of all commands from each user must first be purged from the commands made by users in conflicting user groups. Therefore, the history w has to be be kept and the purged history $p_{G,C_-}(w)$ must be obtainable for each G and C_- in order to produce the *output* $[[w]]_u$. The user model must either be recomputed for every access which is dependent on the group of users G and the set of commands C_-, or several parallel user models have to be kept, each for a static group of users G and set of commands C_-. The shared maintenance of a user model is only possible within a group of noninterfering users (i.e., a group of noninterfering user model clients) whereby all users in that group share the complete information of the group.

Goguen and Meseguer's *noninterference model* makes it possible to separate groups of application systems, each of which maintains a shared user model within a user adaptive system. It is therefore, like the *Chinese wall model* (see above), focused on the users of information (i.e., the user model clients) rather than on the information itself (e.g., on its sensitivity or the purpose of the information request).

1.2.2 Information Flow Control Models

In contrast to the models described in the previous sections, *information flow control models* deal primarily with the information processed within a system. They describe either how information can flow within an information system or which kinds of information flows are prohibited. It is assumed that information flows only within the model described (e.g., in the user modeling component which implements the information flow control model). Information flow between information requesters (e.g., user model clients) is not considered here.

In the following, two well-known information flow control models are presented with examples suitable for user adaptive systems.

The Multi-Level Security Model (Bell-LaPadula).

By relating a set S of *subjects* (i.e., information requesters) to a set O of *objects* (i.e., processed information entities), Bell and LaPadula's multi-level security model (see [Bell and LaPadula, 1976] and [Bell, 1988]) specifies the access to information as well as the flow of information within the system processing the information. Both *subjects* and *objects* are arranged into *security levels*, whereby a *security level* is a pair consisting of a *classification* and a *compartment*.

A *classification* is an element of the totally ordered set C (e.g., $C = \{unclassified, sensitive, very\text{-}sensitive\}$ with the order[16]: *unclassified* $\leq$ *sensitive*, *sensitive* $\leq$ *very-sensitive*). A *compartment* is an element of the power set 2^N with N as the set of all *need-to-know categories* which describe the content of an *object* or the content a *subject* is allowed to refer to. For example, a user model can be partitioned into the *need-to-know categories* $N = \{interests, skills, abilities\}$. For the set of *security levels* $L = C \times 2^N$, a *dominance relation* is defined:

$$(c_1, n_1) \leq (c_2, n_2) \Leftrightarrow c_1 \leq c_2 \wedge n_1 \subseteq n_2 \quad c_1, c_2 \in C, n_1, n_2 \in 2^N \qquad (7.1)$$

The security level function $f = (f_S, f_O, f_C) : S \times O \times S \to L^3$ is applied for every subject s requesting access to object o. The function $f_O : O \to L$ assigns each object its security level and $f_S : S \to L$ each subject its security level. The function $f_C : S \to L, f_C(s) \leq f_S(s), s \in S$, allows the subject to choose a security level lower than the possible maximum. The permissible access modes for subject s_i to object o_j are defined by a matrix $M = (m_{i,j}), m_{i,j} \in 2^A, A = \{read, write\}$.

The Bell-LaPadula model is described in terms of a *state machine model* with a *system state* $v \in V = (B, M, f)$. B denotes the set of current access rights for subjects $s_i \in S$, $o_i \in O$, the objects referred to, and $a_i \in A$ the access mode: $b = (s_i, o_i, a_i) \in B$.

A system state v is considered to be secure according to the Bell-LaPadula model if the following three properties are given:

simple security property ("no read up secrecy"): When a subject has *read* or *write* access to an object, then the security level of the

---

[16]reflexive, transitive, antisymmetric

subject dominates the security level of the object (with respect to the dominance relation 7.1).

$$\forall s \in S, o \in O[(s, o, read) \in B \vee (s, o, write) \in B] \Rightarrow f_S(s) \geq f_O(o) \qquad (7.2)$$

This condition ensures that operations can only be performed for objects subdominant to the subject's security level. For example, the following access modes are:

valid:	$(s_1, o_1, read)$	$f_S(s_1) = (unclassified, \{interests, skills\})$
		$f_O(o_1) = (unclassified, \{interests\})$
valid:	$(s_2, o_2, write)$	$f_S(s_2) = (very\text{-}sensitive, \{abilities\})$
		$f_O(o_2) = (sensitive, \{abilities\})$
not valid:	$(s_3, o_3, read)$	$f_S(s_3) = (very\text{-}sensitive, \{abilities\})$
		$f_O(o_3) = (sensitive, \{interests\})$

The condition enforces that subjects can only access information with the same or a lower security level. Through the combination of *classifications* and *need-to-know categories*, it is possible to partition a user model into classes in which the information flow can be restricted to one direction (e.g., from *sensitive* to *very-sensitive*) within this class (e.g., *abilities*).

∗-property ("no write down secrecy"): When a subject has *read* access to one object, then the security level of another object for the *write* access must not be lower than the subject's security level for the *read* operation.

$$\begin{aligned} (s, o_1, read) \in B \Rightarrow f_C(s) \geq f_O(o_1) \quad &\text{and} \\ (s, o_2, write) \in B \Rightarrow f_C(s) \leq f_O(o_2) \quad &s \in S, o_1, o_2 \in O : \end{aligned} \qquad (7.3)$$

This property specifies that information derived through *read* access to an object of a specific security level cannot flow to another object on a security level which is subdominant with respect to the dominance relation (see Expression 7.1). For instance, the *write* requests are:

valid:	$(s_1, o_1, write)$	$f_C(s_1) = (unclassified, \{interests\})$
		$f_O(o_1) = (unclassified, \{interests\})$
not valid:	$(s_2, o_2, write)$	$f_C(s_2) = (very\text{-}sensitive, \{skills, abilities\})$
		$f_O(o_2) = (sensitive, \{skills, abilities\})$

The condition prevents confidential information from flowing to a subdominant security level to which application systems which cannot be trusted to keep information confidential also have access. Preventing this kind of information flow can be useful for two reasons. First, user modeling agents employ procedures which maintain the integrity of the user model (see *Chapter 7.2*), and this sometimes entails modifying user model entries (e.g., entries of different classes).

The *-property ensures that this is only possible if there is no information flow to classes on a lower security level. Second, neither such intentional information flows, nor unintentional, accidental information flows (e.g., due to an application system error) are permitted unless they are compliant with the model[17].

discretionary security property: All requested access modes must be specified in the matrix M.

$$\forall s_i \in S, \forall o_j \in O, \forall op \in A : (s_i, o_j, op) \in B \Rightarrow op \in m_{i,j} \qquad (7.4)$$

While the previous two properties describe the potential flow of information within the security model, this property describes how an object (i.e., a user model entry) is related to a subject (i.e., an application system) through particular access modes.

Using the terminology of the Bell-LaPadula's *state machine model*, all *secure* transactions (i.e., transactions which transform a *secure* state v_i into a *secure* state v_{i+1}) starting from an initial *secure* state v_0 result in a *secure* system (state v_{i+1}). All transactions are considered to be *secure* if they comply with the three properties described above.

With the Bell-LaPadula security model, it is possible to build a *classification* and *need-to-know categories* which characterize user model entries as well as user model clients (i.e. application systems). The *simple security property* (see Expression 7.2) and the *-property* (see Expression 7.3) specify the possible information flow within the *security levels* of the user model. The particular access modes for user model clients to user model entries can be defined by an access control matrix (see Expression 7.4) which relates each subject to an object. The definition of particular access modes enhances the definition of the possible information *flow* with a specification for concrete information *access*. This model is therefore useful for specifying a compartmentalized user model (see Figure 5.1 on p. 55) and for assigning grades of confidentiality to the user model entries in the compartments.

The Lattice Model of Secure Information Flow (Denning).

In Denning's information flow control model (see [Denning, 1976], [Denning, 1982, Chap. 5]) the *information flow* (denoted by $\rightarrow$) is described as reduced *entropy*[18] of the object to which information flows.

---

[17] Because all components involved in the security model have to comply with such conditions, these models are often called *mandatory* security models (MAC models).

[18] See [Shannon, 1949], [Blahut, 1987], or [Denning, 1982] for *entropy* and *conditional entropy*.

An information flow from the variable $x_{s'}$ to the variable $y_{s'}$

$$x_{s'} \to_\alpha y_{s'} \tag{7.5}$$

is given when, through a state transition from state s to state s' (caused by a command sequence α, $s \vdash_\alpha s'$), new information about $x_{s'}$ can be obtained (i.e., reduction of conditional entropy) from $y_{s'}$:

$$H_{y_{s'}}(x_{s'}) \leq H_{y_s}(x_s) \tag{7.6}$$

.

For example, in a user model[19] in the state s with the set of formulas:

$$R_s = \{ \quad P_1(a) \vee P_1(b) \vee P_1(c) \vee P_1(d), P_2(a) \vee P_2(b), \\ P_2(a) \to P_1(a) \vee P_1(b), P_2(b) \to P_1(c) \vee P_1(d), \tag{7.7} \\ \forall A, B, i : P_i(A) \wedge P_i(B) \Rightarrow A = B \quad \} $$

and $x = P_1$ and $y = P_2$, x_s has an entropy (in bit, with $p(x_s)$ as the probability distribution of x_s):

$$H(x_s) = -\sum_{x_s} p(x_s) ld(p(x_s)) = -(\frac{1}{4}ld\frac{1}{4} + \frac{1}{4}ld\frac{1}{4} + \frac{1}{4}ld\frac{1}{4} + \frac{1}{4}ld\frac{1}{4}) = 2$$

After inserting the predicate $P_2(a)$ through α, the state changes:

$$R_{s'} = \{ \quad P_1(a) \vee P_1(b), P_2(a), \\ P_2(a) \to P_1(a) \vee P_1(b), P_2(b) \to P_1(c) \vee P_1(d), \tag{7.8} \\ \forall A, B, i : P_i(A) \wedge P_i(B) \Rightarrow A = B \quad \} $$

and so does the entropy of $x_{s'}$:

$$H(x_{s'}) = -(\frac{1}{2}ld\frac{1}{2} + \frac{1}{2}ld\frac{1}{2} + 0 + 0) = 1$$

The conditional entropy of x in state s (in absence of information about y_s) is:

$$H_{y_s}(x_s) = H(x_s) = 2 \quad \text{(bits)}$$

---

[19] For this example, the user model consists of a set of first order logic formulas, see [Pohl, 1998, Chap. 3].

and with knowledge of $y_{s'}$:

$$H_{y_{s'}}(x_{s'}) = -\sum_{x_{s'}} p_{y_{s'}}(x_{s'}) ld(p_{y_{s'}}(x_{s'})) = -(\frac{1}{2}ld\frac{1}{2} + \frac{1}{2}ld\frac{1}{2} + 0 + 0) = 1$$

Because (see inequation 7.6):

$$H_{y_{s'}}(x_{s'}) = 1 \leq H_{y_s}(x_s) = 2$$

an information flow exists from the variable $x_{s'}$ to the variable $y_{s'}$ ($x_{s'} \rightarrow_\alpha y_{s'}$, see Expression 7.5). Hence, a user modeling component which only has knowledge about the value of $y_{s'}$ (i.e. P_2) has a lower uncertainty about the (probable) value of x_s (i.e. P_1) after the state transition through the command sequence α.

In Denning's information flow control model, a *flow policy* is defined by arranging *security classes* in a lattice[20] $(SC, \leq, \oplus, \ominus)$, where $\leq$ defines a dominance relation[21], $\oplus$ the *least upper bound* operator ($\forall x, y \in SC : x \oplus y \in SC$), $\otimes$ the *greatest lower bound* operator ($\forall x, y \in SC : x \otimes y \in SC$). There is also a supremum $sup(SC)$ and an infimum $inf(SC)$.

Each object o is assigned to a *security class* $sc(o) \in SC$. An information flow $x_s \rightarrow_\alpha y_{s'}$ is allowed, if

$$sc(x_s) \leq sc(y_{s'}) \tag{7.9}$$

For example, in a specific user adaptive system the security classes *interest_consumer* $\in SC$, *interest_producer* $\in SC$, *interest_maintainer* $\in SC$, and *interest_supervisor* $\in SC$ can be ordered by the dominance relation:

$$
\begin{array}{rcl}
interest\_maintainer & \leq & interest\_consumer \\
interest\_maintainer & \leq & interest\_producer \\
interest\_consumer & \leq & interest\_supervisor \\
interest\_producer & \leq & interest\_supervisor
\end{array}
\tag{7.10}
$$

With $P_{1,2}$ (see Expression 7.7) as objects, the information flow $x_{s'} \rightarrow_\alpha y_{s'}$ is:

---

[20] See [Denning, 1982, Chap. 5] or [Birkhoff, 1962] for a definition.
[21] reflexive, transitive, antisymmetric

valid:	$sc(P_1) = interest\_producer$	$sc(P_2) = interest\_supervisor$
not valid:	$sc(P_1) = interest\_producer$	$sc(P_2) = interest\_maintainer$
not valid:	$sc(P_1) = interest\_consumer$	$sc(P_2) = interest\_maintainer$

The information flow control model describes only which kinds of information flows are allowed within a system but does not specify which actions (e.g., *read, write*) can be performed by subjects on specific objects. It is therefore less stringent than the Bell-LaPadula model. It is also more flexible in its definition of valid information flows because it does not classify user model clients by security levels. Rather, it concentrates on the processed information by grouping user model entries into *security classes* which are arranged in a lattice. Information might flow according to the *dominance relation* (see Expression 7.10) in the direction of the *supremum* of the lattice (e.g., *interest_supervisor* in Expression 7.10).

The model describes in a declarative manner how to verify the validity of an information flow which was induced by a state transition from state s to state s' via a command sequence α ($s \vdash_\alpha s'$). It focuses on the probable values of variables (for instance, on the values of the user model entries P_1 and P_2) rather than on subjects (i.e., user model clients) and the commands they are allowed to give to a user model (e.g., *insert*). Since the concrete commands (or command sequences α) which lead to permissible information flows are not described explicitly by the model, automatic procedures for checking the feasibility of the command (sequence) to be carried out cannot be employed. Rather, the command (sequence) must be carried out on the user model and afterwards retracted if an invalid information flow occurs. This strategy usually involves expensive computations, particularly the calculation of conditional entropy, and command sequences which are not retractable may exist.

Because concrete commands are not described within the information flow model, it is applicable for non-compartmented or sub-symbolic representation mechanisms. However, it is not generally applicable to all user models because of the limitations of the user modeling systems which host them (see above). The information flow control model also has to be implemented within the user modeling system in order to be able to calculate entropies. Thus, a *security model* based on Denning's *information flow control model* must be adjusted to each individual user modeling system.

1.2.3   Access Control Models

The *security models* discussed above defined the information flow within an information system either by grouping conflicting information into mutually exclusive access classes or by specifying the permissable effects between information classes. These *security models* focus either on the relationship between particular information objects (e.g., user model entries) by grouping them into (conflicting) information classes with no information flow permitted between them, or they focus on defining permissable information flows between information classes. An exception is Bell and LaPadula's multi-level security model (see *Chapter 7.1.2.2*) where, in addition to the description of the possible information flows, subjects are related to objects by access modes through an access control matrix (see Expression 7.4 on p. 112). This access control matrix will be described in detail in the following section.

Via a matrix, all objects in an information system can be related to the subjects by access modes which are granted to a given subject on an object (e.g., *read, delete*). When requirements concerning the confidentiality of the objects are strong, most of the matrix's elements will be empty because only few access modes are defined. Hence, the matrix can be broken down into access control lists (with focus on the objects) or capability lists (with focus on the subjects). In both of these methods subjects and objects are related *directly* by access modes. The *role-based access control model* enhances the access matrix model (and the lists into which it can be broken down) by introducing an abstract entity (i.e., a role) which groups access modes. Subjects and objects are no longer related by concrete access modes but by a collective term for these modes (i.e., a role).

In the following sections, the different *access control models* are described.

The Access Matrix Model.

The access matrix model developed by Harrison, Ruzzo, and Ullman (HRU model, [Harrison et al., 1976]) relates each subject s_i ($s_i \in S$) and each object o_j ($o_j \in O$) of an information system through a set of access modes $m_{i,j} \subseteq R$ (e.g., $R = \{read, write, create, delete\}$). The relation is denoted by the matrix $M = (m_{i,j})$. The validity of a request (s_i, o_j, op) with $op \in R$ is given by the following equivalence:

$$(s_i, o_j, op) \text{ valid} \iff op \in m_{i,j} \tag{7.11}$$

For a user adaptive system with application systems $appl_1, appl_2, \ldots,$ $appl_n \in S$, the set of objects $O = \{entry_1, entry_2, entry_3, entry_4, \ldots,$ $entry_m\}$, and the set of rights $R = \{a, u, i, d\}$, (e.g., $a = ask, u =$

update, $i = insert$, $d = delete$) an example of an access control matrix is given below:

$$M = \begin{pmatrix} \{u\} & \{u\} & & \{u,a,i,d\} & \cdots & \{u\} \\ \{u,a,i\} & \{u,a,i\} & & \{u,a,i,d\} & \cdots & \{u,a,i\} \\ \vdots & \vdots & \vdots & \vdots & \vdots & \vdots \\ \{u,a,i,d\} & \{u,a,i,d\} & \{u,a,i,d\} & \{u,a,i,d\} & \cdots & \{u,a,i,d\} \end{pmatrix}$$

(7.12)

In addition to the matrix described here, the HRU model makes it possible for subjects to alter the matrix M in order to modify the relation between subjects and rights (i.e., *discretionary*[22] *access control model, DAC model*) which is, however, not relevant for user modeling purposes.

Capability Lists and Access Control Lists.

For user adaptive systems in which a high degree of separation (i.e., noninterference) between different application systems is demanded (see CONT-DIV, CONT-SEP in Figure 5.1 on p. 55) the matrix $M = (m_{i,j})$ (see above) is sparse (for instance, subject A is not related with a right to objects $o \in cont(B)$ and subject B is not related with a right to objects $o \in cont(A)$).

A *capability list* cl_{s_i} for a subject s_i is a set of pairs containing all rights applicable for s_i:

$$cl_{s_i} = \{(o_j, m_{i,j}) \mid m_{i,j} \neq \emptyset, 1 \leq j \leq m\}$$

(7.13)

The capability list for s_i contains all non-empty sets of the row i of matrix M and their relation to objects (e.g., $cl_{appl_1} = \{(entry_1, \{u\}),$ $(entry_2, \{u\}), (entry_4, \{u,a,i,d\}), \ldots, (entry_m, \{u\})\}$). Ordered according to objects (instead of according to subjects), *access control lists* can be obtained which specify which subjects are allowed to perform operations for a given object o_j:

$$acl_{o_j} = \{(s_i, m_{i,j}) \mid m_{i,j} \neq \emptyset, 1 \leq i \leq n\}$$

(7.14)

For example, the access control list for object $entry_3$ is: $acl_{entry_3} = \{\ldots, (appl_n, \{u,a,i,d\})\}$.

---

[22]The relation of access modes can be modified at the users' *discretion*.

Breaking down the access control matrix reduces the storage and retrieval effort for sparse matrices but does not offer more opportunities
than the access matrix model does.

The next section describes an access control model which extends
the relationship between subjects and objects through access modes to
include an additional entity.

1.2.4   Role-Based Access Control Model

The security models proposed in the previous sections relate subjects
(e.g., user model clients) to objects (e.g., entries in a user model) through
permissions (i.e., permissible access to objects). The semantics of permissions (e.g., *read, write*) are fixed within the respective model and
cannot be changed.

In the *role-based access control model* (*RBAC model*, see [Sandhu
et al., 1996], [Sandhu and Bhamidipati, 1997], and [Sandhu et al., 1999])
permissions are grouped by *roles*. These roles are abstract entities for
which names and semantics can be chosen and changed by the designer
of the access control model. Permissions[23] describe different modes of
access (e.g., to a user model). This flexibility in defining and grouping
permissions through roles means that RBAC is not bound to a particular access policy (see the previous sections in this chapter) though it
still supports important principles [Sandhu et al., 1996, p. 40]:

"Although the RBAC concept is policy neutral, it directly supports
three well-known security principles:

- *Least privilege*: Only those permissions required for the tasks performed by the same user in the role are assigned to the role.

- *Separation of duties*: Invocation of mutually exclusive roles can be
  required to complete a sensitive task, such as requiring an accounting
  clerk and an account manager to participate in issuing a check.

- *Data abstraction*: Instead of the read, write, execute permissions typ-
  ically provided by the operating system, abstract permissions, such
  as credit and debit for an account object, can be established."

The above-mentioned principles support the confidentiality of information. For the purpose of user modeling, the principles are explained by
examples:

---

[23]For instance, two permissions *read-identifying* and *read-anonymous* can distinguish read
access to user model entries which make it possible either to identify the user or to maintain
his anonymity.

- *Least privilege*: Application systems which are only dependent on particular information classes of the user model (e.g., information concerning the user's skills *or* interests) should be able to access only that information class which is intended for them. Also, within that class, only access modes which are necessary for the functioning of the application system should be granted. For a particular application system, *read* access may be adequate but not the modes *delete* or *modify*.

- *Separation of duties*: For a user model which is divided into parts containing anonymous and personal data, two different roles which collect access modes to anonymous data and access modes to personal data can be defined. Application systems may be assigned to one of these roles but not to both in order to prevent the linkage of anonymous and personal data. With *dynamic separation of duty*, an application system is prevented from using two separated roles in one session, *static separation of duty* prevents application systems from using two separated roles at any time.

- *Data abstraction*: Through authorization (see below), user model clients are assigned to roles which collect access modes to user model entries. The user model clients are therefore no longer related directly to user model entries as they were in the security models described in the previous sections. By defining roles, the authorization can abstract from concrete user model entries (compare the enumerated entries in Matrix 7.12 on p. 117). For instance, the role *interest consumer* may collect all access modes necessary to acquire knowledge about the user's interests without specifying the concrete user model entries.

By means of roles, different access modes can be assigned to subjects (i.e., user model clients, denoted as *users* in the model of [Sandhu et al., 1996]) which can vary with different information requests (denoted as *sessions*). The role-based access control model is formulated set-theoretically, making straightforward implementation and verification possible. The base reference model $RBAC_0$ is given by [Sandhu et al., 1996, p. 42] (examples will be given in a later section):

RBAC₀

- U, R, P, and S (users, roles, permissions, and sessions);
- $PA \subseteq P \times R$, a many-to-many permission-to-role assignment relation;
- $UA \subseteq U \times R$, a many-to-many user-to-role assignment relation;

- $user : S \rightarrow U$, a function mapping each session s_i to the single user $user(s_i)$ (constant for the session's lifetime); and

- $roles : S \rightarrow 2^R$, a function mapping each session s_i, to a set of roles
  $roles(s_i) \subseteq \{r|(user(s_i), r) \in UA\}$ (which can change with time) and
  session s_i has the permissions $\cup_{r \in roles(s_i)}\{p|(p, r) \in PA\}$.

For role-based access control models whose roles describe intersecting permission sets, role hierarchies in which permissions are passed along the hierarchy via inheritance can be introduced . This leads to the extended model $RBAC_1$ given in [Sandhu et al., 1996, p. 42] (examples will be given in a later section):

$RBAC_1$

- U, R, P, S, PA, UA, and $user$ are unchanged from $RBAC_0$;

- $RH \subseteq R \times R$ is a partial order on R called the role hierarchy or role dominance relation, also written as $\geq$; and

- $roles : S \rightarrow 2^R$ is modified from $RBAC_0$ to require
  $roles(s_i) \subseteq \{r|(\exists r' \geq r)[(user(s_i), r') \in UA]\}$ (which can change with time) and
  session s_i has the permissions $\cup_{r \in roles(s_i)}\{p|(\exists r'' \leq r)[(p, r'') \in PA]\}$.

A further extension can be made through $RBAC_2$ [Sandhu et al., 1996, p. 44] which allows for integration of arbitrary predicates whose truth values are contingent on their compliance with constraints (e.g., mutual exclusion of roles for one user in the same session or in all sessions, i.e., dynamic or static separation of duty, see above and [Sandhu, 1998], [Kuhn, 1997], [Simon and Zurko, 1997]). In order to fulfill the information request, the necessary access modes must be present and the predicates must be true.

Role-based access control models are policy neutral. Nevertheless, because of their flexibility and expressiveness, several policies, and thereby security models, can be modeled by RBAC. Nyanchama and Osborn (see [Nyanchama and Osborn, 1995], [Osborn, 1997], and [Sandhu, 1996b]) describe the emulation of a mandatory access control model (see *Chapter 7.1.2.2*). Sandhu and Munawer [Sandhu and Munawer, 1998] show how a discretionary access model (see *Chapter 7.1.2.3*) can be represented by RBAC, and Barkley [Barkley, 1997] shows how access control lists (see *Chapter 7.1.2.3*) can be expressed by RBAC.

The role-based access control model makes it possible to implement several of the policies which are mandatory in the *security models* described in *Chapter 7.1.2*, and to vary these policies according to the requirements[24] of particular user adaptive systems. The role-based access control model is also flexible enough to support a changing number of user model clients through data abstraction.

1.2.5 Applicability of Security Models to User Modeling

This section compares the *security models* presented in the previous sections and rates their applicability for the purpose of user modeling. With respect to general information systems, the *security models* described here have been compared by Pernul [Pernul, 1995] and others (e.g., [Dobson and McDermid, 1989], [Gollmann, 1999], [Landwehr, 1997], [McLean, 1987], [Pernul, 1994], [Pernul and Tjoa, 1992], [Sandhu, 1996a], and [Summers, 1997]).

Security models are just as important for user adaptive systems as they are for general information systems. Depending on the domain and structure of the user adaptive system, the mode of cooperation between different application systems (e.g., application system *A* and application system *B* in Figure 5.1 on p. 55) using a shared user model, and the demands of the user being modeled, different security models are appropriate.

Noninterference models are most appropriate when several application systems maintaining a common user model need to be separated completely (see CONT-DIV, CONT-SEP in Figure 5.1 on p. 55).

The *Chinese Wall security policy* provides a formalism for specifying *conflict classes* (e.g., *cont(A)* and *cont(B)* in Figure 5.1 on p. 55) from which a specific user model client can choose to access information from only one of the conflicting classes. An assignment of particular conflicting classes to user model clients is not made by the *Chinese Wall security policy*. The client choosing one class out of a set of conflicting

---

[24]For instance, the described *security models* focus either on the requirement for confidentiality *or* on the requirement for integrity (see *Chapter 7.2.2.1*). For user models, an orientation either on confidentiality or on integrity would both yield negative results. In the first case, user model clients which are classified to handle confidential information are not able to correct user model information which is accessible to user model clients which are classified to handle less confidential information – the integrity of user model information on lower confidentiality levels can therefore not be maintained by clients on higher confidentiality levels. In the latter case, clients which are considered to foster the integrity better must be able to supersede a greater set of user model information than clients which are less reliable – therefore clients on a high integrity level will keep their information less confidential. For user modeling purposes, a mixture of these two orientations will be suitable which affords a security model that can adapt to varying policies.

classes (for instance, $cont(A)$) determines for itself which classes are to be excluded for further requests (for instance, all classes which conflict with $cont(A)$). Thus, it is not possible with the *Chinese Wall security policy* to prevent access to a class of sensitive information for a particular client.

The Goguen and Meseguer *noninterference model* makes it possible to separate user model clients maintaining a common user model by assigning clients to groups. In addition to noninterference of clients, noninterference of commands (e.g., the insertion of user model entries) can also be formulated within the model. When combined with one another, particular commands issued by particular clients can be defined as being noninterfering with other clients (i.e., the execution of these commands cannot be detected by other application systems). Crucial for the noninterference model is the history of all issued commands starting from an initial state and the ability to purge commands from the history. User modeling components usually don't keep a history of all executed commands. However, even if they did, it is likely that a history purged by arbitrarily chosen commands would result in an inconsistent state of the user modeling component. This danger would be particularly great for conflict classes which are not static (for instance, when clients change or join a conflict class).

In their *multi-level security model* Bell and LaPadula provide means for classifying user model entries and application systems according to content classes and sensitivity levels. Furthermore, the model defines the permissible information flow in order to prevent information from becoming accessible in content classes which were not assigned or on sensitivity levels which are lower than expected. The *no write down property* supports confidentiality within a user adaptive system but has two consequences which are counterproductive[25]: First, application systems in which the user trusts (i.e., application systems on a high sensitivity level) are unable to supersede (e.g., *update, delete*) entries made by application systems on a lower sensitivity level. This means that trusted application systems are not allowed to correct user model entries made by untrusted application systems. Second, untrusted application systems are not allowed to acquire knowledge of *any* user model entry made by an application in which the user places greater trust. These characteristics lower the trustworthiness of the user model entries and consequently diminish the quality of the user adaptive system.

---

[25]The conflict between confidentiality and integrity inherent in such security models is discussed in [Wiseman, 1991] and on p. 120. Possible ways of resolving this conflict are explored in *Chapter 7.2.2.4* and *Chapter 7.1.2.4*.

Using Denning's *information flow model*, it is possible to specify permissible information flows by arranging security classes in a lattice. This allows for a more flexible security policy – in contrast to the multi-level security model where the security policy is mandatory. Nevertheless, an information flow between classes caused by a command sequence can be detected only by a tremendous amount of computation (see the comparatively simple example on p. 113).

Common to the noninterference, multi-level security, and information flow models is the fact that the defined security policy must be enforced by the user modeling system. For example, the noninterference model relies on the history of commands and on their virtual execution after being purged of certain commands. This can only be done, if at all, by the user modeling system. The multi-level security model presumes that information is not processed outside the component implementing the security model. Otherwise it would be possible to retrieve information belonging to a security level $f_C(s)$ and insert that information on a security level $f'_C(s)$ subdominant to $f_C(s)$ (thereby violating the *-property, see Expression 7.3 on p. 111). For the information flow control model, it is essential to calculate the conditional entropy for all user model entries before each state transition of the user modeling component. Because inferences within the user modeling component influence the conditional entropy of a user model entry (see example 7.10 on p. 114), the calculation can only be performed within this component.

To be implemented within a user modeling system, these security models must be adapted to the specific representation and inference techniques of the particular user modeling system. They are therefore not independent of the user modeling system employed.

For the majority of user adaptive systems, it is appropriate to focus on the interface of the user modeling component with the user adaptive system. Controlling the communication between application systems and the user modeling component makes it possible to specify the joint maintenance of a shared user model through selective access to information. This approach makes no assumptions about the internal structure and information processing of the user modeling component and is therefore generally applicable.

The role-based access control makes it possible to develop simple and intuitive security models as well as to emulate many well-known security models. The balance between security requirements and convenient use can be achieved on different levels of granularity (e.g., different structures of the role hierarchy) – which is especially important for user adaptive systems in which a user protecting his user model is included in the system.

The role-based access control model implemented here and its potential for user modeling purposes will be discussed in the next section.

1.3   Confidentiality through the Role-Based Access Control Model

In the previous section the role-based access control model was described and compared with other well-known security models. Because it is independent of a given policy and is flexible in supporting a changing number of application systems, we recommend this access control model for use within user adaptive systems.

This section offers examples of policies which apply to the use of user model entries by application systems and are expressed as role-based access control models (RBAC models).

User models often collect data on the interests of their users in order to provide adaptive application systems with a basis for personalized information supply. While "some application systems only make use of the user's interests stored in the user model"[26] (i.e., they are *interest consumers*), "other application systems have to insert or update entries in the user model" (i.e., they are *interest producers*). "A certain set of permissions is common to all application systems" (e.g., contacting the user model, *interest maintainer*) and "all permissions must be available for a supervisor" which must be able to correct the user model entries (for instance, the user, *interest supervisor*).

Given the competencies described above for the roles[27] *interest_consumer*, *interest_producer*, *interest_maintainer*, and *interest_supervisor*, a hierarchy of roles can be arranged where permissions[28] are propagated (i.e., *inherited*) along the hierarchy in the direction of the arrows:

---

[26]Common requirements of user adaptive systems used for the examples in this section are enclosed in quotation marks.
[27]See also the *security classes* of example 7.10 on p. 114.
[28]Permissions for this example are defined on pp. 128 and 136.

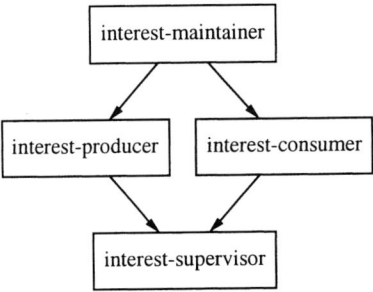

Figure 7.2. Role hierarchy arranging roles according to competencies

In the terminology of $RBAC_1$ (see *Chapter 7.1.2.4*), the role hierarchy is given by:

$$RH = \{ \quad (interest\_supervisor, interest\_producer), \\ (interest\_supervisor, interest\_consumer), \\ (interest\_producer, interest\_maintainer), \\ (interest\_consumer, interest\_maintainer) \quad \} \tag{7.15}$$

where the elements of RH represent the *dominance relation*: $(a, b) \in RH : a \geq b$.

For many user adaptive systems, there are different implementations for a type of application system (e.g., different implementations for a news reader exist as representatives for *interest_consumer*) and different implementations "can be on different user's trust levels" depending on their reliability, the implementer, the availability of the source code, etc.

To illustrate, we have chosen three *trust levels*: *untrusted* (no assurances regarding the trust level of the implementation can be given), *trusted* (the implementation is assumed to be trustworthy, e.g., based either on experience or on recommendation), *inspected* (the trustworthiness of the implementation has been proven, e.g., by inspection of the source code).

Through ordering the three levels (*inspected* $\geq$ *trusted* $\geq$ *untrusted*) a second hierarchy is established which is orthogonal to the classification shown in Figure 7.2. A combination of these two orthogonal hierarchies (e.g., *interest_consumer_tr* represents a "trusted interest consumer") is shown in Figure 7.3:

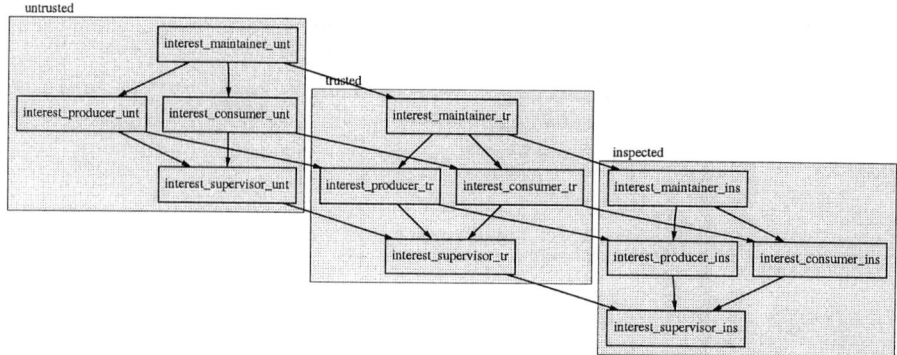

Figure 7.3.   Layered role hierarchy grouped by trust levels

The roles in the figure are grouped by trust levels. Within one trust level group (e.g. *trusted*, a hierarchy similar to that of Figure 7.2 on p. 125 can be recognized). Arrows between roles in different groups represent the way in which permissions are passed (*inherited*) between hierarchies on different trust levels. The role hierarchy for the example in Figure 7.3 is denoted by:

$$
\begin{aligned}
RH_1 = \{ \quad & (interest\_maintainer\_unt, interest\_maintainer\_tr), \\
& (interest\_maintainer\_tr, interest\_maintainer\_ins), \\
& (interest\_producer\_unt, interest\_producer\_tr), \\
& (interest\_producer\_tr, interest\_producer\_ins), \\
& (interest\_consumer\_unt, interest\_consumer\_tr,), \\
& (interest\_consumer\_tr, interest\_consumer\_ins), \\
& (interest\_supervisor\_unt, interest\_supervisor\_tr), \\
& (interest\_supervisor\_tr, interest\_supervisor\_ins), \\
& (interest\_maintainer\_unt, interest\_producer\_unt), \\
& (interest\_maintainer\_unt, interest\_consumer\_unt), \\
& (interest\_producer\_unt, interest\_supervisor\_unt), \\
& (interest\_consumer\_unt, interest\_supervisor\_unt), \\
& (interest\_maintainer\_tr, interest\_producer\_tr), \\
& (interest\_maintainer\_tr, interest\_consumer\_tr), \\
& (interest\_producer\_tr, interest\_supervisor\_tr), \\
& (interest\_consumer\_tr, interest\_supervisor\_tr), \\
& (interest\_maintainer\_ins, interest\_producer\_ins), \\
& (interest\_maintainer\_ins, interest\_consumer\_ins), \\
& (interest\_producer\_ins, interest\_supervisor\_ins), \\
& (interest\_consumer\_ins, interest\_supervisor\_ins) \quad \}
\end{aligned}
\tag{7.16}
$$

The same hierarchy as depicted in Figure 7.3 and denoted by RH_1 in Equation 7.16 is shown in Figure 7.4 where roles are not grouped by trust levels (see Figure 7.3), but by competencies:

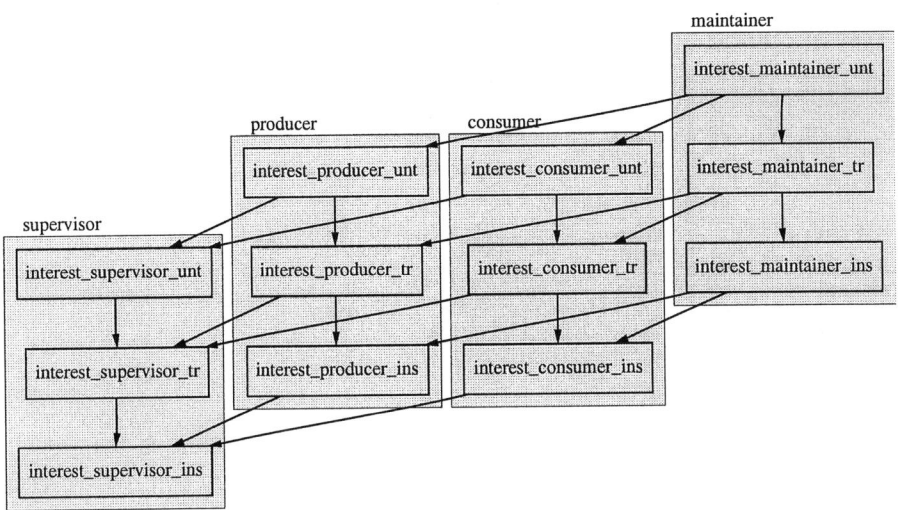

Figure 7.4. Layered role hierarchy grouped by competencies

So far, competencies required when manipulating assumptions about the user's interests have been defined (see Figure 7.2). The hierarchy of competencies was extended by including different trust levels (see Figure 7.3) resulting in a general hierarchy which can be applied to all user adaptive systems dealing with user interests.

To be more intelligible for users, the role hierarchy can be further extended to include roles describing more specific (exemplary) classes of application systems (e.g., *WWW-news-service*, *news-reader*, and *model-owner*):

$$RH_2 = RH_1 \cup \{ \quad (interest\_producer\_unt, WWW\text{-}news\text{-}service),$$
$$(interest\_consumer\_tr, news\text{-}reader),$$
$$(interest\_supervisor\_ins, model\text{-}owner) \quad \}$$
$$(7.17)$$

With respect to the roles of the hierarchy RH_2 a *permission-to-role assignment*[29] PA (see $RBAC_0$ on p. 119) can be depicted in the following way:

---

[29]More precisely: permission names are related to role names.

$$PA = \{ \quad (interest\_maintainer\_unt, update),$$
$$(interest\_maintainer\_tr, insert),$$
$$(interest\_consumer\_tr, ask\text{-}if),$$
$$(interest\_producer\_tr, delete\text{-}one), \qquad\qquad (7.18)$$
$$(interest\_consumer\_ins, ask\text{-}all),$$
$$(interest\_producer\_ins, delete\text{-}all) \quad \}$$

The permission-to-role assignment[30] is motivated by the following requirements of a common user adaptive system :

update	"All application systems are allowed to update user model entries."
insert	"Only trusted application systems are allowed to insert new entries."
ask-if	"Some of the trusted application systems are allowed to acquire knowledge about particular interests."
delete-one	"Some of the trusted application systems are allowed to delete particular interests. "
ask-all	"Some of the inspected application systems are allowed to acquire knowledge about all interests."
delete-all	"Some of the inspected application systems are allowed to delete all interests."

The distribution of permissions and the way they are passed along the hierarchy RH_2 to the specific roles of RH_2, which were added to RH_1 in Equation 7.17, can be depicted in the following way:

---

[30]Permission names are motivated by KQML performatives, see *Chapter 6.2.2.*

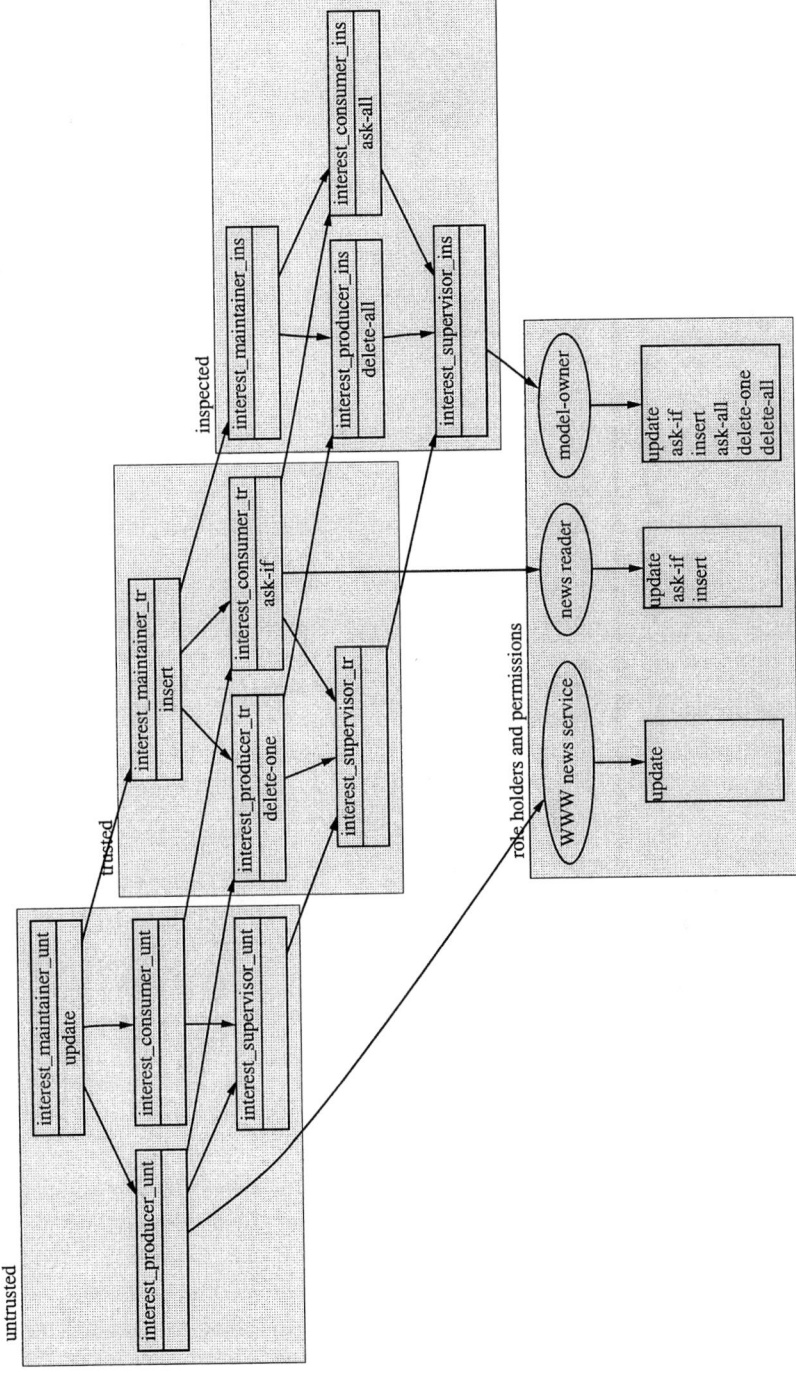

Figure 7.5. Role hierarchy with permission inheritance

To complete the role-based access control model $RBAC_1$ (see p. 120) for this example, the

- set of users (i.e., application systems) is defined as $U = \{appl1, appl2\}$,

- the *user-to-role assignment* relation
  $UA = \{(appl1, WWW\text{-}news\text{-}service), (appl2, news\text{-}reader)\}$,

- and the function *roles* as the maximum of all applicable roles for two sessions[31] s_{appl1} and s_{appl2}:
  $roles(s_{appl1}) = \{WWW\text{-}news\text{-}service\}$ and $roles(s_{appl2}) = \{news\text{-}reader\}$ are defined.

This gives us the permission sets $P_{s_{appl1}} = \{update\}$ and $P_{s_{appl2}} = \{update, ask\text{-}if, insert\}$. In the next section, this example will also be discussed in connection with the implementation we developed for role-based access control in user modeling.

Another example of a role hierarchy[32] that can be applied to user adaptive systems is given in [Schreck, 1997b] where the motivation for defining roles can be traced to different kinds of agents (i.e., application systems) embedded in a user adaptive system:

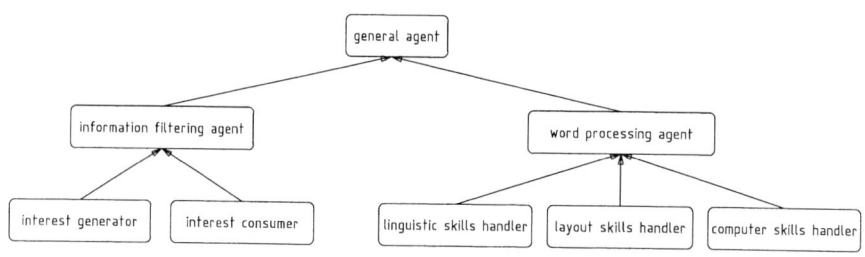

Figure 7.6.   Role hierarchy concerning agents

Modeling characteristics valuable for *information filtering* and *word processing* usually underly different mechanisms and domains of user modeling (see *Chapter 1*). By analogy, access to the characteristics should be defined and administered in the different and independent domains which are best qualified for this task (e.g., in *trust centers*). The follow-

---

[31]Sessions are defined in the following section.
[32]Arrows are in opposite direction.

ing figure depicts the situation where two role hierarchies[33] reference[34] roles of a third hierarchy containing roles general to both domains:

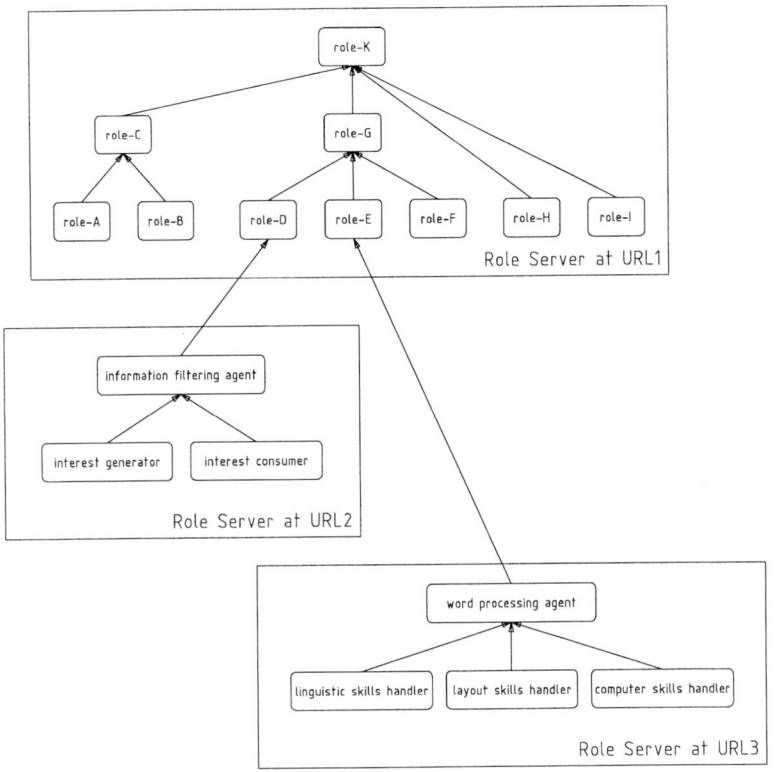

Figure 7.7. Role hierarchies spanning different domains

By dividing role hierarchies into different areas of responsibility, which extends the model $RBAC_2$, the *delegation of administration* and *scalability* required in *Chapter 5.1.2* can be achieved. The *flexibility* of the role arrangement means that expectations regarding *confidentiality* and its *grade* can be met and constraints which are included in $RBAC_2$ (e.g., static or dynamic separation of duty) can be applied. The most important feature of our proposed model is its *user orientation*; it is intelligible even to users who wish to protect their own user model (see the specific roles in Figure 7.5 which were added to RH_1 in Equation 7.17 on p. 127).

---

[33]Arrows are in opposite direction.
[34]See next section for the definition of reference.

1.4   Implementation of a Role-Based Access Control Model

This section describes an implementation developed in this work in order to define and enforce a role-based access control model (see $RBAC_0$ on p. 119) within a user adaptive system. As a basis, the $RBAC/Web$ *implementation*[35] of NIST[36] is used (see [Barkley et al., 1997], [Ferraiolo et al., 1999], and [Sandhu and Park, 1998]), making the following possible:

- definition of the set of application systems U and the set of roles R (see the reference model $RBAC_0$ on p. 119), and the role hierarchy RH (see the reference model $RBAC_1$ on p. 120 and Equation 7.15),

- definition of constraints regarding role hierarchies (e.g., static and dynamic separation of duty, p. 119),

- definition of user-role assignment (i.e., the relation UA, see the reference model $RBAC_0$, p. 119 and p. 130),

- specification of maximum cardinality for a role (i.e., the maximum number of application systems which can assume a particular role),

- visualization of role hierarchies and user assignment, and

- convenient use via a WWW interface.

After being identified and authenticated[37] by RBAC/Web, the role administrator is able to define users[38], roles, a role hierarchy (i.e., inheritance of permissions, see RH_1 on p. 126), maximum cardinality of roles, and the mutual exclusion of roles (e.g., separation of duty).

The following figure shows the role administrator's interface with values for the definition of the exemplary role hierarchy RH_1 (see Equation

---

[35] RBAC/Web Release 1.1, http://csrc.nist.gov/rbac/
[36] National Institute of Standards and Technology, Maryland, USA
[37] The identification and authentication of the role administrator is handled via the web server.
[38] *Users* of the RBAC model correspond to application systems for the scope of this work, but might also include the user of the user adaptive system.

7.16 on p. 126) used in the previous section:

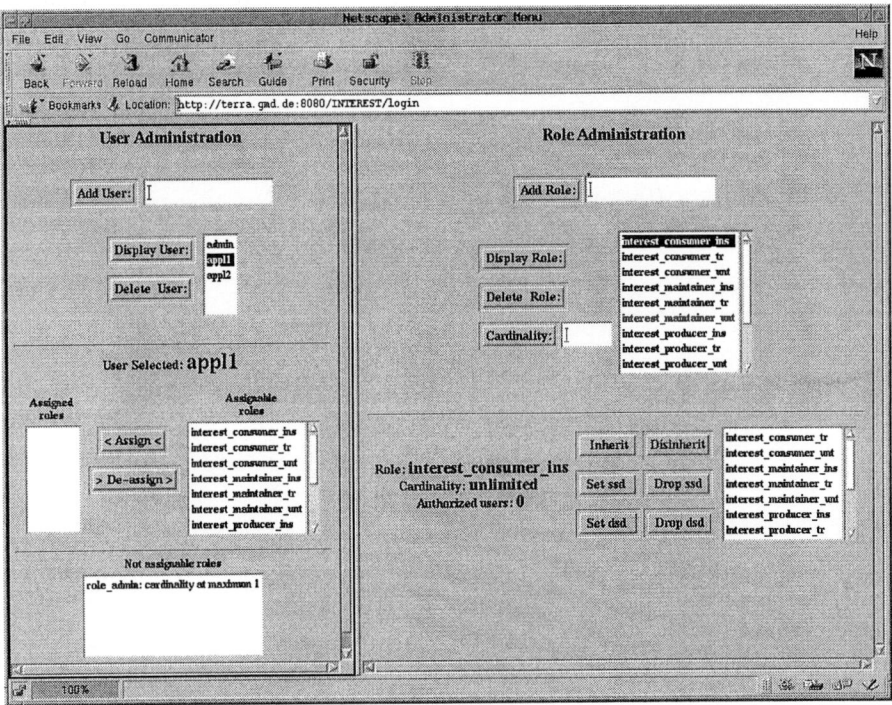

Figure 7.8. RBAC/Web user interface for role definition

The defined role hierarchy (e.g., RH_1) can also be represented in graphic form (see also Figure 7.3 on p. 126 and Figure 7.4 on p. 127):

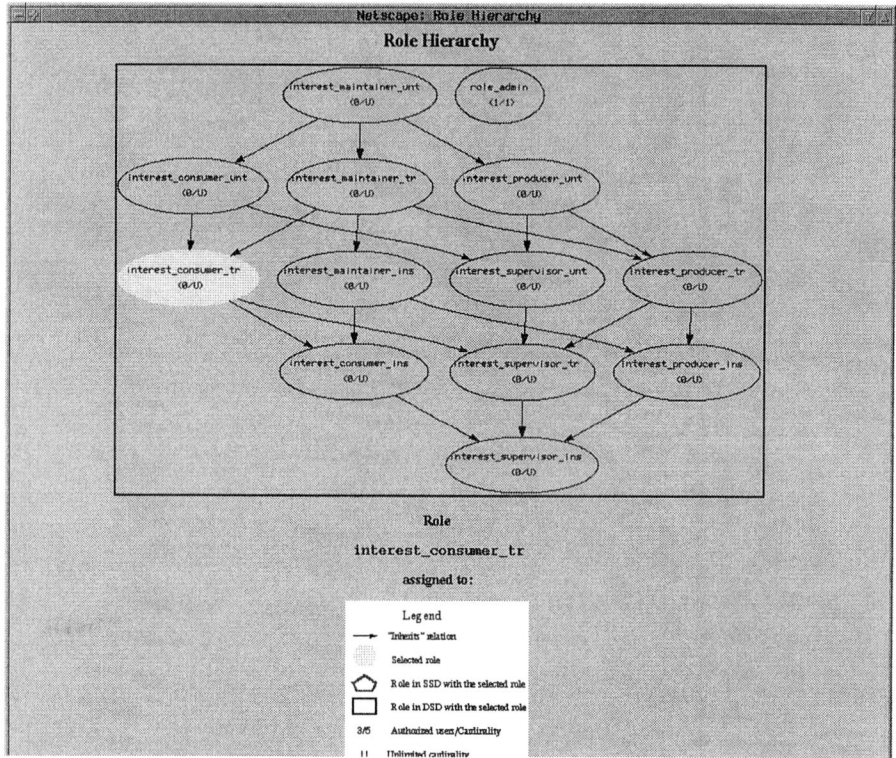

Figure 7.9. RBAC/Web user interface for graphic representation of a role hierarchy

In Figure 7.5 on p. 129 the role hierarchy RH_1 (see Equation 7.16 on p. 126) was enlarged by the specific roles *WWW-news-service, news-reader*, and *model-owner* to create the role hierarchy RH_2 (see Equation 7.17 on p. 127), providing the user with role names suitable for his domain. In Figure 7.7 on p. 131 a role hierarchy was put together by referencing RBAC models from different domains. An analogous division can be made for RH_2 in which the exemplary $domain_{interest}$ contains[39] RH_1 and is administered by experts in interest modeling. The roles $RH_2 \setminus RH_1$ can be arranged in a second $domain_{IntAppl}$ which can be maintained by another role administrator or by the user himself. With different instances of the RBAC/Web implementation, differ-

---

[39]The domain contains not only independent role hierarchies but independent RBAC models (see $RBAC_0$, $RBAC_1$, and $RBAC_2$ in *Chapter 7.1.2.4*).

ent RBAC models can be managed and addressed by different URLs[40]. Through this small extension to the RBAC/Web implementation, it is possible to associate different RBAC models (as described above, for instance, those in the domains $domain_{interest}$ and $domain_{IntAppl}$) in order to be able to link different RBAC models. In Figure 7.11 on p. 136 the string $interest\_consumer\_tr@INTEREST\text{-}Server$ is a reference to $domain_{interest}$ which establishes an inheritance relation between the role $interest\_consumer\_tr$ of $domain_{interest}$ to the role $news\text{-}reader$ of $domain_{IntAppl}$ (see Figures 7.5 and 7.7). Thereby, the permissions assigned to role $interest\_consumer\_tr$ in $domain_{interest}$ also apply to $interest\_consumer\_tr@INTEREST\text{-}Server$ in $domain_{IntAppl}$ which transfers these permissions to the role $news\text{-}reader$ (see Figure 7.10):

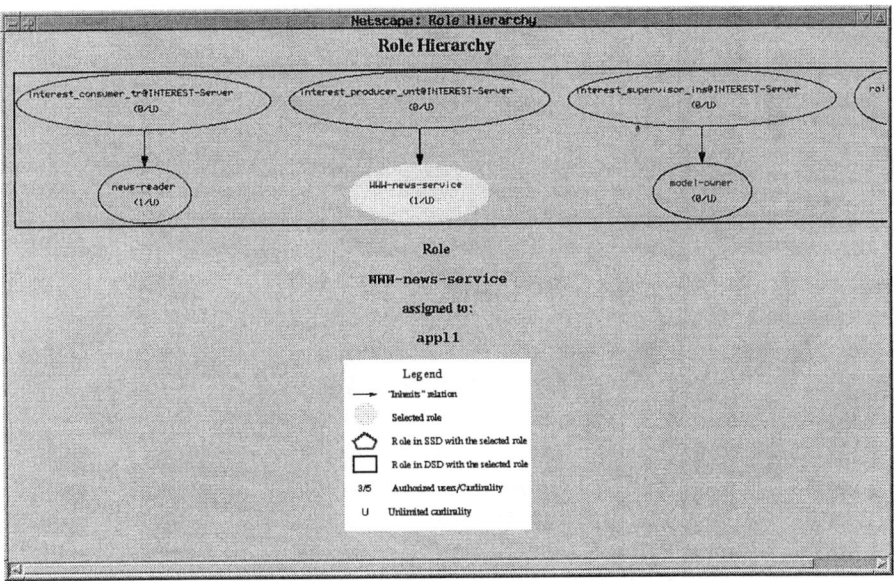

Figure 7.10. RBAC/Web user interface for graphic representation of user-role assignment

The RBAC/Web implementation also assists in managing the user-role assignment UA (see $RBAC_0$ on p. 119). Figure 7.11 shows the interface for the user-role assignment UA (see p. 130) for $domain_{IntAppl}$ in which *appl1* can assume the role $WWW\text{-}news\text{-}service$:

---

[40]Compare the URLs of Figures 7.8 and 7.11:
$domain_{interest}$ at `http://terra.gmd.de:8080/INTEREST/login`
$domain_{IntAppl}$ at `http://terra.gmd.de:8080/OFFICEAPPLICATION/login` .

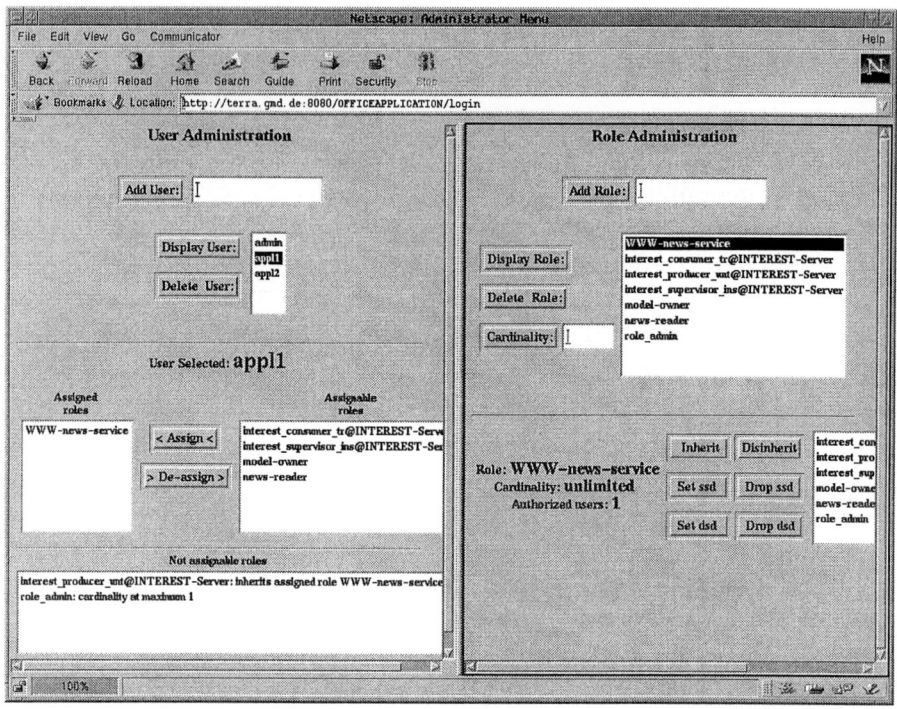

Figure 7.11. RBAC/Web user interface for user assignment

Since the RBAC/Web implementation supports only the arrangement[41] of roles into a hierarchy and the assignment[42] of users to roles, it was necessary to add the assignment[43] of permissions to roles, the inheritance of permissions along the role hierarchy and the functions[44] *user* and *roles* to RBAC/Web in order to achieve an implementation which is able to enforce the RBAC model in a user adaptive system.

The term *permission* used in the previous sections is defined here as a pair consisting of the *permission name*[45] and the *permission definition*. On the basis of the permission definition, access requests from components of the user adaptive system can be verified by the RBAC model. Access requests consist of KQML messages[46] which are compared with *regular expressions* which specify the kind of access (e.g., getting knowledge of the data without modifying it) as well as the data affected. For

---

[41] See the definition of the relation *RH* on p. 120.

[42] See the definition of the relation *UA* on p. 119.

[43] See the definition of the relation *PA* on p. 119.

[44] See p. 119.

[45] See Equation 7.18 on p. 128.

[46] See *Chapter 6.2.2.*

user models, it is appropriate to specify classes of data affected rather than single items. In Figure 7.12 an example[47] for a permission definition is given which specifies the permission *ask-if* (see Equation 7.18 on p. 128) as a KQML *ask-if* performative which refers, for example, in the BGP-MS user modeling shell system, to the partition *SBUB* (see [Kobsa and Pohl, 1995] and [Pohl, 1998]):

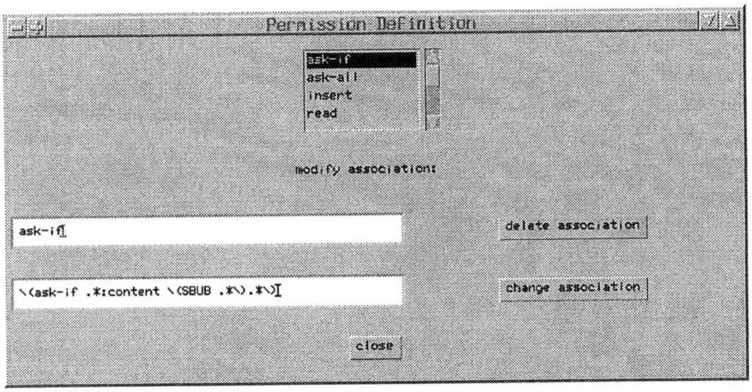

Figure 7.12. A definition of permission

With a complete set of permissions P and roles R, the permission-to-role assignment (i.e., the relation PA on p. 119) can be established. The figure shows the assignment of the permissions *insert* and *update* to the role *interest_consumer_tr*:

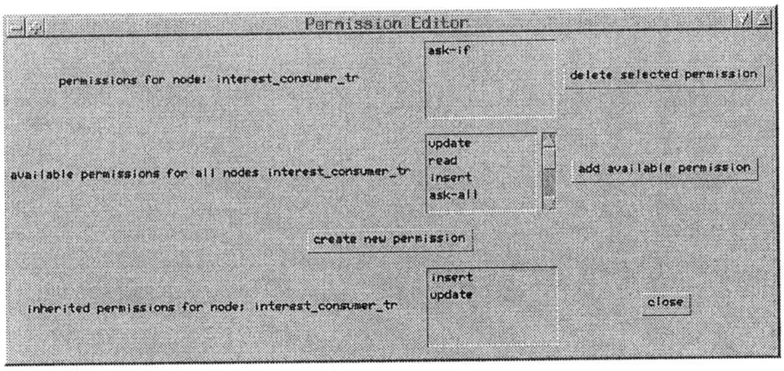

Figure 7.13. Permission-to-role assignment

With the interfaces depicted in Figures 7.12, 7.13, and 7.14, the developer of the RBAC model is able to authorize (see *Chapter 5.2.1*) the

---

[47]See *Chapter 8.2* for further examples.

roles and to represent graphically the way permissions are passed on through inheritance within the role hierarchy.

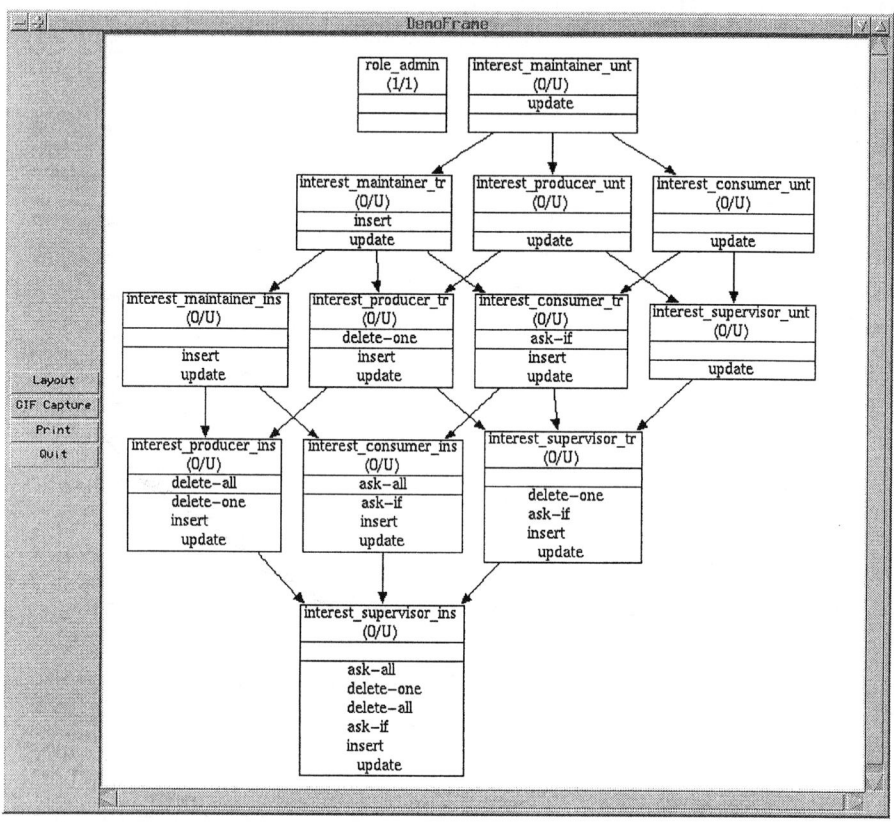

Figure 7.14.   Graphic representation of the permission-to-role assignment

As shown in the previous figures, extensions to the RBAC/Web implementation are necessary to support the combination of different RBAC models in different domains by means of reference to roles of different domains. A further extension permits the definition of permissions and their assignment to roles (i.e. authorization). By comparing[48] an access request with a permission, the compliance of the access request with the RBAC model can be validated[49]. With this implementation, we are able to define and enforce a security model which supports the confidentiality

---

[48]In this implementation, a session s_i (see $RBAC_0$ on p. 119) lasts for one access request and $user(s_i)$ results in the name of the (possibly authenticated) sender of the SKQML message. The maximum set of possible roles is applied for $user(s_i)$.
[49]See also the example described in *Chapter 8.2* on p. 164.

of user model entries (described by an RBAC model) in a user adaptive system.

1.5 Motivation for Roles in RBAC

In *Chapter 7.1.3* the role-based access control model was defined with respect to the potential clients of user models (e.g, *news-reader*) and their assignment to *roles* (i.e., the members of the set R). The examples for roles given in several equations[50] were motivated by access modes to information and by trust in the information requester. These examples in no way limit the proposed RBAC model to a specific policy. Common to examples[51] of RBAC models is that the definition of roles and their hierarchy is motivated by the information requesters (i.e., members of the set U) thereby specifying the *context* (e.g., *information filtering*) in which the requested information may be used. Another way of controlling access to information is to define the RBAC model according to *content-dependent* aspects [Summers, 1997, p. 130]:

> "**Context-dependent and content-dependent access control.** An access decision may use information about the context in which the decision is made. This may be environment information (time of day, for example), subject attributes (such as location, job responsibilities, or history of other accesses), and object attributes (such as file size or creation date). Access control using such information is called *context-dependent*. *Content-dependent* control uses information in the object being accessed. Content-dependent control is especially relevant for database systems, where the data is structured enough to be used in access decisions."

Particularly in user adaptive systems, data (i.e., information about the user being modeled) is structured to support processing, for instance, to support inference mechanisms (see BGP-MS *partition hierarchies*, [Kobsa and Pohl, 1995], [Pohl, 1998]). The same or similar structures might be used as a basis for defining the role hierarchy (see example of *Chapter 8.2*).

Given a user model with an internal structure describing the content of the data, the role definition can be motivated by the content's structure. In the case of user modeling it is logical to define the roles of the RBAC model according to the user's roles. A very general example from role theory for a user's roles[52] is given in [Oeser and Harary, 1966, p. 100]:

---

[50]See Equations 7.15 on p. 125, 7.16 on p. 126, and 7.17 on p. 127.

[51]See [Ferraiolo et al., 1999], [Gavrila and Barkley, 1998], [Goh and Baldwin, 1998], [Lawrence, 1993], [Moffett, 1998], [Nyanchama and Osborn, 1994], [Sandhu et al., 1996], and [Sandhu and Park, 1998].

[52]In contrast to this simple example, Zurfluh argues that persons might assume up to 100 roles in interaction with their environment [Zurfluh, 1998, p. 50].

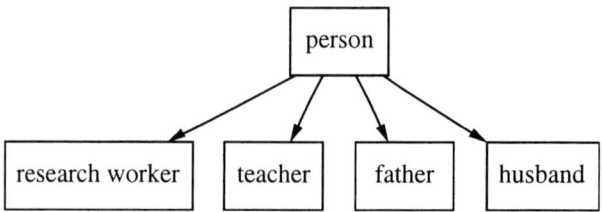

Figure 7.15.   Example of a user's roles

For the purpose of user modeling, the user's roles must be more specific to provide an effective basis for the role-based access control model. The user's general *customer* role might be further subdivided into the roles *anonymous customer* and *identified customer*. This division can improve the user's privacy while interacting with a user adaptive system of the electronic commerce domain. For example, an application system might access information treated by the *anonymous customer* role in order to offer advice based on the user's personal characteristics to the user who is trying to select a product. Information treated by the *identified customer* role should only be accessible to the application system after the user has decided to a carry out a transaction which requires identification (e.g., delivery of products or payment).

Another example of the different roles a user can assume while interacting with a user adaptive system is given in [Jones, 1989, Chap. 2] where combinations of the *patient* and *agent* roles are discussed with respect to a medical information system.

1.6   Summary

The previous sections covered solutions for *secrecy in user modeling*. It was shown that secrecy of the user modeling information can be achieved through anonymization and through encryption of data. For the encryption of user modeling data, the means for exchanging user model entries in electronic networks were extended to include the *Secure Sockets Layer*. This implementation also makes it possible to authenticate the information exchanged, thereby supporting information integrity, as we will see in a section below.

Confidentiality of user model information which is shared by several user model clients, was covered as a weaker form of secrecy. Several *security models* which have been explored in the security literature were presented and their applicability and advantages for user modeling purposes were described and exemplified.

From the security models presented here, the role-based access control model was chosen for implementation because of its flexibility and applicability for a wide range of user adaptive systems. As an access control model, it can assure both the confidentiality of the user modeling information and its integrity even though it may not be possible to ensure both simultaneously for each user adaptive system.

The definition of the role hierarchy within the role-based access control model was motivated by the usage context of the user modeling data (i.e., context-dependent access control, see Equation 7.17 on p. 127). It was also shown that the motivation for the definition of a hierarchy according to the users' roles while interacting with a user adaptive system (i.e., content-dependent access control) can support the user's privacy.

2. Solutions for Integrity

In the previous section (see *Chapter 7.1*) solutions for the complex of *secrecy* were explored. As another constituent of *security* in user modeling, *integrity* and the ways of meeting its requirements will be dealt with in this section.

As far as possible, measures and methods will be described which are compliant with the requirements listed in *Chapter 5.2*. In addition, mutually exclusive ways of meeting integrity requirements are discussed. It will become evident that, due to the influence of factors which determine the integrity of the particular user adaptive system and user modeling system, general solutions like those described in *Chapter 7.1* which can be applied to the majority of user adaptive systems, do not exist.

For this reason, solutions which advance integrity will often be discussed with respect to a particular user modeling system where appropriate.

2.1 External Integrity

External integrity is considered from the perspective of user model clients (i.e., application systems) which make use of the user model information. Solutions for providing external integrity (see *Chapter 5.2.1*) cannot be discussed in general because of the dependence on the user adaptive system and its domain. Instead we will focus on exemplary solutions implemented in several user modeling systems.

2.1.1 Consistency

The user adaptive system can only provide steady adaptations to the user if the user model is consistent (i.e., does not contain contradictory user model entries). The assurance of consistency is covered in the literature on several user modeling shell systems, for example, in GUMS [Finin, 1989] or in UMT [Brajnik and Tasso, 1994, p. 41]:

"More precisely, a *possible user model* is a consistent set of assertions, including all known premises, a maximal set of known assumptions, and all the assertions derived from these premises and assumptions through notified inferences."

Other user modeling shell systems are able to interpret an inconsistency as a misconception and can inform the application system of the discrepancy between the current state and the ideal state. For instance, in BGP-MS, the *alert-from-bgp-ms* is sent (*notified*) to the application in order to signal a *misconception* [Kobsa and Pohl, 1995, p. 70]. The ability to prevent or detect and process inconsistencies is dependent on the user modeling system used to maintain the user model. Due to the varieties of user modeling systems, neither a general solution nor an enumeration of all particular solutions can be given within the scope of this book. Further specific solutions can be found in descriptions of user modeling shell systems (see Table 1.1 on p. 13).

2.1.2   Correctness

User modeling systems often employ *production systems* (e.g., *knowledge-based systems*, see [Genesereth and Nilsson, 1987], [Nilsson, 1980], or [Ullman, 1988]) which infer new assumptions about the user from a set of given assumptions and rules. The validity of the inferred (i.e., newly generated) assumptions must be correct, not only with respect to the calculus utilized in the production system (e.g., predicate calculus, see [Pohl, 1998, Chap. 3] and [Davis, 1993]) but also with respect to the domain of the user adaptive system.

The correctness of the calculus can be verified for most systems. The correctness of an inferred user model entry is contingent on the assumptions *and* the rules represented within the production system. The validity of an inferred entry can be verified by the user being modeled and the developer of the user modeling system. The latter is able to interpret the inferred syntactic entity (i.e., the inferred user model entry) and the former is able to compare the validity of this interpretation with the facts of the domain. The facts of the domain are often accessible only to the users (e.g., their interests or goals). Therefore, means must be provided for the user to verify the correctness of the user model (and the user modeling system). Several user modeling systems provide means for *inspection* and *correction* (see [Paiva et al., 1995] and [Cook and Kay, 1994, p. 145]):

"There are many potential benefits from making a user model accessible to the user it describes. This is on the grounds of the user's right to access information about themselves, the accountability it enforces on the programmer creating and using the model and the benefit of having the user verify or correct the information in the user model."

Nevertheless, the possibility for inspection and correction is no substitute for the required correctness of the user model.

2.1.3 Adequacy

The adequacy of a user model is defined in *Chapter 5.2.1* as the co-existence of *completeness* and *correctness*. Since completeness can only be given for domains which can be formalized to a sufficient extent (e.g., the production rules for assumptions must be explicit) and correctness often requires the user's cooperation, adequacy of a user model is only possible for limited areas of user adaptive systems.

2.1.4 Timeliness

A particular user model entry can change its value caused by many factors, for example:

update: The application system can update the user model entry, thereby changing its value. The timeliness of the updated user model from the perspective of the updating application system is obvious. For other application systems utilizing the same (shared) user model, the update will go unnoticed. Several user modeling systems provide a notification mechanism which informs the application systems about changes of particular user model entries (see the notifications (`alert-from-bgp-ms :retracted-assumption ...`) and (`alert-from-bgp-ms :inferred-assumption ...`) in BGP-MS, [Kobsa and Pohl, 1995, Chap. 2.6]).

update consequence: The update or insertion of a user model entry can influence another user model entry or a set of entries, for instance, by stereotype activation (see the notification (`alert-from-bgp-ms :stereotype-change ...`) [Kobsa and Pohl, 1995, Chap. 2.6]). Both the applications system doing the updating and the other application systems sharing a user model must be notified of this change.

internal mechanisms: User model entries can also be modified by internal mechanisms of the user modeling system which can include information from other user models (e.g., clustering algorithms, learning techniques, aging of attributes, normalization of values, see [Orwant, 1995]). The application systems must be informed of this change as well.

user intervention: Including the user in the maintenance of user model entries also causes changes. User interventions are usually independent of the application system's actions with respect to time. For example, there are several systems in which the user's corrections have the highest priority. In the um system, e.g., [Kay, 1995, p. 172]:

> "The reliability is ordered:
>
> given > rule > observation > stereotype.
>
> If two pieces of evidence have the same reliability, we accept the most recent."

This list of factors by which a user model entry's value can change describes changes caused by explicit actions either by application systems or by the user. Exceptions are *internal mechanisms* of the user modeling system which can operate on a regular basis or only after the input set of user model entries (i.e., the set of user model entries which is not achieved by inference) has changed (e.g., aging of interests, stereotype manipulation).

Not included in our enumeration nor in most user adaptive systems is the change of the domain and the application systems. User model entries in user user modeling systems which employ symbolic representation mechanisms [Pohl, 1998] summarize *concepts* to which they refer by their designator[53]. In many domains, the relation between *designator, intention,* and *extension* is not constant with respect to time (e.g., compare the change of the designator "gopher" to "WWW" with only minor changes to the intention and extension of the concept, changing headlines of news referring to the same story, or often unchanged *subject* lines for news in newsgroups with completely changed content).

2.1.5   Authorization

As described in detail in *Chapter 7.1.2* authorization of application systems can be established in various ways. By means of an access control model, responsibility of application systems for areas of the user model can be expressed and enforced through the assignment of access modes (i.e., permissions) to application systems.

2.1.6   Identification

Chapters 4 and 6 cover various levels of identification ranging from *super-identification* to *anonymity* (see *Chapter 4.1.1*). With the proposed implementations (*KQMLmix* and *SKAPI*) the complete range of identification can be provided in user adaptive systems. *Super-identification, identification,* and *latent identification* can be established through *SKAPI* as well as through *SKQML* (see *Chapter 7.1.1.2* and *Chapter*

---

[53] A concept can be defined as the triple $(designator, intention, extension)$.

6.2.2). *Pseudonymous identification, anonymous identification,* and *anonymity* can be established by *SKQML* and the *KQMLmix* implementation (see *Chapter 6.2.3*).

2.1.7 Authentication

The *SKAPI* implementation also makes it possible to authenticate the communication partners (e.g., the application systems and the user modeling agent) through means provided by the *Secure Sockets Layer (SSL)* via certificates (see Table 7.1 on p. 98). In the same manner, the content of exchanged data is authenticated while in transit (i.e., by means of the MD5 algorithm, see p. 97 and [Hirsch, 1997]).

Because *SKAPI* operates on a low layer (see Table 6.6 on p. 92) and is transparent to the application system, information about the authenticity of the content is not provided to the application system after the authenticity has been proven. Once an authenticated message has been successfully accepted by the user model, the authenticity cannot be subsequently proven (e.g, to another application system).

The proof of origin (i.e., the authenticity) of a particular user model entry is important for many scenarios – for example, when an application system needs to be certain that an authoritative application system has awarded a particular level of expertise to the user, or to the user wants to ascertain which application system has inserted or modified an entry. With the *:signature* value of *SKQML* (see *Chapter 6.2.3.1*), the application system is able to authenticate the sender of a message as well as the authenticity of the message's content. The *:signature* value of the message can be stored with the entry in the model and provided to other application systems or the user for further proofs of authenticity of the user model entry (see [Schreck, 1997b]).

2.1.8 Accountability

The accountability of user model clients for user model entries can be established in different ways. For identified user model clients (see above and *Chapter 4.1.1*), the assignment of user model entries to clients can be established by the user modeling agent. For anonymous user model clients, the origin of a particular user model entry can be established based on the signature which has to be kept with the user model entry (see *Chapter 6.2.2.2*). With the latter method it is not necessary to rely on the user modeling agent's assignment of user model entries to clients, because the signature of an entry can be checked without resorting to the user modeling agent. Not only can the inserting user model client be ascertained with respect to a particular user model entry, but it can also be determined whether the user model entry has been modified since its insertion (e.g., through processes carried out by the user modeling agent).

Through accountability of user model clients, the user is able to re-trace the client which inserted or changed particular user model entries. This enables the user to evaluate user model clients (i.e., application systems) and to modify the authorization (see above). The accountability of clients is also the basis for the supervision of the user adaptive system.

2.1.9   Supervision

Different aspects of the supervision of the user model and its processes have been treated by several user modeling shell systems. Kay argues not only for accessibility to the user but also for simplicity of user model entries:

> "Accessibility of the user model is a critical aspect of um's design. If a user model is to be *effectively* accessible, the user must be able to understand it. One strategy for achieving this is to strive for simplicity at all levels." [Kay, 1995, p. 179]

Simplicity of user model entries requires an understandable terminology and a clear presentation (e.g., similar to that presented in *Chapter 8.5*). However, simplicity of the rules of the production system often runs counter to its expressive power (see [Pohl, 1998, Chap. 5]). For simple representation styles and inference procedures, viewer components which visualize user model entries and their justification (frequently depicted as chains of rules) are possible. The um toolkit [Kay, 1995, p. 181] of-fers possibilities for viewing an *explanation* of a user model entry and its *justification* as well as for modifying the entry by choosing one of three possible values. Doppelgänger provides a natural language inter-face which allows for inspection and correction of user model entries via email [Orwant, 1994]. TAGUS[54] proposes a method for *externalizing* a user model so that it can also be inspected and corrected outside the user modeling shell system [Paiva et al., 1995]. The externalization of the model contains both assertions about the user and chains of rules used to generate inferred assertions.

Supervision consists of more than just inspection and correction of user model entries. It also includes means for acquiring information about the complete user adaptive system's manner of processing, in-cluding:

- monitoring the information flow to and from the user model,

---

[54] *Theory and Applications for General User/Learner-modeling Systems*

- adjusting the amount of (or even disabling) user modeling activity within the user adaptive system, and

- establishing accountability for modifications of user model entries to application systems in order to judge the reliability of these systems.

2.2 Internal Integrity

In this section solutions are presented which meet the requirements for internal integrity of user models and user modeling systems as outlined in *Chapter 5.2.2*. Due to their dependence on the mechanisms implemented in the user modeling systems, these solutions will often be discussed in regard to measures provided by particular systems implemented.

2.2.1 Data Integrity

Integrity of the data processed in a user modeling system is essential for the *correctness* and *consistency* of a user model (see *Chapter 7.2.1.2* and *Chapter 7.2.1.1*). The integrity of the user model is dependent on the user modeling system implementing the model, its representation mechanisms, its inference procedures, and its robustness when confronted with unexpected data. Several methods have been developed in user modeling systems to avoid inconsistencies. For instance, BGP-MS allows the insertion of an entry only if it is consistent with the current set of entries and rules [Pohl, 1998, Chap. 7.2.1]. Because all requests sent from application systems to BGP-MS are evaluated only by means of the set of entries and rules, no dependencies between the entries and inferred assertions need be maintained. TAGUS also checks the consistency of an expression to be inserted and uses furthermore an auxiliary system which maintains the dependencies between entries and their derivations (see [Paiva and Self, 1994b] and [Paiva and Self, 1994a]). The um system provides *resolvers* which to try identify the source of an inconsistency and provide extensible procedures to dissolve the inconsistency [Kay, 1995, Chap. 3.4]. The UMT system has the special component *Consistency Manager* which receives notifications of inconsistencies from the *Model Manager* in order to dissolve them [Brajnik and Tasso, 1994, p. 43].

So far we have explored ways in which the user modeling system and the user can supervise data integrity. However, there are aspects of data integrity which are beyond the scope of the representation and inference mechanism of the user modeling system, and therefore not under its supervision. Particularly in user modeling, data integrity is endangered when several application systems maintain a shared user model. User model entries from different application systems can be inserted into the user model. These entries, while appearing to be consistent with respect to the representation and inference mechanism employed by the user modeling system, might actually be inconsistent when considered within the domain (e.g., the consecutive insertion of an assertion and its converse by different application systems). For the conservation of data integrity on this level, different *integrity models* have been developed in the area of *security in information systems* (without regard to user modeling).

Clark and Wilson's informal integrity model [Clark and Wilson, 1987] focuses on *well-formed transactions* and *separation of duty*. *Well-formed transactions* are defined which have partial recourse to an entity (e.g., the user) capable of validating the transaction with respect to the domain. By *separation of duty*, scenarios can be constructed in which application systems control each other.

Biba's formal integrity model of [Biba, 1977] resembles the BellLaPadula security model (see *Chapter 7.1.2.2*) with the exception of the *-property (see Expression 7.3 on p. 111) which is inverted. Only more trusted subjects are allowed to create objects which are accessible to less trusted subjects. Thereby, trusted subjects are able to correct data when its integrity has been weakened by untrusted subjects but not vice versa.

Common to most integrity models is the reduced importance of confidentiality of the processed data. Obviously, this is valid for Biba's integrity model which inverts the *dominance relation*[55] with respect to the Bell-LaPadula model, thus making objects on a higher trust level accessible to subjects on a lower trust level. When two lattices are required to represent independent *security classes*[56], e.g., with one lattice depicting confidentiality and another referring to integrity of the user model information, the problem can be solved by combining the two lattices. This results in a more complex lattice which satisfies both integrity and confidentiality requirements [Sandhu, 1993, p. 16].

None of these integrity models has been employed for the protection of data integrity within user models so far. A partial improvement for data integrity can be achieved through access control models[57] which allow for authorization[58], thus granting distinct permissions (e.g., modification of user model entries) to application systems. By means of access control, the access policy can be adapted to enhance the integrity *and* confidentiality of the user model information ([Summers, 1997, p. 116]):

---

[55]See p. 110.
[56]See p. 114.
[57]See *Chapter 7.1.2.3* and *Chapter 7.1.4*.
[58]See *Chapter 7.2.1.5*.

"Access control is the process of ensuring that all access to resources is authorized access. Access control enforces the fundamental security principle of authorization. It supports both confidentiality and integrity."

2.2.2 System Integrity

The hardware and software used in implementing the user modeling system must provide integrity with respect to the functionality required by the user adaptive system. User adaptive systems present no additional requirements to the hardware and the underlying software (see *Chapter 5.3*).

Regardless of how reliable the infrastructure is, certain user modeling techniques endanger system integrity. For instance, the BGP-MS user modeling shell system is implemented in the LISP programming language which is considered to be sufficiently documented and tested, and is able to recover from many exceptions. For logical inferences, the OTTER[59] theorem prover is employed (see [McCune, 1994] and [Pohl, 1998, p. 148]). Since the first-order predicate calculus is undecidable[60], a set of user model entries passed on to OTTER could throw the system into a state of unterminated process despite the reliability of the infrastructure. In BGP-MS, a time limit, which terminates the resolution process without having achieved a conclusion about the application system's request, prevents this from happening.

2.2.3 Transition Integrity

Essential for user modeling servers serving several users and/or several application systems is *concurrency control*. Through concurrency control, processes caused by synchronous requests from independent application systems are rearranged, thereby avoiding the possible negative effects of synchronous processes. User modeling systems which are based on a *database management system* can take advantage of several ways for ensuring concurrency control of the database management system (e.g., isolation, atomicity, transactions, locking, deadlock prevention, rollback, recovery, see [Castano et al., 1994], [Summers, 1997], [Ullman, 1988], [Maier, 1983], and [Cook and Kay, 1994]). User modeling systems which act as a user model(ing) server (see [Fink, 1998], [Fink, 1999], and [Fink et al., 2002]) and implement their particular data management techniques must provide similar security features.

The BGP-MS user modeling shell system, which was extended to include the capability to serve several application systems and users [Pohl

---

[59]organized techniques for theorem-proving and effective research
[60]See [Genesereth and Nilsson, 1987].

and Höhle, 1997], avoids concurrency by serializing application systems' requests via the serialization of KQML message processing within the communications module.

In order to specify the information flow within the system, several *security models* (see *Chapter 7.1.2.2*) are described in terms of system states and transitions between these states. *Security models* have not been employed in user modeling systems so far. Kay describes the information flow within the um system in terms of *transitions* [Kay, 1995, p. 151]:

> "[...] This means that we can support the machine's ability to model users if we improve the transition of helpful information towards the $machine_{private}$ area at the right of the figure.
>
> One way to do this is by improving the machine's skill in making clever interpretations of the user's shared space. This corresponds to the transition:
> $$user_{shared} \rightarrow machine_{private} \text{ "}$$

This informal and mandatory model of information flow is only used to explain the um system; it is not implemented within the system in order to ensure that only permissible transitions take place. Nevertheless, it demonstrates the applicability of *security models*, particularly *information flow control models*, within user models. The integrity of user models which are compliant with formalized information flow models can be enforced with the procedures described in *Chapter 7.1.2.2* and *Chapter 7.2.2.1*.

2.2.4   Inference Integrity

User modeling systems often include *production systems* which extend a given set of user model entries to cover new assertions about the user by means of inference, statistics, and machine learning (see Orwant quotation on p. 12 and the example on p. 112). User modeling systems employ production systems to a different degree, thus establishing a compromise between the user model's expressive power and computational effort (see [Orwant, 1995], [Pohl, 1998], and [Schauer, 1997]).

With the assignment of a (possibly shared) responsibility[61] of particular application systems for distinct user model entries or areas of a user model, constraints which did not apply previously are imposed on the user model and the user modeling system. For user model entries newly generated by means of the production system, the responsibility must also be defined. Because most *security models* rely on a classification of the newly generated user model entry (e.g., a *security level* for the

---

[61]See *Chapter 5.1.2.*

Bell-LaPadula model[62], or an additional column in the access control matrix model, see Equation 7.12 on p. 116), the new entry must also be classified – automatically – by the production system.

If the new entry is inferred on the basis of user model entries from only one of the defined areas, the classification for the inferred entry could be derived from the classification of the area involved (e.g., the same classification). For instance, if the set R_s (see Equation 7.7 on p. 113) and the predicate $P_2(a)$ (see Equation 7.7 on p. 113) descend from the same area, the inferred formula $P_1(a) \vee P_1(b)$ (see Equation 7.8 on p. 113) can be assigned to this area as well. Problems arise when entries descending from different areas are used for inference. For instance, if P_1 is available in $cont(A)$ (see Figure 5.1 on p. 55), P_2 in $cont(B)$, and the production rule $P_2(a) \rightarrow P_1(a) \vee P_1(b)$ applies in both areas, the transition from R_s to $R_{s'}$ (see Equation 7.8 on p. 113) through inference makes it possible to ascertain the presence of $P_1(a) \vee P_1(b)$ in $cont(A)$ for an application system which is only allowed to access $cont(B)$. Assuming that all production rules are known to the application systems and P_1 was not modified within the transition, application systems allowed to access $cont(A)$ are also capable of ascertaining $P_2(a)$.

Inference procedures using user model entries of different areas of access, regardless of how the area is specified by the different security models, require a classification function which assigns a newly generated user model entry to an area. Secure user models must not only provide procedures for consistent, correct, and timely inferences but also for the assurance that only intended inferences are possible (see the research literature on security of knowledge-based systems, [Berson and Lunt, 1987a], [Berson and Lunt, 1987b], [Garvey and Lunt, 1991], [Morgenstern, 1987], [Morgenstern, 1988], [Tener, 1991], and [Thuraisingham, 1990]).

With the role-based access control model proposed in *Chapter 7.1.3*, the user modeling system can determine without restriction the set of user model entries (e.g., $cont(A)$ and $cont(B)$, see above) supporting the inference of new user model entries. The classification of a newly generated entry (e.g., into $cont(A)$ or $cont(B)$) is not specified by the access control model and is therefore dependent on the user modeling system.

The previous paragraphs covered the inference integrity (i.e., the assurance that inferences that are intended can be drawn but not unintended inferences) of production systems (with an example of an unin-

---

[62]See *Chapter 7.1.2.2.*

tended inference within a knowledge-based system). User models often lack complete information about a user due to the demand for implicit construction (see Rich quotation on p. 30). To complete a user model, analogical inferences can be employed by a user modeling server which infer missing entries from information acquired from other user models (see [Orwant, 1995] and [Kobsa et al., 2000]). For instance, a typical question for a user model with the characteristics A and the unknown characteristic B is: "How many other users who show characteristics A also show characteristic B?"

For this reason, the relevant user model entries from the different user models can be collected and stored in a manner suitable for replying to statistical inquiries supporting analogical reasoning. The statistical inquiries should only provide information about the *average user* and should not make it possible to ascertain more about the characteristics of a particular user than is allowed. Knowledge of a unique combination of characteristics of an anonymous user can give clues for deanonymiza-tion[63]. As a simple example of a statistical database, characteristics of several users are collected in the following (relational) table, whereby users are identified by *pseudonyms*[64]:

Table 7.3.   Example of a statistical database

#	pseudonym	age	browser	advertisements	characteristic Z
1	a	[,20]	N	y	a
2	b	[21,30]	N	n	b
3	c	[21,30]	S	y	c
4	d	[31,40]	IE	n	d
5	e	[21,30]	N	y	a
6	f	[31,40]	IE	n	a
7	g	[21,30]	IE	y	a
8	h	[41,50]	N	n	a
9	i	[50,]	S	y	a
10	k	[31,40]	N	n	a
11	l	[21,30]	N	y	a
12	m	[21,30]	IE	n	a

For the above question the function $count(A \wedge B) = n$ is given to determine the number of users in the table which show characteristic A and B. With the request $count(age = [50,]) = 1$ a unique characteristic is found in the table which makes it possible to ascertain all other

---

[63]See *Chapter 6.1.2.*
[64]See *Chapter 4.4.*

characteristics for that pseudonymous user, for instance $count(age = [50,] \wedge browser = S) = 1$, $count(age = [50,] \wedge advertisements = y) = 1$, etc. To ensure that the characteristics of a user with a unique combination of characteristics cannot be ascertained, the function $count$ can be limited to values which do not enable it to recognize a unique combination of characteristics:

$$count(A \wedge B) = n, 0 < n_{min} \leq n \leq n_{max} < N \qquad (7.19)$$

With the values $n_{min} = 2, n_{max} = 10, N = 12$ set for this example, the previous requests cannot be satisfied.

Unfortunately, this restriction can be evaded by transforming the request. The following example answers the question whether a user characterized by $A = (age = [21, 30] \wedge browser = N \wedge advertisements = n)$ also has the characteristic $B = (Z = b)$. Despite the limitation of Equation 7.19, it can also be ascertained that the combination of characteristics is unique. Therefore, A is decomposed into $A = A_1 \wedge A_2$ for which $count(A_1 \wedge \overline{A}_2)$ and $count(A_1)$ can be determined:

$$n_{min} \leq count(A_1 \wedge \overline{A}_2) \leq count(A) \leq n_{max} \qquad (7.20)$$

$T = A_1 \wedge \overline{A}_2$ is called *individual tracker* and can be found for most statistical databases (see [Denning et al., 1979, p. 80] and [Denning, 1982, Chap. 6.3]). With the two satisfiable counts

$$count(A) = count(A_1) - count(T) \qquad (7.21)$$

$$count(A \wedge B) = count(T \vee (A_1 \wedge B)) - count(T) \qquad (7.22)$$

the request can be satisfied [Denning, 1982, Chap. 6.3].

The method for answering statistical queries which should not be answerable (see Equation 7.19) is as follows: First, a test is conducted to determine whether A describes a unique relation of Table 7.3 where $A_1 = (age = [21, 30] \wedge browser = N)$ and $A_2 = (advertisements = n)$ and by Equation 7.21:

$$count((age = [21, 30] \wedge browser = N) \wedge advertisements = n)$$

$$\begin{aligned} = \quad & count(age = [21, 30] \wedge browser = N) \\ & -count((age = [21, 30] \wedge browser = N) \wedge advertisements = y) \end{aligned} \qquad (7.23)$$

$$= \quad 3 - 2$$

A therefore denotes a unique combination and can be used for inference of characteristic B by Equation 7.22:

$$count((age = [21, 30] \wedge browser = N \wedge advertisements = n) \wedge (Z = b))$$

$$= \quad count((age = [21, 30] \wedge browser = N \wedge advertisements = y)$$
$$\vee((age = [21, 30] \wedge browser = N) \wedge (Z = b)))$$
$$-count((age = [21, 30] \wedge browser = N) \wedge advertisements = y)$$

$$= \quad 3 - 2$$

$$(7.24)$$

The example uses an *individual tracker* for the *positive compromise* of the statistical database (concerning the user known by the pseudonym b) which must be found for every user (i.e. row) of the table. For many databases there is a *general tracker* which can be used for requests affecting arbitrary rows of the table (see [Denning et al., 1979, p. 83] and [Denning, 1988, p. 348]).

Several techniques have been developed to protect statistical databases from similar attacks (see [Castano et al., 1994, Chap. 5], [Hinke et al., 1997], [Adam and Wortmann, 1989], and [Pernul and Luef, 1992]):

- the *lattice model* [Denning and Schlörer, 1983],

- *conceptual clustering* [Chin and Ozsoyoglu, 1981],

- *query set size control* (partially described above, see [Fellegi, 1972] and [Chin, 1978]),

- *cell suppression* [Cox, 1980],

- *data swapping* (see [Schlörer, 1981] and [Reiss, 1980]),

- *non-overlapping queries* [Dobkin et al., 1979],

- *data perturbation* [Matloff, 1986], etc.

Despite their complexity, all techniques are alike in their inability to protect data from all attacks simultaneously. Inference integrity in statistical databases therefore depends on the combination of several techniques [Castano et al., 1994, p. 339]:

"In general, we can conclude that no single protection technique alone provides high security and low information loss at low cost. Moreover, no technique that can prevent both exact and partial compromise exists. Since no one technique is superior to another in all aspects, the choice of suitable protection technique(s) should be guided by the protection requirements and the characteristics of the environment protected."

2.2.5 Constraint Integrity

Several constraints can be imposed on the user model which are collateral rather than being central to user modeling. For instance, the anonymity[65] requirement is a constraint which actually limits the user model's range of functions, e.g., by limiting data sets from which inferences can be drawn.

Particularly with regard to the constraints of *environmental anonymity*[66] (e.g., that the characteristics of more than one user must be maintained within the user modeling server) and *contextual anonymity* (e.g., as a very minimum requirement, no unique combination of characteristics within all user models should be observable, see *Chapter 6.1.2* and *Chapter 7.2.2.4*) no single user model can ascertain whether the requirements are met. Anonymity often benefits from an *anonymity set* of similar entities which prevents a single entity from being singled out. For this reason, user modeling servers (see [Orwant, 1995], [Pohl, 1998], [Fink, 1998], and [Fink and Kobsa, 2001]) are advantageous, because they could ensure that a survey of all user models will not lead to the formation of a unique combination of characteristics for a particular user. Unfortunately, this runs counter to Allen's demand (see p. 11) for *differentiation* across users.

2.2.6 Semantic Integrity

Semantic integrity of a user model has so far been considered only to the extent that it is important for user model developers (see *system integrity*[67] and *data integrity*[68]). The user modeling systems which are described in the literature offer no possibilities for users to specify *semantic constraints* on their characteristics (for instance, "My characteristics regarding skills should only be processed if they don't deviate from the mean by 30%.").

Whether the semantic integrity of the user model data can be preserved depends on the domain of the user adaptive system and the means provided by the user modeling system; means for ensuring semantic integrity cannot be discussed in general.

2.2.7 Alteration Integrity

Ways of using authorization to protect user model entries from alteration were discussed in *Chapter 7.2.1.5* and in *Chapter 7.1.2*. In a

---

[65] See *Chapter 4.4* and *Chapter 7.2.2.4*.
[66] See *Chapter 6.1.1*.
[67] See *Chapter 7.2.2.2*.
[68] See *Chapter 7.2.2.1*.

similar manner, user models which do not authorize application systems are able to detect changes of particular attributes by monitoring the *authenticity* (see above) of the entries via *signatures*[69].

2.3   Summary

In contrast to *Chapter 7.1*, where general measures for ensuring secrecy were proposed, this chapter has offered no general solutions for meeting the requirements for *integrity in user modeling*. Rather, solutions which have been implemented in user modeling systems were presented for the particular requirements described in *Chapter 5.2*.

The integrity of a user model was broken down into external integrity (regarding the application of the user model by a user adaptive system) and internal integrity (regarding solutions provided by the user modeling system). It was shown that factors which improve the confidentiality of a user model (e.g., identification, authentication, and authorization) also help to improve its external integrity. Other solutions for the requirements regarding consistency, correctness, adequacy, functionality, timeliness, accountability, and supervision were discussed with regard to examples taken from particular user modeling systems.

Measures for improving the internal integrity of a user model through data integrity, system integrity, and inference integrity were discussed in connection with production systems which enhance the set of user model entries by inferring further assumptions about the user. We have shown that few attempts have been made to support these types of integrity within implemented user modeling shell systems, despite the fact that they are crucial for the user's privacy. However, when security models are employed, the confidentiality of user model information and its integrity can be maintained (e.g., through Biba's integrity model) and in some cases, confidentiality and integrity can be maintained simultaneously. Concerning the security models proposed in *Chapter 7.1.2*, the most suitable ones to support both the confidentiality and the integrity of the user model are access control models and the role-based access control model which was described in detail.

Ways of meeting the requirements for transition integrity, constraint integrity, semantic integrity, and alteration integrity are dependent on the particular user modeling system and were therefore not discussed in detail.

---

[69]See *Chapter 6.2.2* and p. 79.

IV

Discussion

Chapter 8

SELECTED USER MODELING COMPONENTS

This chapter covers several components of user modeling systems which deal with security and privacy requirements. *Doppelgänger* and *BGP-MS* will be presented as two instances of user modeling servers with different focuses. As examples, the security features implemented in these systems will be described and the ways in which the respective designs can affect security will be discussed.

Another component called *User Model Reference Monitor* is included here to combine the three solutions which were described in detail in the previous part. This reference monitor gives an overview of their interaction and their applicability for particular security requirements in user modeling.

The *AVANTI system* is a user adaptive system especially designed to handle sensitive information about users. It is presented here as an example of an application of the proposed solutions and the limits of previously available solutions for security and anonymity.

A brief description of the current *Platform for Privacy Preferences Project (P3P)* shows how security measures can support the user's privacy. The dependence of privacy on security, which was posited in the introduction, is illustrated by the definition of *policies* for data usage. The access control model described in the previous part can be used to specify the required access control for user model clients.

1.   Doppelgänger

Doppelgänger, the "generalized tool for gathering, processing, and providing information about users" consists at its core "of a server, a toolkit of learning techniques, and a database of user models" (see [Orwant, 1994], [Orwant, 1995], and [Orwant, 1996]). Data gathered from *sensors* (both hardware and software) is stored and augmented by machine learning techniques and statistical methods in order to provide application systems with a *pragmatic model*[1] of the user.

In addition to sensors and application systems, the user is also given considerable attention as a part of the user adaptive system. Special interfaces which allow for inspection and modification of user model entries (see *Chapter 7.2.1.2* and [Orwant, 1994, p. 152]) are included in the design. The inclusion of the user has also been considered in the design phase of the interface to the user modeling server [Orwant, 1994, p. 155]:

> "The underlying principles of interface design in DOPPELGÄNGER are as follows:
>
> - Let the user know what the system is doing.
>
> - Let the user choose the degree of interactivity with the system: different amounts will be appropriate at different times.
>
> - Model the user's understanding of the system's operation, and provide explanations appropriate to that level. If in doubt, simplify.
>
> - Provide an interface that highlights the unusual inferences and actions made by the system.
>
> - Integrate communications between the user and the user modeling system into normal daily activities."

The listing above shows the user's ability to supervise[2] the system, for instance, through knowledge about *what the system is doing* and the ability to *choose the degree of interactivity*.

By means of analogical modeling, *Doppelgänger* is also able to supply application systems with meaningful information[3] about the user if the user model is incomplete (see Orwant quotation on p. 12). However, means for ensuring the limitation of possible inferences[4] and anonymity have not been implemented. As a user modeling server which hosts models of many users and which employs a variety of statistical methods, *Doppelgänger* could check for unique combinations of user model entries which allow for deanonymization and could prevent such combinations (see *Chapter 7.2.2.5*).

Aspects of confidentiality and integrity (i.e., authentication and authorization) have also been emphasized as a basis for the user's privacy [Orwant, 1995, p. 110]:

---

[1] See [Kay, 1991], [Kay, 1993], and [Strachan et al., 1997].
[2] See *Chapter 7.2.1.9*.
[3] See *Chapter 5.2.1* and *Chapter 7.2.2.4*.
[4] See *Chapter 7.2.2.4*.

"An integral part of the *user modeling system as server* paradigm are safe-guards for notions of data security and privacy. Potentially harmful, sensitive, or damaging information is stored in DOPPELGÄNGER, and in an environment where many workstations are making use of network services, users and applications might be able to falsify their identity to a remote service. This is a serious risk and requires some means of access control."

From the *levels of anonymity*[5], *identification* and *super-identification* have been implemented by means of the *Kerberos* authentication system (see [Steiner et al., 1988] and [Summers, 1997, p. 487]). Through the *Kerberos* authentication system, the identity of an application system, the user, and also the user modeling server can be authenticated while information is exchanged between them. It is not possible for an application system to authenticate a particular user model entry after it has been accepted by *Doppelgänger*. In contrast to this, with the proposed extensions to the KQML language (i.e., *SKQML*[6]), the proof of origin is available to the user model by means of the *:signature* value which can be stored with the user model entry. With this value, another application system is able to verify without the help of the user modeling system that a user model entry has been inserted by a particular application system (and has not been modified in the meantime).

The *confidentiality*[7] of the user model can be attained by assigning the user model entries to four categories [Orwant, 1995, p. 110]:

Users modeled by DOPPELGÄNGER can control the access to any and all parts of their user model, tagging them entirely private, entirely public, or a gray area in between, which can be expressed as either "everyone but certain users," or "no one but certain users".

As a basis for the access control model, the *Andrew File System* (see [Ohio State University, 1998] and [Summers, 1997, p. 542]) has been included in the implementation. The *Andrew File System* uses *access control lists*[8] to relate user model entries and user model clients by access modes, thereby *authorizing* user model clients. The user interface defining the authorization, which is essential for an effective assignment of the clients' responsibility for parts of the user model, is not described in the literature (compare the description for the authorization through the role-based access control model, Figures 7.11 – 7.14 on pp. 136 – 138). With the four categories *private, entirely public, everyone but cer-*

---

[5]See *Chapter 4.1.1.*
[6]See *Chapter 6.2.2.*
[7]See *Chapter 5.1.2* and *Chapter 7.1.2.*
[8]See p. 117.

tain users[9], and *no one but certain users*, an access control model[10] can be established which allows for the definition of simple requirements regarding *confidentiality*[11] while several user model clients are maintaining a (shared) user model. Using this access control model, groups of application systems (for instance, "no one but certain users") can be related to single user model entries. In [Sandhu, 1997], it is shown that access control by groups is less flexible and more complicated to manage than the role-based access control model described in the previous part.

Secrecy of the user model data while in transit from sensors to the user model server or from the user model server to the application system has been implemented by means of *encryption*[12]. For encryption, the PGP encryption algorithm [Garfinkel, 1995] has been used to protect the communication carried out via electronic mail.

In addition, *secrecy* through temporary *denial of access*[13] to the user model has been implemented by giving the user not only *computational ownership* (as in the solutions proposed in *Chapter 6.2* or *Chapter 7.1.1.2*) but also *physical ownership* [Orwant, 1995, p. 110]:

> "Another method of guaranteeing privacy is to ensure that the user retains not only computational ownership of the data [...], but physical ownership as well. To this end, DOPPELGÄNGER can store user models on PCMCIA cards as well as on disks."

The *timeliness*[14] of inferences and membership in *communities* in *Doppelgänger* is given by a recalculation on a daily basis.

Among the user modeling servers discussed in this book, *Doppelgänger* combines the highest number of security mechanisms. As described above, it provides mechanisms for ensuring the secrecy of user model information while in transit between *Doppelgänger* and the application systems, a basic access control model for authorization, means for supervision, and the ability to cope with incomplete information about the user. Further mechanisms which improve the system's security could be added to *Doppelgänger*, for instance, a more detailed access control model for defining the user's demands regarding confidentiality of the user model information, a decentralized mechanism for authentication (in contrast to the Kerberos system), and means for protecting the

---

[9] *Users* corresponds in this context to *user model clients*, e.g., application systems.

[10] This access control model does not distinguish different access modes (for instance, *read, write*) and is therefore not suitable for defining requirements regarding confidentiality *and* integrity (see *Chapter 7.2.2.1*).

[11] See *Chapter 5.1.2* and *Chapter 7.1.2*.

[12] See *Chapter 5.1.1.2*.

[13] See *Chapter 5.1.1*.

[14] See *Chapter 7.2.1.4*.

authenticity of each user model entry. In addition, mechanisms which support the users' anonymity, and thereby their privacy, could be added, for instance, through prevention of deanonymization of user model entries, limitation of possible inferences, and the inclusion of anonymous remailers[15].

2.   BGP-MS

The *BGP-MS*[16] user modeling shell system "can assist interactive software systems in adapting to users based on assumptions about their knowledge, beliefs, and goals" [Kobsa and Pohl, 1995, p. 4]. Knowledge about the user can be represented and processed via various formalisms: *terminological, first-order*, and *modal logic* [Pohl, 1998, Chap. 6]. *BGP-MS* was expanded to a user modeling server which can host models of several users maintained by different application systems [Pohl, 1998, p. 199]. Pohl and Höhle suggest the *domain-based user modeling* by which user model entries do not relate application systems and users (i.e., an *(A,U) environment*) but domains and users (i.e., a *(D,U) environment*), see [Pohl and Höhle, 1997, p. 412] and [Pohl, 1998, Chap. 7.3.3]):

> "Therefore, the (A,U) environments, which were suggested above as containers for run time UMKBs, should better be regarded as (D,U) environments that store the assumptions about a user U concerning a domain D together with other domain-specific data. There is no reason to constrain an application A_i to one domain only; user modeling data could be modularized into several domains $D_1,...,D_n$. Vice versa, there is no reason to constrain a domain to be used by one application only."

Domains as well as *views* (see [Kobsa and Pohl, 1995, Chap. 4] and [Pohl, 1998, Chap. 2.3.3]) as implemented in *BGP-MS* allow for the shared[17] maintenance of parts of the user model. Domains as well as views of *BGP-MS* can directly be mapped to *roles* of the proposed *role-based access control model*[18]. In the following, this mapping is given for the example of [Pohl and Höhle, 1997, p. 413]:

> For a more illustrative example, imagine two applications "Adaptex" (a text processor) and "IntelliDraw" (a drawing tool), which both employ a centralized BGP-MS instance for user modeling. They make use of the domains "text-processing" and "vector-graphics", respectively, and share the domain "printing".

---

[15]Anonymous remailers can be used with PGP to achieve some of the mechanisms provided by the KQMLmix component (see p. 69 and *Chapter 6.2.3*) for procedural anonymity.
[16]Belief, Goal, and Plan Maintenance System
[17]See the modes CONT-SEP, CONT-INCL, and CONT-SHAR in Figure 5.1 on p. 55.
[18]See *Chapter 7.1.4*.

The notation of the role-based access control model[19] for this example is given by:

$$
\begin{aligned}
U \;&=\; \{Adaptex,\ IntelliDraw\} \\
R \;&=\; \{text\text{-}processing,\ vector\text{-}graphics,\ printing\} \\
P \;&=\; \{tp\text{-}ask,\ tp\text{-}tell,\ vg\text{-}ask,\ vg\text{-}tell,\ pr\text{-}ask,\ pr\text{-}tell\} \\
UA \;&=\; \{(Adaptex,\ text\text{-}processing),\ (IntelliDraw,\ vector\text{-}graphics)\} \\
RH \;&=\; \{(printing,\ text\text{-}processing),\ (printing,\ vector\text{-}graphics)\} \\
PA \;&=\; \{(text\text{-}processing,\ tp\text{-}ask),\ (text\text{-}processing,\ tp\text{-}tell), \\
&\qquad (vector\text{-}graphics,\ vg\text{-}ask),\ (vector\text{-}graphics,\ vg\text{-}tell), \\
&\qquad (printing,\ pr\text{-}ask),\ (printing,\ pr\text{-}tell)\}
\end{aligned}
$$

$$(8.1)$$

Permissions[20] regarding KQML messages sent from the application system to *BGP-MS* are defined as:

$$
\begin{aligned}
PD = \{ \ &(tp\text{-}ask,\ \texttt{"\textbackslash(ask-if\ .*:domain\ text-processing.*\textbackslash)"}), \\
&(tp\text{-}tell,\ \texttt{"\textbackslash(tell\ .*:domain\ text-processing.*\textbackslash)"}), \\
&(vg\text{-}ask,\ \texttt{"\textbackslash(ask-if\ .*:domain\ vector-graphics.*\textbackslash)"}), \\
&(vg\text{-}tell,\ \texttt{"\textbackslash(tell\ .*:domain\ vector-graphics.*\textbackslash)"}), \\
&(pr\text{-}ask,\ \texttt{"\textbackslash(ask-if\ .*:domain\ printing.*\textbackslash)"}), \\
&(pr\text{-}tell,\ \texttt{"\textbackslash(tell\ .*:domain\ printing.*\textbackslash)"}) \ \}
\end{aligned}
$$

$$(8.2)$$

For a given (sample) message,

```
m = (ask-if :sender Adaptex :content (...) :domain text-processing ...)
```

the authorization[21] of the sender is determined as follows:

1　determining the user: $u = user(\mathtt{m}) = Adaptex$

2　determining the set of roles assigned to user u: $rs' = \{r' \mid (u, r') \in UA\} = \{text\text{-}processing\}$

3　enhancing the set of roles with roles which inherit to the roles within rs' :
$rs = rs' \cup \{r \mid (r, r') \in RH, r' \in rs'\} = \{text\text{-}processing,\ printing\}$

4　determining the set of permissions for all roles within rs :
$ps = \{p \mid (r, p) \in PA, r \in rs\} = \{tp\text{-}ask,\ tp\text{-}tell,\ pr\text{-}ask,\ pr\text{-}tell\}$

5　checking whether at least one permission definition ($pd \in PD$) for the permission $p \in ps$

---

[19]See $RBAC_1$ on p. 120, *Chapter 7.1.3*, and *Chapter 7.1.4*.
[20]See Figure 7.12 on p. 137.
[21]See *Chapter 7.1.3* and *Chapter 7.1.4*.

matches the message m (for this example, the permission definition (*tp-ask*, `"\(ask-if .*:domain text-processing.*\)"`) matches the message)

6 if a match can be found, process the message.

The above example illustrates the *authorization* of application systems for parts of the user model (in this example, *domains*). By means of authorization, the responsibility of several application systems for parts of a user model can be defined and enforced. The *confidentiality* of particular user model entries can thereby be established. In this simple example, user model entries of the domain *text-processing* can only be read or modified by application systems which are authorized via their assignment to the respective role (e.g., the *Adaptex* application system). A similar protection exists for the user model entries of the domain *vector-graphics*. This example represents the *mode of cooperation* CONT-SHAR (see Figure 5.1 on p. 55) with the user model entries of the *printing* domain in the intersection of $cont(A)$ and $cont(B)$, for this example, $cont(Adaptex)$ and $cont(IntelliDraw)$. In the above example, the application systems *Adaptex* and *IntelliDraw* can share information from the *printing* domain but not information from the *text-processing* and *vector-graphics* domains.

The role-based access control model not only supports confidentiality but can also be applied to improve the *integrity* of the user model information. To extend the example above, we can add another role *supervisor*

$$R' = R \cup \{supervisor\} \tag{8.3}$$

which can be assumed by an application system *KnowledgeUpdate* of which the user (or the developer of the user adaptive system) is convinced that it improves the integrity of the entries of all three domains by keeping them up to date. An enhancement of the permission assignment

$$PA' = PA \cup \{ \begin{array}{l} (supervisor,\ tp\text{-}tell), (supervisor,\ vg\text{-}tell), \\ (supervisor,\ pr\text{-}tell) \end{array} \} \tag{8.4}$$

enables the application system *KnowledgeUpdate* to update all entries in the three domains without acquiring knowledge about the insertions made by other application systems. Thereby, it is able to improve the integrity of the user model without weakening confidentiality.

The *secrecy* of the data while in transit between the application system and *BGP-MS* can be secured by means of SKAPI[22] through encryption.

---

[22]See *Chapter 7.1.1.2.*

Authentication of the application systems and the user model server, and the *authenticity* of the exchanged user model entries can also be guaranteed. Like *Doppelgänger*, *BGP-MS* supports *identification* and *super-identification*. For *BGP-MS*, super-identification is provided by means of X.509 certificates which can be issued by different trust centers. The components of the user adaptive system can choose freely among trust centers to verify their identity. This process model therefore offers more flexibility than the Kerberos system (see the previous section). Using the SKQML[23] keyword *:signature*[24], the user model entries could also be authenticated by other application systems. Furthermore, *BGP-MS* is able to support *procedural anonymity* through *sender anonymity* as well as through *receiver anonymity*[25] if it is connected to the application system by a mix network[26].

As a user model server, *BGP-MS* could also provide *environmental* and *content-based anonymity* if means for detecting a unique combination of user model entries and other identifying entries were added.

The *confidentiality* of the user model information can be protected by the proposed role-based access control model[27]. This model has been proposed[28] because of its general applicability as a filter which controls the information flow between the user model and the application systems. It is therefore not dependent on internal mechanisms of the user modeling system. With respect to a particular user modeling system, improvements to this access control model can be made. Moreover, it might be advantageous to replace the proposed (external) access control model with another (internal) *security model*[29]. The strong inferential capabilities of *BGP-MS* (for instance, the ability to process modal logic expressions, see [Pohl, 1998, Chap. 5.2.6], [Pohl, 1998, Chap. 6.3.4], [Schreck, 1995], and [Simon, 1995]) would permit the user modeling system to define the desired information flow between parts of the user model by internal means of the user modeling system[30].

---

[23]See *Chapter 6.2.2.*

[24]The value of this keyword (see p. 79) must also be stored with the user model entry and must be retrievable for application systems.

[25]See *Chapter 4.1.3* and *Chapter 6.2.5.*

[26]See *Chapter 6.2.6,* and *Chapter 8.3.*

[27]See the above example and the following section.

[28]See *Chapter 7.1.2.5.*

[29]See *Chapter 7.1.2.*

[30]A discussion of the matter of inference security in knowledge-based systems (for instance, a logic-based system like *BGP-MS*) would exceed the scope of this book. The reader interested in the implementation of a knowledge-based system with inference control based on logic should refer to [Berson and Lunt, 1987b], [Cuppens, 1992], [Cuppens, 1993], [Cuppens and Trouessin, 1994], [Garvey and Lunt, 1991], [Gallaire et al., 1984], [Morgenstern, 1987], [Morgenstern, 1988], [Pernul, 1994], [Rowe, 1989], and [Su and Ozsoyoglu, 1987].

Measures for increasing the *external integrity* of BGP-MS (e.g., consistency, timeliness, authorization, identification, and authentication) are described above and in *Chapter 7.2.1*. Measures for increasing *internal integrity* (e.g., data, system, transition, and inference integrity) are described in *Chapter 7.2.2*.

Supervision measures (e.g., inspection and correction) are not emphasized by *BGP-MS*. However, a function is provided which returns all user model entries, thereby enabling the application system to conduct a dialog with users about their user model.

A detailed description of all features of the user modeling shell system *BGP-MS* can be found in [Kobsa and Pohl, 1995] and [Pohl, 1998].

3. User Model Reference Monitor

The *User Model Reference Monitor*[31] is not discussed here as a component implemented within a user adaptive system, but rather as an illustration of the interplay of the implementations developed in the previous part. Each of the three implementations *SKAPI*[32], *KQMLmix*[33], and the *role-based access control model*[34] is suited to different requirements[35] of user adaptive systems and should be regarded as an initial set of modules which are applicable to a wide range of user adaptive systems. Depending on the user's and developer's requirements for the adaptive system and the user modeling agent, a different range of security measures is adequate. For instance, a user adaptive system with only *one* user might provide *procedural* and *content-based* anonymity. While *environmental* anonymity cannot be guaranteed with only one (identifiable) user, measures for the two other types[36] of anonymity might turn out to be futile, thus causing unnecessary effort (for instance, computational effort for encryption, user effort for configuration, latency, etc.) without providing a benefit. Similar considerations have to be taken into account for the limiting conditions of other security measures and their reciprocal action[37]. This is often only possible with respect to the user adaptive system and the user modeling agent employed. Only a few general so-

---

[31]See [Longley and Shain, 1987] for the definition of a *reference monitor*: "In computer security, a security control concept in which an abstract machine mediates access to objects by subjects. [...]".

[32]See *Chapter 7.1.1.2*.

[33]See *Chapter 6.2.2.1*.

[34]See *Chapter 7.1.4*.

[35]See *Chapter 4* and *Chapter 5*.

[36]See *Chapter 4.1.3*.

[37]See, for instance, the necessity of *super-identification* for anonymity emerging through the mix technique (see *Chapter 6.2.3.3*) or the conflict between *confidentiality* and *integrity* discussed in *Chapter 7.1.2.5*.

lutions are feasible. These concentrate on the connection between the application system and the user model (for instance, by manipulating the information flow between them through access control and anonymization) without considering internal features of the systems. With respect to the design of the user adaptive system, the user model, and the user's demands for security and privacy the necessary security features for a given user adaptive system should be discussed on a case-by-case basis.

In the following paragraphs, the interaction of the three implementations will be discussed and a suggestion for arranging them between the user adaptive application system (*UM client* in Figure 8.1) and the user model will be made. This arrangement can serve as a default security architecture for user adaptive systems and can be modified or extended according to the requirements of the particular user adaptive system.

In Figure 6.5 on p. 91 we showed how application dependent anonymization techniques[38] and application independent anonymization by means of the KQMLmix[39] component must be combined in a user adaptive system. The following figure focuses on the application independent anonymization[40], super-identification[41], encryption[42], authorization[43] and includes further components necessary for basic security services (for instance, a certificate directory) which are described in the following figure:

---

[38]For instance, *Anonymizers, LPWA, Anonymous Remailers, Onion Routing*, and *Crowds* (see *Chapter 6.1.3*).

[39]See *Chapter 6.2.2.1*.

[40]See the righthand side of Figure 6.5 on p. 91.

[41]See *Chapter 6.2.3.1, Chapter 7.1.4*, and *Chapter 7.2.1.6*.

[42]See *Chapter 5.1.1.2* and *Chapter 6.2.3.1*.

[43]See *Chapter 5.1.2, Chapter 5.2.1, Chapter 7.1.2.4*, and *Chapter 7.2.1.5*.

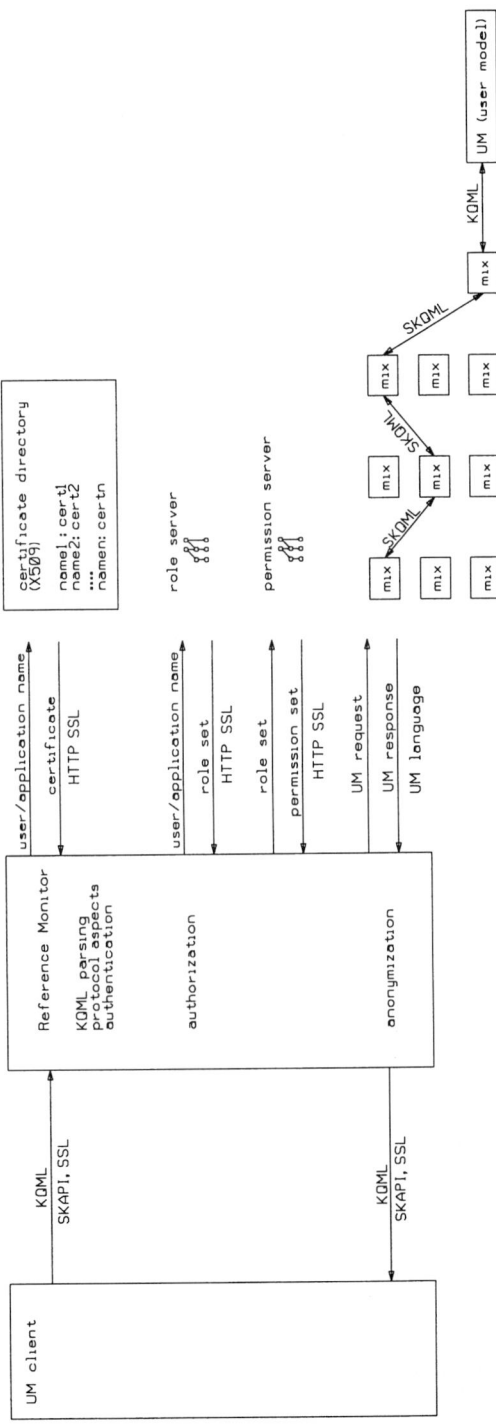

Figure 8.1. User Model Reference Monitor

UM client: The client of a user model (UM) can be either one or several user adaptive application systems or the user. The UM clients as well as the UM are connected[44] to the *User Model Reference Monitor* via an electronic network and operate on a TCB[45].

certificate directory: The certificate directory contains an X.509 certificate[46] for the UM and for each UM client which can be used to verify their identity. It can also be used to verify the authenticity of the information which is exchanged between the UM clients and the *User Model Reference Monitor.*

role server: The role server provides an interface for the definition of the roles for a role-based access control model[47] and the arrangement of roles[48] into a hierarchy[49]. Furthermore, it manages the assignment[50] of clients to roles. Since the role server is based on a common web server[51], communication can take place with encryption and authentication by means of SSL[52]. With the (authenticated) name or pseudonym of the UM client, the roles which have been assigned[53] to it are ascertained.

permission server: The permission server, which is also based on a common web server, handles the relation PA[54] of the role-based access control model $RBAC_1$[55]. For a given set of roles (see above), the set of permissions assigned to the roles and to roles inheriting to them can be determined by this server. For each permission in the set, the *permission definition*[56] is ascertained and the set of permission definitions is returned to the *User Model Reference Monitor.* If the UM client's request matches[57] one of the permission definitions, the request is authorized and can be processed.

---

[44]For instance, through TCP/IP, p. 96.

[45]*Trusted computing base*, see [Pfleeger, 1989] and [Summers, 1997].

[46]See Table 7.1 on p. 98.

[47]See *Chapter 7.1.4.*

[48]See Figure 7.8 on p. 133.

[49]See Figure 7.9 on p. 134.

[50]See Figure 7.10 and the relation UA as described in the role-based access control model $RBAC_1$ on p. 120.

[51]See *Chapter 7.1.4.*

[52]See p. 97.

[53]See Figure 7.8 on p. 133 and the example on p. 164 for the definition and processing of the assigned roles and *Chapter 7.1.5* for the rationale of the role hierarchies.

[54]See p. 120, Figure 7.12 on p. 137, and Figure 7.14 on p. 138.

[55]See p. 120.

[56]See p. 136 and Figure 7.13 on p. 137.

[57]See the example on p. 164.

mix: By connecting the *User Model Reference Monitor* through a mix network with the user model, procedural anonymity can be achieved. The mix network[58] consists of KQMLmix[59] components which provide sender anonymity as well as receiver anonymity.

User Model Reference Monitor: It manipulates the information flow between the UM clients and the user model. It can be placed between the UM clients and the UM which exchange UM entries via KQML[60]. Since it imposes no demands on the internal mechanisms of the user modeling agent which hosts the UM, it is applicable to a wide range of such systems. It performs the following actions:

- Parsing of the KQML messages: Messages from UM clients must be accepted and parsed.

- Handling of protocol aspects: The message has to be stored and either be answered with the reply by the UM or with an error message.

- Authentication: The sender of the message (and its content) can be authenticated through *super-identification* by means of certificates. Also, senders acting under a (controlled or uncontrolled) pseudonym can be authenticated if their certificate contains the pseudonym[61]. If no authentication is demanded, this step can be omitted.

- Authorization: The compliance of the UM client's request with the definitions for access to the UM entries is verified[62].

- Anonymization: The routing of KQML messages containing the user model entries through a mix network[63] provides *procedural anonymity*. Thereby, the relationship between the identity of the user (i.e., the *User Model Reference Monitor* instance) and the user model is hidden.

user model (UM): The user model processes only requests which are authenticated, authorized, dispatched, and anonymized by the *User Model Reference Monitor*.

Using a mix network to isolate the *User Model Reference Monitor* and the user model ensures procedural anonymity or procedural pseudonymity

---

[58]See *Chapter 6.2.6.*
[59]See *Chapter 6.2.2.1.*
[60]See *Chapter 6.2.2.1.*
[61]See (11) and (12) in Table 7.1 on p. 98.
[62]See the example on p. 164.
[63]See *Chapter 6.2.6.*

of the user (model client) against the user model. As long as *content-based* and *environmental anonymity*[64] are also given, the user's identity cannot be ascertained by the user model (or the user modeling agent). Alternatively, the mix network could be used to isolate the UM client from the *User Model Reference Monitor* which hides the user's identity from the UM client. Both methods can be combined to hide the user's identity from both components (see Figure 6.5 on p. 91).

As the *User Model Reference Monitor* described in this section can enhance the security of user adaptive systems without making far-reaching presuppositions about the user modeling agent, it can be applied to a wide range of agents exchanging information about the user by KQML messages. For reduced security requirements, several components may be omitted, for instance, the encryption through SSL, the certificate directory, authorization through the access control model, or the mix network. Single components can be provided either as software packages (e.g., for encryption and authentication) to be included into user model clients or as services (e.g., authorization of information requests or anonymization of exchanged messages).

---

[64]See *Chapter 4.1.3* and *Chapter 6.1.*

4.   The AVANTI system

An example of a user adaptive system in which the *User Model Reference Monitor* (see previous section) can be applied is the *AVANTI* system [Fink et al., 1997] to be described below. It provides user adapted hypermedia information about a metropolitan area (e.g., about public services, transportation, sights) for a variety of users with different needs (e.g., tourists, citizens, time-restricted visitors, travel agency clerks, and people who are elderly, vision-impaired, or wheelchair-bound).

An initial amount of user information is gathered by an interview which is carried out prior to using the system. Further information about the current user is collected during the interaction with the system by the *Hyperstructure Adaptor* and processed by the *User Model Server* (i.e., the *BGP-MS* user modeling shell system, see *Chapter 8.2*). Based on the assumptions about the user, the content as well as its presentation is adapted to the user. An overview of the system's architecture is given in Figure 8.2 (see [Fink et al., 1997] for a description of all system components).

The *AVANTI* system can be used by means of a common web browser (see the top left corner of Figure 8.2) as well as by means of a specially-developed user interface which has been adapted for users with certain kinds of physical disabilities (i.e, the *AVANTI web browser*, see the top right corner, [Stephanidis et al., 1998], and [Stephanidis et al., 1997]). In both cases, the information which is collected and processed within the system might be considered as sensitive by the user. Therefore, measures have been proposed which maintain the system's security and protect the privacy of the user being modeled [Fink et al., 1997, Chap.6].

If used with a common web browser, anonymous or pseudonymous access to the system can be achieved for the user by the services described in *Chapter 6.1.3* (e.g., through *Anonymizers*, *LPWA*, *Crowds*, *Onion Routing*, or also *KQMLmix*, see Figure 6.5 on p. 91). If no anonymity is required (or possible) for the user, the secrecy of the information exchanged between the web browser and the *Hyperstructure Adaptor* can be secured through such well-known technologies as the *Secure Sockets Layer* (SSL, see p. 97). The secrecy of the information exchanged between the *Hyperstructure Adaptor* and the *User Model Server* can be ensured by the SKAPI[65] implementation which permits end-to-end encryption of the communication and authentication of the involved components.

---

[65]See *Chapter 7.1.1.2.*

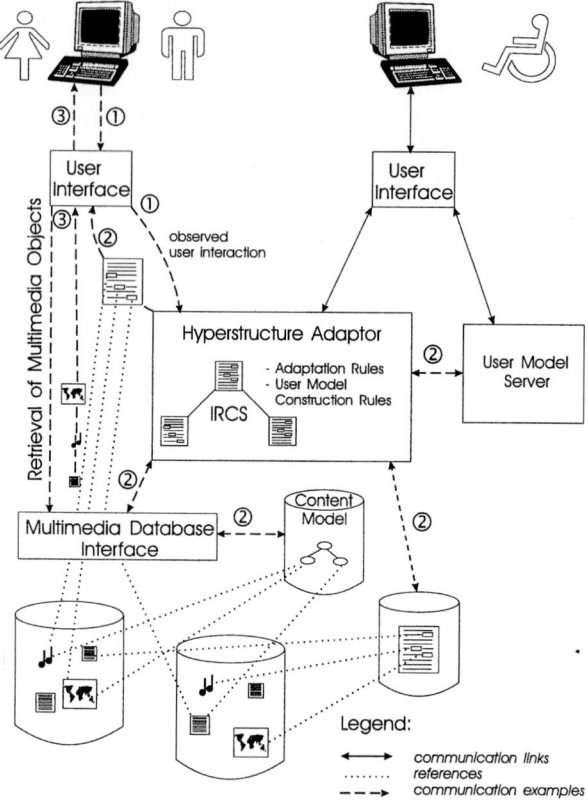

Figure 8.2. The AVANTI user adaptive system

Assuming that only *one Hyperstructure Adaptor* is connected to *one User Model Server*, an encrypted tunnel which is independent of the application system's protocol can be established by such implementations as the *Secure Shell*[66] or *IPv6*[67].

If the system is accessed through the *AVANTI web browser*, information flows occur not only between the browser and the *Hyperstructure*

---

[66]The *Secure Shell* (see http://www.ietf.org/html.charters/secsh-charter.html, http://www.openssh.org/, and http://www.ssh.org) provides a proxy over a TCP socket for the communication partner. Communication over a network is performed in encrypted form by means similar to the *Secure Sockets Layer* (SSL, see p. 97). The application system is neither able to change the X.509 certificate which it expects of its communication partner nor is it able to access information about it – which is possible with SKAPI (see p. 96). Likewise, the *User Model Server* must either establish a distinct *Secure Shell* proxy for each communication partner (i.e. a *Hyperstructure Adaptor*) or use the same cryptographic keys for all of them. This approach is therefore only appropriate for a very simple structure of the user adaptive system.

[67]See [Fink et al., 1997], [Huitmea, 1996], and the comments on the *Secure Shell*.

Adaptor but also between the browser and the *User Model Server* (see Figure 8.2). The *AVANTI web browser* monitors the user's interaction and reports anomalies to the *User Model Server* (e.g., *user idle* or *high error rate* [Stephanidis et al., 1997]). Based on this information, assumptions inserted by the *Hyperstructure Adaptor*, and inferences drawn by the *User Model Server*, further assumptions are forwarded (*notified*) to the *AVANTI web browser* by the (shared) user model in order to adapt the browser to the user's needs. Therefore, the two information flows from the *Hyperstructure Adaptor* and the *AVANTI web browser* must be coordinated before being processed by the *User Model Server*.

The services discussed in *Chapter 6.1.3* are not sufficient for this purpose for several reasons. With *Onion Routing*[68], the physical network address of the *User Model Server* must be known to the *Hyperstructure Adaptor* and to the *AVANTI web browser* and vice versa. Therefore, *procedural anonymity* cannot be present because *receiver anonymity*[69] is not given for the browser with respect to the *User Model Server*. This means that the *User Model Server* is able to determine the network node[70] on which the browser is running, which may in turn provide hints to the user's identity. Using the KQMLmix[71] component, it is possible to provide not only *sender anonymity* but also *receiver anonymity* by means of the *:RPI*[72] keyword which allows the *User Model Server* to send replies and notifications to a browser whose network address (and thereby user's identity) is not known.

If the *AVANTI* system contains not only one application system (i.e., the *Hyperstructure Adaptor*), but several systems which share a common user model on a per user basis, the *User Model Reference Monitor*[73] is particularly valuable. Included as a filter which manipulates the information flow between the *User Model Server* and its clients (for instance, several instances of the *Hyperstructure Adaptor* and the *AVANTI web browser*), it can ensure the secrecy of the exchanged information, verify the authorization of the different clients and anonymize the relationship between the users and their user models. This approach is also appropriate if the *AVANTI* system is only part of a broader user adaptive system with the same (shared) user model.

---

[68] See *Chapter 6.1.3*.
[69] See *Chapter 6.2.5*.
[70] See the KQML example on p. 75.
[71] See *Chapter 6.2.3*.
[72] See *Chapter 6.2.2.2* and *Chapter 6.2.5*.
[73] See *Chapter 8.3*.

5.   The Platform for Privacy Preferences Project (P3P)

In the previous chapters[74] proposals for advancing the security of user adaptive systems were made. Although no concrete *policies*[75] for the processing of data within user adaptive systems were formulated, ways of defining and enforcing security requirements were discussed as a basis for the formulation of policies which would enhance the user's privacy[76]. Examples of *policies* for dealing with user model data were given along with descriptions of well-known *security models* (see *Chapter 7.1.2*) and an access control model was proposed (see *Chapter 7.1.3*, *Chapter 7.1.5*, and *Chapter 8.2*).

The *Platform for Privacy Preferences Project (P3P)*[77] enables *user agents* (i.e., implementations compliant with the P3P specification) to take advantage of a previous agreement or to negotiate on behalf of the user with adaptive application systems (e.g., web servers) in order to reach an agreement between the application system's requirements and the user's preferences concerning his user model and its use (see [Reagle and Cranor, 1999] and [Cranor, 1998]).

The P3P specification defines the following data categories ([P3P, 2002, Chap. 3.4] and [P3P, 2002]) as a basis for a *content-dependent*[78] access control model:

```
category =  "<physical/>"    | ; Physical Contact Information
            "<online/>"      | ; Online Contact Information
            "<uniqueid/>"    | ; Unique Identifiers
            "<purchase/>"    | ; Purchase Information
            "<financial/>"   | ; Financial Information
            "<computer/>"    | ; Computer Information
            "<navigation/>"  | ; Navigation and Click-stream Data
            "<interactive/>" | ; Interactive Data
            "<demographic/>" | ; Demographic and Socioeconomic Data
            "<content/>"     | ; Content
            "<state/>"       | ; State Management Mechanisms
            "<political/>"   | ; Political Information
            "<health/>"      | ; Health Information
            "<preference/>"  | ; Preference Data
            "<location/>"    | ; Location Data
```

---

[74]See *Chapter 6* and *Chapter 7*.

[75]Some policies have been given as examples, for instance, the *Chinese Wall Security Policy* (see p. 107), the *mandatory security model* of Bell and La-Padula (see p. 110), and the *flow policy* of the Denning model (see p. 114). Nevertheless, the proposed *role-based access control model* (see *Chapter 7.1.2.4*) is policy neutral (see the quotation on p. 118).

[76]See *Chapter 2*.

[77]The *Platform for Privacy Preferences Project* is being carried out by the World Wide Web Consortium (see http://www.w3c.org/TR/P3P/) in cooperation with several software companies.

[78]See *Chapter 7.1.5*.

```
"<government/>    |  ; Government-issued Identifiers
"<other-category>" ; Other
```

In order to structure the *user data*, a hierarchy is defined for which the first level and the respective *category* are given in the following table (for instance, `user.home-info.postal.postalcode` represents the postal code of the user's home address, see [P3P, 2002, Chap. 5.6.1]):

Table 8.1. P3P user data structure

	Short display name	Category
user.name	User's Name	physical, demographic
user.bdate	User's Birth Date	demographic
user.login	User's Login Information	uniqueid
user.cert	User's Identity certificate	uniqueid
user.gender	User's gender	demographic
user.employer	User's Employer	demographic
user.department	Department or division of organization where user is employed	demographic
user.jobtitle	User's Job Title	demographic
user.home-info	User's Home Contact Information	physical, online, demographic
user.business-info	User's Business Contact Information	physical, online, demographic

In the negotiation phase, proposals which describe the affected user data (i.e., the *category*) and intended use (e.g., personalization of service, market research, etc.) are exchanged. As soon as an agreement has been reached, the proposal can be assigned to a proposal ID (`propID`, [Reagle and Cranor, 1999, p. 51]) for further use. The combination of application system, proposal, and *user agent* can be summarized by a temporary or session ID (`TUID`, see *transaction pseudonym* in *Chapter 4.2.1*) which is valid for the current session for maintaining state (i.e., the relationship between the application system and the *user agent* in the current session). It can also be extended to a pairwise or site ID (`PUID`, see *application pseudonym* in *Chapter 4.2.1*) which makes the combination persistent and reusable for further sessions, thus avoiding renegotiation of the achieved agreement. Furthermore, a P3P *user agent* might manage different sets of *user data* (i.e. *personae*) which are suitable to represent different user roles ([Reagle and Cranor, 1999, p. 54], see also *Chapter 7.1.5* and p. 24):

> "Some user agents might also allow users to specify multiple *personae* and associate a different set of data element values with each persona. Thus, users might specify different work and home personae, specify different personae for

different kinds of transactions, and even make up a set of completely fictitious personae. By storing the data values that correspond to each personae in their repository, users will not have to keep track of which values go with each personae to maintain persistent relationships with services."

With the P3P proposal, it would be possible to negotiate with the adaptive application systems about which user data should be used in the adaptation process. Agreements can be stored as temporarily or permanently associated with an application system which establishes either a *transaction pseudonym* or an *application pseudonym* (see *Chapter 4.2.1*). The *categories* defined with the P3P proposal can be mapped directly to the role-based access control model which can provide the enforcement of the privacy requirements defined by the user (for instance, to exchange no information in the *physical* or *uniqueid categories*).

Unfortunately, the P3P specification does not mention in detail:

Authentication: The required method by which application systems are identified and authenticated (see *Chapter 7.1*).

Authorization: The procedure which assigns distinct access modes (e.g., *read, write, update*, etc.) to application systems, propIDs, TUID, PUID, or *personae* (see *Chapter 7.1.2*).

Secrecy: The user's expectation regarding the secrecy of the data while it is being transported (see *Chapter 5.1* and *Chapter 7.1*) and stored on the application system's side.

Anonymity: While *transaction pseudonyms* and *application pseudonyms* are provided for pseudonymity, no requirements regarding *procedural* and *environmental anonymity* (see *Chapter 4.1.3*) are specified. *Content-based anonymity* is considered in the specification via the *categories of user data* (see Table 8.1 on p. 177).

P3P is therefore of only limited value in closing the gap between the security mechanisms offered (e.g., access control) and the user's expectations regarding privacy. In addition to the other aspects of security that were discussed in chapters 2, 4, and 5, the above-mentioned aspects are especially important from the user's point of view and should also be taken into account in the definition of privacy preferences.

Wolf and Pfitzmann (see [Wolf, 2001], [Wolf and Pfitzmann, 1999], and [Pfitzmann et al., 1998]) propose a user interface which is intended to assist the user in defining *protection goals for communication* (for instance, *confidentiality, anonymity, integrity,* and *accountability*) and which offers only plausible combinations of these *protection goals* for general purpose information systems. As described in [Wolf and Pfitzmann, 1999], the user interface can define but not enforce the *protection goals* in an information system. Lau et al. [Lau et al., 1999] describe a *privacy interface* which enables users to define which bookmarks for web pages should be *private* and which should be *public*. They summarize the experience they gained while designing different versions of the *privacy interface* [Lau et al., 1999, p. 94]:

"In summary, our experience has led to the following general conclusions:

- Privacy interfaces should facilitate the creation, inspection, modification, and monitoring of privacy policies.

- Privacy policies should apply automatically to objects as they are encountered.

- One way of achieving these goals is the use of an intensional [sic] representation of privacy policies."

Chapter 9

SUMMARY AND CONCLUSION

In the introduction, the importance of security in user modeling was emphasized for several reasons. First, user adaptive systems process user-related information (i.e., personal data) in order to adapt to the user's characteristics. The processing of user related information is subject to mandatory and voluntary regulations (e.g., laws and guidelines) which demand security mechanisms. Second, the secrecy or confidentiality of personal information is crucial for many users when deciding whether or not to use a user modeling system.

Two complementary approaches to security in user modeling have been described in this book. The anonymization or pseudonymization of the user's information processed in a user adaptive system reduces it to data which cannot be traced to an identifiable person. This means that there is no longer any rationale for many of the laws and user concerns summarized in the introduction. Measures for providing super-identification, identification, pseudonymity, and anonymity were described. Furthermore, several types of anonymity (*environmental, content-based*, and *procedural anonymity*) in user adaptive systems were explored.

The second approach follows the prevailing definition of security as being composed of secrecy, integrity, and availability. Because the requirements regarding availability of user modeling systems do not go beyond those of general information systems, they have not been covered here. Factors pertaining to secrecy and integrity have been considered in detail from the perspective of user modeling. Secrecy of the user's information was examined from the perspective of secrecy through denial of access, involving encryption and anonymity, and secrecy through selective access, which deals with the confidentiality of information shared between particular application systems. Selective access was discussed with regard to well-known security models, such as noninterference models, information flow control models, and access control models. With these models, both the confidentiality and the integrity of the user model can be advanced through the authorization of application systems for particular areas of the user model, though not simultaneously. From the perspective of the application system, the integrity of a user model was analyzed as external integrity; i.e., internal details of the user modeling system were not considered. The discussion of internal integrity covered the factors of integrity which depend on the user modeling system and its particular representation and inference mechanisms.

Proposals for meeting the security requirements described in chapters 4 and 5 were dealt with in relation to the particular aspects on which the security measures focus (e.g., anonymity, confidentiality, and integrity). Security measures can also be categorized according to the number of components involved. In the following table, some of the security measures presented in this book are divided into three groups according to the number of components which are necessary for their implementation. *Unilateral security measures* can be applied on the side of the user model itself, *bilateral security measures* require an additional component, and for *multilateral security measures* several components of the system must act jointly (see Table 9.1):

Table 9.1.   Grouping security measures according to the number of components involved

Type of security measure	Examples	Covered in chapter
unilateral	access control	5.1.2, 7.1.2
	identification	4, 6
	content-based anonymity	4.1.3, 6.1.2
	authorization	5.2.1, 7.1.2, 7.2.1.5
	internal integrity	5.2.2, 7.2.2
	noninterference	7.1.2.1
	information flow control	7.1.2.2
bilateral	authentication of communication partners	5.2.1, 7.2.1.7, 7.1.1.2
	secrecy of communication	5.1.1.2, 7.1.1
	super-identification	4.1.1, 6.2.6, 7.1.1.2, 7.2.1.6
multilateral	certificates	6.2.3.1, 4.1.1, 7.1.1.2
	procedural anonymity	4.1.3, 6.1.3, 6.2
	environmental anonymity	4.1.3, 6.1.1
	confidentiality	5.1.2, 7.1.2, 7.1.3
	external integrity	5.2.1, 7.2.1

Within this book, three new methods for increasing the security of user modeling systems have been presented. First, extending the KQML Application Programmer's Interface to include the Secure Sockets Layer (SKAPI) makes possible encrypted and authenticated communication between the components of a user adaptive system without appreciably modifying them. Second, by applying SKQML and integrating the KQMLmix implementation into the application system, procedural anonymity and pseudonymity can be achieved to various degrees. Furthermore, user model entries can be stored with a proof of their origin and integrity which was not possible with the previously available implementations. Third, the implementation of a role-based access control model (RBAC model) enables us to assign areas of responsibility on a user model to application systems, thereby making it possible to define and to satisfy the user's requirements for confidentiality and integrity of the data. The interaction of these three implementations was demonstrated by combining them via the *User Model Reference Monitor* which interconnects application systems with the user model. This combination can serve as a default security architecture for user adaptive systems. It can be modified or extended according to the requirements of the particular user adaptive systems. Single components of this architecture can be provided either as software packages (e.g., to be used locally) or as services (e.g., of trust centers).

The roles of the RBAC model used in the *User Model Reference Monitor* can be defined with respect to the application systems which could potentially request user information, thereby establishing a context-dependent access control. The roles can be defined equally well with respect to the users' roles they assume when interacting with the user adaptive system, thereby establishing a content-dependent access control. The RBAC model is therefore more flexible than any of the previously proposed access control models for user modeling (e.g., the access control model used in *Doppelgänger*).

The discussion of selected user modeling components depicts the applicability of security measures within user adaptive systems. Two well-known user modeling servers (*Doppelgänger* and *BGP-MS*) have been discussed and their security features were pointed out. Also, the security measures these servers provide were compared with those described in this book. The *AVANTI* system was introduced as a representative of user adaptive systems which process sensitive user information and security measures for this system were proposed. From this proposal, it is clear that previously available means for security (e.g., for encryption) and for anonymity (e.g., the means for establishing procedural anonymity as described in *Chapter 6.1.3*) were not adequate to meet the requirements of user modeling which have been considered in this book. The description of the basics of the Platform for Privacy Preferences Project (P3P) showed that P3P is suitable only for the definition of usage policies of personal information and the negotiation about these policies through the user (agent) and user adaptive application systems. P3P neither supports the security of a user model(ing agent) (e.g., its secrecy or integrity) nor does it provide means for the anonymization of the user model(ing agent). Therefore, P3P cannot replace the solutions we presented but it can be included in the proposed security architecture (see *Chapter 8.3*), for instance, as part of the (role based) access control model by establishing a role hierarchy with the data categories introduced with P3P (see p. 176).

The requirements for security in user modeling systems have been analyzed on the basis of a user adaptive system which consists of a user model, several application systems maintaining the model, and the user, whereby the system operates on several trusted computing bases. Obviously, for a user adaptive system which is under the complete control of the user or which has only one affected application system, moderate security requirements may be sufficient. For instance, the requirements for anonymity can be overstated in an electronic commerce scenario in which the user has to be identified, either for billing or for the delivery of goods.

The predominance of logic-based approaches in user modeling has also influenced the focus of this book. Several examples of so-called *security models* have been formulated for logic-based user modeling systems. This is partly because the mechanisms of these models lend themselves to the compartmented representation of many such systems, and partly because the mechanisms are less applicable to other approaches, for instance for sub-symbolic representation systems such as neural networks. Further development of the models described (for instance, Denning's information flow control model) or analysis of other security models should be carried out in order to provide appropriate security models for those user modeling systems whose internal structure is not as explicit as that of symbolic systems (e.g., user modeling systems based on sub-symbolic representation mechanisms).

Several conclusions can be drawn from an analysis of the additional security requirements for user modeling systems. Security is a composite of a multitude of concepts, most of which can only be applied to a limited extent to a given user modeling system. Furthermore, security is expensive both in terms of computational effort and in terms of design considerations. Designing security features to be included in an existing user modeling system usually involves considerably more effort than creating a new system which can be shaped to fit the security requirements. For some user adaptive systems, particular combinations of security requirements cannot be fulfilled or can be met only to a limited degree due to contradictions inherent to the system (e.g., confidentiality vs. integrity, complexity of modeling vs. intelligibility and supervision, inferential power vs. inference security). Contradictions of this kind should be identified in the design phase of the system and the requirements for security and user modeling must be balanced against each other. There are also several requirements which cannot be imposed onto all of the user modeling systems (e.g., content-based anonymity, consistency, or internal integrity).

In addition to augmenting a user adaptive system with security measures which are specifically designed for user modeling mechanisms, we have introduced a second approach toward safeguarding the user's privacy. Anonymization and pseudonymization reduce the user's information to data to which reduced requirements apply, as it cannot be traced to a person. Despite the effort involved in anonymization (e.g., computational effort for encryption, consecutive checks for possible deanonymization), this approach is potentially very valuable, because it introduces a qualitative improvement where only a gradual improvement could otherwise be achieved.

Two counter-intuitive conclusion can also be drawn: First, the centralization of users' information within a user modeling server can be valuable if not necessary for anonymization. Only knowledge about all user models can prevent unique combinations of user model entries which would facilitate deanonymization. Second, super-identification is necessary for the anonymization process using the mix method.

The security considerations covered in this book included instrumental factors which enable the system designer and/or the user to define and enforce specific procedures (e.g., access control, authentication, encryption). Furthermore, descriptive factors were discussed (for instance, integrity, environmental anonymity) which are dependent on the employed user modeling system and on its representation and inference methods, and which cannot be modified by users according to their preferences. Nevertheless, these considerations are important for an assessment of the system's security and its ability to protect the user's privacy.

The specifications of the Platform for Privacy Preferences Project point to ways in which the described solutions can be applied in defining and enforcing *privacy preferences*. The role-based access control model in particular provides a basis for converting specified privacy preferences into decisions about access to the user model as well as making it possible to define access modes more flexibly (for instance, through access permissions for anonymous user information only if the underlying system supports all or several types of anonymity). On this basis, the user's privacy preferences can be evaluated more thoroughly.

From the Platform for Privacy Preferences Project the advantages of a structured and standardized user model (e.g., a hierarchical data structure and categories as in P3P) for the intelligibility as well as for the underlying security mechanisms are also clear. However, user models often employ more complex representation and inference methods in order to support adaptivity. User models which employ production systems need to be analyzed with particular care to determine whether access control models are sufficient or information flow control models must be added (within the user modeling systems).

In addition to the proposed access control models which allow for a qualitative decision about the admissibility of an application system's request, quantitative regulations can be used in specifying the amount of information which might be exchanged between an application system and the user model. For example, an application can be endowed with a certain sum in a virtual currency, from which the user model deducts a fee for each request the application system submits. In this way, an economic access control could be achieved which would force the application system to make frugal use of information despite its authorization to access particular information, and would facilitate refined access control and evaluation of the adaptive application system on the basis of the amount transferred.

References

[Abe, 1998] Abe, M. (1998). Universally verifiable mix-net with verification work independent of the number of mix-servers. In [Nyberg, 1998], pages 437–447.

[ACM92, 1992] ACM92 (1992). ACM Code of Ethics and Professional Conduct. Technical report.

[ACS, 2002] ACS (2002). Australian computer society code of ethics. Technical report.

[Adam and Wortmann, 1989] Adam, N. R. and Wortmann, J. C. (1989). Security-control methods for statistical databases: A comparative study. *ACM Computing Surveys*, 21(4):515–556.

[Allen, 1990] Allen, R. B. (1990). User models: theory, method, and practice. *International Journal of Man-Machine Studies*, 32(5):511–543.

[Amann and Kessler, 1993] Amann, E. and Kessler, V. (1993). Sicherheitsmodelle in Thoerie und Praxis. In Spies, P. P., editor, *Europäischer Informatik Kongreß Architektur von Rechensystemen, Euro-ARCH '93, München, 18.-19. 10.*, pages 242–254. Springer.

[Anonymous, 1996] Anonymous (1996). Risks of anonymity. *Communications of the ACM*, 39(12):162.

[Art Technology Group, 2001] Art Technology Group (2001). ATG Dynamo e-Business Platform. http://www.atg.com/products.

[Aucsmith, 1998] Aucsmith, D., editor (1998). *Information Hiding, Second International Workshop, Portland, Oregon, April 14-17.* Springer, Berlin, Heidelberg, New York.

[Barkley, 1997] Barkley, J. (1997). Comparing simple role based access control models and access control lists. In [RBAC97, 1997], pages 127–132.

[Barkley et al., 1997] Barkley, J. F., Cincotta, A. V., Ferraiolo, D. F., Gavrilla, S., and Kuhn, D. R. (1997). Role based access control for the world wide web. In *Proc. 20th National Information System Security Conference, NIST/NSA*.

[Bauknecht et al., 1998] Bauknecht, K., Büllesbach, A., Pohl, H., and Teufel, S., editors (1998). *Sicherheit in Informationssystemen, Proceedings der Fachtagung SIS'98, Universität Hohenheim, Germany, 26.-27.3.* Hochschulverlag AG ETH Zürich.

[BCS, 2002] BCS (2002). British computer society code of conduct. Technical report.

[BDSG90, 1990] BDSG90 (20. Dezember 1990). Gesetz zur Fortentwicklung der Datenverarbeitung und des Datenschutzes. *BGBl. I*, page 2954.

[Bell and LaPadula, 1976] Bell, D. and LaPadula, L. (1976). Secure computer systems: Unified exposition and multics interpretation. Technical Report MTR 2997, MITRE Corporation, Bedford MA.

[Bell, 1988] Bell, D. E. (1988). Concerning "modeling" of computer security. In [SSP88, 1898], pages 8–13.

[Berson and Lunt, 1987a] Berson, T. A. and Lunt, T. F. (1987a). Multilevel security for knowledge-based systems. In [SSP87, 1897], pages 235–242.

[Berson and Lunt, 1987b] Berson, T. A. and Lunt, T. F. (1987b). Security considerations for knowledge-based systems. In *Third Annual Expert Systems in Government Conference, Washington, D.C., October*, pages 266–271.

[Berthold et al., 2000] Berthold, O., Federrath, H., and Köhntopp, M. (2000). Project "Anonymity and Unobservability in the Internet". In *Proceedings 10th Conference on Computers, Freedom & Privacy 2000, Westin Harbour Castle, Toronto, Ontario, Canada, April 4-7*, pages 57–68.

[Berthold et al., 2001] Berthold, O., Federrath, H., and Köpsell, S. (2001). Web MIXes: A system for anonymous and unobservable Internet access. In Federrath, H., editor, *Designing Privacy Enhancing Technologies. Proc. Workshop on Design Issues in Anonymity and Unobservability, LNCS 2009*, pages 115–129. Springer, Berlin, Heidelberg, New York.

[Bertino, 1998] Bertino, E. (1998). Data security. *Data & Knowledge Engineering*, 25:199–216.

[Bertino et al., 1996] Bertino, E., Kurth, H., Martella, G., and Montolivo, E., editors (1996). *Computer Security - ESORICS 96, Proc. 4th European Symposium on Research in Computer Security, Rome, Italy, September 25-27*. Springer.

[Biba, 1977] Biba, K. (1977). Integrity considerations for secure computer systems. Technical Report Report MTR 3153, MITRE Corporation, Bedford MA.

[Biddle and Thomas, 1966] Biddle, B. J. and Thomas, E. J. (1966). *Role Theory: Concepts and Research*. John Wiley & Sons.

[Birkhoff, 1962] Birkhoff, G. (1962). *Lattice Theory*. American Mathematical Society.

[Biskup et al., 1994] Biskup, J., Morgenstern, M., and Landwehr, C. E., editors (1994). *Database Security, VIII: Status and Prospects, Proceedings of the IFIP WG11.3 Working Conference on Database Security, Bad Salzdetfurth, Germany, August 23-26*. Elsevier Science Publishers.

[Bizer and Bleumer, 1997] Bizer, J. and Bleumer, G. (1997). Pseudonym. *Datenschutz und Datensicherheit*, 21(1):46.

[Blahut, 1987] Blahut, R. E. (1987). *Principles and Practice of Information Theory*. Addison-Wesley.

[Blank, 1996] Blank, K. (1996). *Benutzermodellierung für adaptive interaktive Systeme: Architektur, Methoden, Werkzeuge und Anwendungen*. Infix, Germany.

[Borking, 1998] Borking, J. (1998). Einsatz datenschutzfreundlicher Technologien in der Praxis. *Datenschutz und Datensicherheit*, 22(11):636–640.

[Boston Consulting Group, 1997] Boston Consulting Group (1997). eTRUST Internet Privacy Study: Summary of Market Survey Results. Technical report.

[Brajnik and Tasso, 1994] Brajnik, G. and Tasso, C. (1994). A shell for developing non-monotonic user modeling systems. *International Journal of Human-Computer Studies*, 40:31–62.

[Brewer and Nash, 1989] Brewer, D. F. and Nash, M. J. (1989). The chinese wall security policy. In [SSP89, 1989], pages 206–214.

[Brusilovsky, 1998] Brusilovsky, P. (1998). Methods and techniques of adaptive hypermedia. In Brusilovsky, P., Kobsa, A., and Vassileva, J., editors, *Adaptive Hypertext and Hypermedia*, pages 1–43. Kluwer.

[Burns et al., 1992] Burns, A., McDermid, J., and Dobson, J. (1992). On the meaning of safety and security. *The Computer Journal*, 35(1):3–15.

[Campbell, 1995] Campbell, J. R. (1995). A brief database security tutorial: Or the less than Civil War between Ease-of-use and Security, the Battle between Grant and Lee's Privilege, Roles and Rollbacks, MAC DAC and FACT, even Distribution and Replication Maybe. In [ISS95, 1995], pages 740–757.

[Castano et al., 1994] Castano, S., Fugini, M., Martella, G., and Samarati, P. (1994). *Database Security*. Addison-Wesley.

[CC99, 1999] CC99 (1999). The Common Criteria for Information Technology Security Evaluation (Common Criteria Version 2.1, ISO/IEC 15408). Technical report.

[CCS98, 1998] CCS98 (1998). *Fifth ACM Conference on Computer and Communications Security, San Francisco, California, November 2-5*.

[Chang and Keisler, 1990] Chang, C. and Keisler, H. J. (1990). *Model Theory*. North-Holland, 3 edition.

[Chapman and Davida, 1997] Chapman, M. and Davida, G. (1997). Hiding the hidden: A software for concealing ciphertext as innocuous text. In [Han et al., 1997], pages 335–345.

[Chaum, 1988] Chaum, D. (1988). The dining cryptographers problem: Unconditional sender and recipient untracability. *Journal of Cryptology*, 1(1):65–75.

[Chaum, 1981] Chaum, D. L. (1981). Untraceable electronic mail, return addresses, and digital pseudonyms. *Communications of the ACM*, 24(2):84–88.

[Chin, 2000] Chin, D. N. (2000). Empirical evaluation of user models. *User Modeling and User-Adapted Interaction*, to be published.

[Chin, 1978] Chin, F. Y. (1978). Security in statistical databases for queries with small counts. *ACM Transactions on Database Systems*, 3(1):92–104.

[Chin and Ozsoyoglu, 1981] Chin, F. Y. and Ozsoyoglu, G. (1981). Statistical database design. *ACM Transactions on Database Systems*, 6(1):113–139.

[Clark and Wilson, 1987] Clark, D. C. and Wilson, D. R. (1987). A comparison of commercial and military computer security policies. In [SSP87, 1897], pages 184–194.

[Cohn, 1994] Cohn, A. G., editor (1994). *Proc. Eleventh European Conference on Artificial Intelligence ECAI, Amsterdam, The Netherlands, August 8-12.*

[Commission of the European Communities,] Commission of the European Communities. Information technology security evaluation criteria (ITSEC): provisional harmonized criteria, version 1.2. Technical report, Office for Official Publications of the European Communities, Luxembourg.

[Cook and Kay, 1994] Cook, R. and Kay, J. (1994). The justified user model: a viewable, explained user model. In [UM94, 1994], pages 145–150.

[Covington, 1998] Covington, M. A. (1998). Speech acts, electronic commerce, and KQML. *Decision Support Systems*, 22(3):203–211.

[Cox, 1980] Cox, L. (1980). Suppression methodology and statistical disclosure control. *Journal of the American Statistical Association*, 75:377–385.

[Cramer, 1999] Cramer, R. (1999). Introduction to secure computation. In [Damgard, 1999], pages 16–62.

[Cranor, 1998] Cranor, L. F. (1998). Internet privacy: A public concern. *NetWorker*, 2(3):13–18.

[CSFW91, 1991] CSFW91 (1991). *Proc. Computer Security Foundations Workshop, Franconia, New Hampshire, June 18-20.* IEEE Computer Society Press.

[CSFW97, 1997] CSFW97 (1997). *Proc. Computer Security Foundations Workshop, Rockport, Massachusetts, June 10-12.*

[Culnan and Milne, 2001] Culnan, M. J. and Milne, G. R. (2001). The Culnan-Milne survey on consumers & online privacy notices: Summary of responses. In *Interagency Public Workshop: Get Noticed: Effective Financial Privacy Notices, Washington, D.C., Dec. 4, 2001*, pages 47–54.

[Cuppens, 1992] Cuppens, F. (1992). A modal logic framework to solve aggregation problems. In [Landwehr and Jajodia, 1992], pages 315–332.

[Cuppens, 1993] Cuppens, F. (1993). A logical formalization of secrecy. In Gray, J. W., editor, *Proceedings of the Computer Security Foundations Workshop VI, June 15-17*, pages 53–62, Franconia, New Hampshire. IEEE Computer Society Press.

[Cuppens and Trouessin, 1994] Cuppens, F. and Trouessin, G. (1994). Information flow controls vs inference controls: An integrated approach. In [Gollmann, 1994], pages 447–468.

[Damgard, 1999] Damgard, I. (1999). *Lectures on Data Security: Modern Cryptology in theory and Practice, Lecture Notes in Computer Science 1561.* Springer, Berlin, Heidelberg, New York.

[Davis, 1993] Davis, M. (1993). First order logic. In [Gabbay et al., 1993], pages 31–65.

[Dayal and Traiger, 1987] Dayal, U. and Traiger, I. L., editors (1987). *Proc. Association for Computing Machinery Special Interest Group on Management of Data 1987 Annual Conference, San Francisco, California, May 27-29.*

[Denning, 1976] Denning, D. E. (1976). A lattice model of secure information flow. *Communications of the ACM*, 19(5):236–243.

[Denning, 1988] Denning, D. E. (1988). Database security. In Traub, J., editor, *Annual Review of Computer Science*, volume 3, pages 1–22.

[Denning et al., 1979] Denning, D. E., Denning, P. J., and Schwartz, M. D. (1979). The tracker: A threat to statistical database security. *ACM Transactions on Database Systems*, 4(1):76–96.

[Denning and Schlörer, 1983] Denning, D. E. and Schlörer, J. (1983). Inference controls for statistical databases. *IEEE Computer*, 16(7):69–82.

[Denning, 1982] Denning, D. E. R. (1982). *Cryptography and Data Security.* Addison-Wesley.

[DePallo, 2000] DePallo, M. (2000). AARP National Survey on Consumer Preparedness and E-Commerce: A Survey of Computer Users Age 45 and Older. Technical report, AARP, Washington, D.C. http://research.aarp.org/consume/ecommerce.pdf.

[Deswarte et al., 1992] Deswarte, Y., Eizenberg, G., and Quisquater, J.-J., editors (1992). *Computer Security - ESORICS 92, Proc. 2nd European Symposium on Research in Computer Security, Toulouse, France, November 23-25.* Springer.

[Dierstein, 1990] Dierstein, R. (1990). The concept of secure information processing systems and their basic functions. In Dittrich, K., Rautakivi, S., and Saari, J., editors, *Proceedings of the Sixth IFIP International Conference on Computer Security and Information Integrity in our Changing World IFIP/Sec'90, Espoo (Helsinki), Finland, May 23-25*, pages 133–149.

[Diffie and Hellman, 1976] Diffie, W. and Hellman, M. E. (1976). New directions in cryptography. *IEEE Transactions on Information Theory*, IT-22(6):644–654.

[Dobkin et al., 1979] Dobkin, D., Jones, A. K., and Lipton, R. J. (1979). Secure databases: Protection against user influence. *ACM Transactions on Database Systems*, 4(1):97–106.

[Dobson and McDermid, 1989] Dobson, J. E. and McDermid, J. A. (1989). Security models and enterprise models. In [Landwehr, 1989], pages 1–39.

[ECDIR95,] ECDIR95. Directive 95/46/EC of the European Parliament and of the Council of 24 October 1995 on the protection of individuals with regard to the processing of personal data and on the free movement of such data. *Official Journal of the European Communities of 23 November 1995 No L. 281*, page 31.

[Egger, 1993] Egger, E. (1993). Considering privacy-aspects in designing cscw-applications. In Clement, A., Kolm, P., and Wagner, I., editors, *NetWORKing: Connecting Workers In and Between Organizations, Proceedings of the IFIP*

WG9.1 Working Conference on NetWORKing, Vienna, Austria, June 16-18, pages 133–141. North-Holland.

[Eydner and Vergara, 1993] Eydner, G. and Vergara, H. (1993). Die Benutzermodellierungsshell PROTUM basierend auf PROLOG und KN-PART. In Kobsa, A. and Pohl, W., editors, *Arbeitspapiere des Workshops Adaptivität und Benutzermodellierung in interaktiven Softwaresystemen, Berlin, 13.-15.9.93*, pages 136–143, Berlin, Germany. Universität Konstanz, Bericht Nr. 30/93 (WIS-Memo 7).

[Farber and Larson, 1975] Farber, D. and Larson, K. (1975). Network security via dynamic process renaming, october 7-9. In *Fourth Data Communication Symposium*, pages 8–13 – 8–18, Quebec, Canada.

[Fellegi, 1972] Fellegi, I. P. (1972). On the question of statistical confidentiality. *Journal of the American Statistical Association*, 67(337):7–18.

[Ferraiolo et al., 1999] Ferraiolo, D. F., Barkley, J. F., and Kuhn, D. R. (1999). A role-based access control model and reference implementation within a corporate intranet. *ACM Transactions on Information and Systems Security*, 2(1):34–64.

[Finin et al., 1995] Finin, T., Mayfield, J., and Thirunavukkarasu, C. (1995). Secret agents – a security architecture for the KQML agent communication language. In *Intelligent Information Agents Workshop held in conjunction with Fourth International Conference on Information and Knowledge Management CIKM'95, Baltimore*.

[Finin and Weber, 1993] Finin, T. and Weber, J. (1993). Draft specification of the KQML agent-communication language. Technical report.

[Finin, 1989] Finin, T. W. (1989). GUMS - A General User Modeling Shell. In [Kobsa and Wahlster, 1989], pages 411–430.

[Fink, 1998] Fink, J. (1998). Implikationen aus dem Datenbank- und Transaktionsmanagement für anwendungsorientierte Serversysteme zur Benutzermodellierung. In [Timm and Rössel, 1998], pages 7–15.

[Fink, 1999] Fink, J. (1999). Transactional consistency in user modeling systems. In [Kay, 1999], pages 191–200.

[Fink, 2002] Fink, J. (2002). *User Modeling Servers: Requirements, Design, and Implementation*. PhD thesis, Department of Mathematics and Computer Science, University of Essen, Germany, forthcoming.

[Fink and Kobsa, 2001] Fink, J. and Kobsa, A. (2001). A review and analysis of commercial user modeling servers for personalization on the world wide web. *to appear in: User Modeling and User-Adapted Interaction*. http://www.ics.uci.edu/ kobsa/papers/2001-UMUAI-kobsa.pdf.

[Fink et al., 1998] Fink, J., Kobsa, A., and Nill, A. (1998). Adaptable and adaptive information provision for all users, including disabled and elderly people. In *The New Review of Hypermedia and Multimedia, Volume 4*, pages 163–214. Taylor Graham, London.

[Fink et al., 1997] Fink, J., Kobsa, A., and Schreck, J. (1997). Personalized hyper-media information provision through adaptive and adaptable system features: User modelling, privacy and security issues. In [Mullery et al., 1997], pages 459–467.

[Fink et al., 2002] Fink, J., Koenemann, J., Noller, S., and Schwab, I. (2002). Putting personalization into practice. *Communications of the ACM*, 45(5):41–42.

[Flinn and Maurer, 1995] Flinn, B. and Maurer, H. (1995). Levels of anonymity. *Journal of Universal Computer Science*, 1(1):35–47.

[Forrester Research, 1999] Forrester Research (1999). The privacy best practise. Technical report, Cambridge MA.

[Fox, 2000] Fox, S. (2000). Trust and privacy online: Why americans want to rewrite the rules. Technical report, The Pew Internet & American Life Project, Washington, D.C.

[Franz et al., 1998] Franz, E., Graubner, A., Jerichow, A., and Pfitzmann, A. (1998). Einsatz von dummies im Mixnetz zum Schutz der Kommunikationsbeziehungen. In [Bauknecht et al., 1998], pages 65–94.

[Franz et al., 1997] Franz, E., Jerichow, A., and Pfitzmann, A. (1997). Systematisierung und Modellierung von Mixen. In [Müller et al., 1997], pages 171–190.

[Freier et al., 1996] Freier, A. O., Karlton, P., and Kocher, P. C. (1996). The SSL Protocol, Version 3.0. Technical report, Netscape Communications Company.

[Gabbay et al., 1993] Gabbay, D. M., Hogger, C., and Robinson, J. (1993). *Handbook of Logic in Artificial Intelligence and Logic Programming*. Clarendon Press.

[Gabber et al., 1999] Gabber, E., Gibbons, P. B., Kristol, D. M., Matias, Y., and Mayer, A. (1999). Consistent, yet anonymous, web access with LPWA. *Communications of the ACM*, 42(2):42–47.

[Gabber et al., 1997] Gabber, E., Gibbons, P. B., Matias, Y., and Mayer, A. (1997). How to make personalized web browsing simple, secure, and anonymous. In [Hirschfeld, 1997], pages 17–31.

[Gallaire et al., 1984] Gallaire, H., Minker, J., and Nicolas, J.-M. (1984). Logic and databases: A deductive approach. *ACM Computing Surveys*, 16(2):153–185.

[Garfinkel, 1995] Garfinkel, S. (1995). *PGP Pretty Good Privacy*. O'Reilly & Associates.

[Garvey and Lunt, 1991] Garvey, T. D. and Lunt, T. F. (1991). Multilevel security for knowledge based systems. Technical Report SRI-CSL-91-01, Menlo Park, California.

[Gavish and Gerdes Jr., 1998] Gavish, B. and Gerdes Jr., J. (1998). Anonymous mechanisms in group decision support systems communication. *Decision Support Systems*, 23(4):297–328.

[Gavrila and Barkley, 1998] Gavrila, S. I. and Barkley, J. F. (1998). Formal specification for role based access control user/role and role/role relationship management. In [RBAC98, 1998], pages 81–90.

[Genesereth and Nilsson, 1987] Genesereth, M. R. and Nilsson, N. J. (1987). *Logical foundations of artificial intelligence*. Morgan Kaufmann.

[Gesellschaft für Informatik, 1995] Gesellschaft für Informatik (1995). Ethische Leitlinien der Gesellschaft für Informatik. http://www.gi-ev.de/, Germany.

[Goguen and Meseguer, 1982] Goguen, J. and Meseguer, J. (1982). Security policies and security models. In [SSP82, 1982], pages 11–20.

[Goguen and Meseguer, 1984] Goguen, J. A. and Meseguer, J. (1984). Unwinding and inference control. In [SSP84, 1984], pages 75–86.

[Goh and Baldwin, 1998] Goh, C. and Baldwin, A. (1998). Towards a more complete model of role. In [RBAC98, 1998], pages 55–61.

[Goldschlag et al., 1999] Goldschlag, D., Reed, M., and Syverson, P. (1999). Onion routing for anonymous and private internet connections. *Communications of the ACM*, 42(2):39–41.

[Gollmann, 1994] Gollmann, D., editor (1994). *Computer Security - ESORICS 94, Proc. 3rd European Symposium on Research in Computer Security, Brighton, United Kingdom, November 7-9*. Springer.

[Gollmann, 1999] Gollmann, D. (1999). *Computer Security*. John Wiley & Sons.

[Gotterbarn et al., 1999] Gotterbarn, D., Miller, K., and Rogerson, S. (1999). Software engineering code of ethics is approved. *Communications of the ACM*, 42(10):102–107.

[Greer, 1995] Greer, J., editor (1995). *Proc. World Conference on Artificial Intelligence in Education, AI-ED'95*.

[Gülcü and Tsudik, 1996] Gülcü, C. and Tsudik, G. (1996). Mixing email with babel. In [SNDSS96, 1996], pages 2–16.

[GVU's WWW Surveying Team, 1998] GVU's WWW Surveying Team (1998). GVU's Tenth WWW User Survey. http://www.cc.gatech.edu/gvu/user_surveys/survey-1998-10/, Graphics, Visualization, & Usability Center, College of Computing, Georgia Institute of Technology, Atlanta, GA.

[Han et al., 1997] Han, Y., Okamoto, T., and Qing, S., editors (1997). *Information and Communications Security, First International Conference ICIS '97, Beijing, China, November 11-14*. Springer, Berlin, Heidelberg, New York.

[Harrison et al., 1976] Harrison, M. A., Ruzzo, W. L., and Ullman, J. D. (1976). Protection in operating systems. *Communications of the ACM*, 19(8):461–471.

[Herrmann, 1990] Herrmann, T. (1990). Benutzermodellierung und Datenschutz. *Datenschutz und Datensicherung*, 14(7):352–359.

[Hinke et al., 1997] Hinke, T. H., Delugach, H. S., and Wolf, R. P. (1997). Protecting databases from inference attacks. *Computers & Security*, 16(8):687–708.

[Hirsch, 1997] Hirsch, F. J. (1997). Introducing SSL and Certificates Using SSLeay. *World Wide Web Journal*, pages 141–173.

[Hirschfeld, 1997] Hirschfeld, R., editor (1997). *Financial Cryptography, Proc. First International Conference FC'97, Anguilla, British West Indies, February 24-28.* Springer.

[Huitmea, 1996] Huitmea, C. (1996). *IPv6 - The New Internet Protocol.* Prentice-Hall.

[Hunt, 1992] Hunt, C. (1992). *TCP/IP Network Administration.* O'Reilly & Associates.

[IBM, 1999] IBM (1999). IBM Multi-National Consumer Privacy Survey. http://www.ibm.com/services/files/privacy_survey_oct991.pdf.

[IEEE, 2002] IEEE (2002). IEEE Code of Ethics. Technical report.

[IJCAI79, 1979] IJCAI79 (1979). *Proc. Sixth International Joint Conference on Artificial Intelligence IJCAI'79, Volume 2, Tokyo, Japan, August 20-23.*

[International Organization for Standardization, 1995] International Organization for Standardization (1995). Information technology - Open Systems Interconnection - The Directory: Authentication framework. Technical report, Geneva, Switzerland.

[ISS95, 1995] ISS95 (1995). *Proc. 18th National Information Systems Security Conference, Balitmore, Maryland, October 10-13.*

[IuKDG2001, 2001] IuKDG2001 (2001). Gesetz ber den Datenschutz bei Telediensten. http://www.iid.de/iukdg/gesetz/, http://jurcom5.juris.de/bundesrecht/tddsg/.

[IuKDG97, 1997] IuKDG97 (22. Juli 1997). Gesetz zur Regelung der Rahmenbedingungen für Informations- und Kommunikationsdienste (Informations - und Kommunikationsddienste-Gesetz – IuKDG). Bundesgesetzblatt Teil I Nr. 52.

[IuKDG97a, 1997] IuKDG97a (July 22 1997). Federal Act Establishing the General Conditions for Information and Communication Services - Information and Communication Services Act - (Informations- und Kommunikationsdienste-Gesetz - IuKDG).

[Jakobsson, 1998] Jakobsson, M. (1998). A practical mix. In [Nyberg, 1998], pages 448–461.

[Jakobsson, 1999] Jakobsson, M. (1999). Flash mixing. In *PODC '99: Proceedings of the Eighteenth Annual ACM Symposium on Principles of Distributed Computing, May 3-6, Atlanta, Georgia*, pages 83–89.

[Jameson et al., 1997] Jameson, A., Paris, C., and Tasso, C., editors (1997). *User Modeling, Proceedings of the Sixth International Conference UM97, Chia Laguna, Sardinia, Italy, June 2-5.* Springer, Wien, New York.

[Jeon et al., 2000] Jeon, H., Petrie, C., and Cutkosky, M. R. (2000). JATLite: A Java Agent Infrastructure with Message Routing. *IEEE Internet Computing*, 4(2):87–96.

[Jerichow, 1999] Jerichow, A. (1999). *Generalisation and Security-improvement of Mix-mediated Anonymous Communication*. PhD thesis, Department of Computer Science of the Dresden University of Technology, Germany.

[Johnson and Nissenbaum, 1995] Johnson, D. G. and Nissenbaum, H. F. (1995). *Computers, Ethics & Social Values*. Prentice-Hall.

[Jones, 1989] Jones, K. S. (1989). Realism about user modeling. In [Kobsa and Wahlster, 1989], pages 341–363.

[Kahn, 1967] Kahn, D. (1967). *The Codebreakers, The Story Of Secret Writing*. Macmillan.

[Kass, 1991] Kass, R. (1991). Building a user model implicitly from a cooperative advisory dialog. *User Modeling and User-Adapted Interaction*, 1(3):203–258.

[Kay, 1991] Kay, J. (1991). Generalised user modelling shells - a taxonomy. In *Proc. IJCAI Workshop W4: Agent Modeling for Intelligent Interaction, Sydney, Australia*, pages 169–185.

[Kay, 1993] Kay, J. (1993). Pragmatic user modelling for adaptive interfaces. In Schneider-Hufschmidt, M., Kühme, T., and Malinowski, U., editors, *Adaptive User Interfaces: Principles and Practice*, pages 129–148. North-Holland, Amsterdam.

[Kay, 1995] Kay, J. (1995). The um toolkit for cooperative user modelling. *User Modeling and User-Adapted Interaction*, 4(3):149–196.

[Kay, 1999] Kay, J., editor (1999). *User Modeling, Proceedings of the Seventh International Conference UM99, Banff, Canada, June 20 -24*. Springer, Wien, New York.

[Kesdogan, 2000] Kesdogan, D. (2000). *Privacy im Internet, Vertrauenswürdige Kommunikation in offenen Umgebungen*. Vieweg.

[Kesdogan et al., 1998] Kesdogan, D., Egner, J., and Büschkes, R. (1998). Stop-and-go-mixes providing probabilistic anonymity in an open system. In [Aucsmith, 1998], pages 83–98.

[Kessler, 1992] Kessler, V. (1992). On the chinese wall model. In [Deswarte et al., 1992], pages 41–54.

[Kobsa, 1990] Kobsa, A. (1990). User modeling in dialog systems: Potentials and hazards. *AI & Society*, 4:214–231.

[Kobsa, 1991] Kobsa, A. (1991). Utilizing knowledge: The components of the sb-one knowledge representation workbench. In Sowa, J., editor, *Principles of Semantic Networks: Exploration in the Representation of Knowledge*, pages 457–486. Morgan Kaufmann.

[Kobsa, 2001a] Kobsa, A. (2001a). Generic user modeling systems. *User Modeling and User-Adapted Interaction*, 11(1-2):49–63.
http://www.ics.uci.edu/~kobsa/papers/2001-UMUAI-kobsa.pdf.

[Kobsa, 2001b] Kobsa, A. (2001b). Tailoring privacy to users' needs
(invited keynote). In Bauer, M., Gmytrasiewicz, P. J., and Vassileva, J., editors, *User Modeling 2001: 8th International Conference*, pages 303–313. Springer, Berlin, Heidelberg, New York.
http://www.ics.uci.edu/~kobsa/papers/2001-UM01-kobsa.pdf.

[Kobsa, 2002] Kobsa, A. (2002). Personalized hypermedia and international privacy. *Communications of the ACM*, 45(5):64–67.
http://www.ics.uci.edu/~kobsa/papers/2002-CACM-kobsa.pdf.

[Kobsa et al., 2000] Kobsa, A., Koenemann, J., and Pohl, W. (2000). Personalized
hypermedia presentation techniques for improving online customer relationships.
Technical report.

[Kobsa and Pohl, 1995] Kobsa, A. and Pohl, W. (1995). The user modeling shell
system BGP-MS. *User Modeling and User-Adapted Interaction*, 4(2):59–106.

[Kobsa and Wahlster, 1989] Kobsa, A. and Wahlster, W., editors (1989). *User Models in Dialog Systems*. Springer, Berlin, Heidelberg, New York.

[Konstan et al., 1997] Konstan, J. A., Miller, B. N., Maltz, D., Herlocker, J. L., Gor-
don, L. R., and Riedl, J. (1997). Grouplens: Applying collaborative filtering to
usenet news. *Communications of the ACM*, 40(3):77–87.

[Kuhn, 1997] Kuhn, D. R. (1997). Mutual exclusion of roles as a means of implementing separation of duty in role-based access control systems. In [RBAC97, 1997],
pages 23–30.

[Labrou and Finin, 1997] Labrou, Y. and Finin, T. (1997). A proposal for a new
KQML specification. Technical report, Computer Science and Electrical Engineering Department, University of Maryland, Baltimore County.

[Lamersdorf and Merz, 1998] Lamersdorf, W. and Merz, M., editors (1998). *Trends
in Distributed Systems for Electronic Commerce, Proc. International IFIP/GI
Working Conference TREC'98, Hamburg, Germany, June 3-5*, Berlin, Heidelberg,
New York. Springer.

[Landwehr, 1989] Landwehr, C. E., editor (1989). *Database Security, II: Status and
Prospects. Result of the IFIP WG 11.3 Workshop on Database Security, Kingston,
Ontario, Canada, 5-7 October 1988*. North-Holland.

[Landwehr, 1997] Landwehr, C. E. (1997). Protection (security) models and policy.
In [Tucker Jr., 1997], pages 1914–1928.

[Landwehr and Jajodia, 1992] Landwehr, C. E. and Jajodia, S., editors (1992).
*Database Security, V: Status and Prospects. Results of the IFIP WG 11.3 Work-
shop on Database Security, Shepherdstown, West Virginia, 4-7 November 1991*.
North-Holland.

[Lau et al., 1999] Lau, T., Etzioni, O., and Weld, D. S. (1999). Privacy interfaces for information management. *Communications of the ACM*, 42(10):88–94.

[Lawrence, 1993] Lawrence, L. G. (1993). The role of roles. *Computers & Security*, 12(1):15–21.

[Leveson, 1995] Leveson, N. G. (1995). *Safeware: system safety and computers.* Addison-Wesley.

[Lin and Qian, 1998] Lin, T. and Qian, S., editors (1998). *Database Security XI: Status and Prospects, IFIP TC11 WG11.3 Eleventh International Conference on Database Security, Lake Tahoe, California, 10-13 August 1997.* Chapman & Hall.

[Lindsay and Price, 1991] Lindsay, D. and Price, W., editors (1991). *Information Security, Proceedings of the IFIP TC11 Seventh International Conference on Information Security: Creating Confidence in Information Processing, IFIP/Sec '91.* North-Holland.

[Linton et al., 1999] Linton, F., Joy, D., and Schaefer, H.-P. (1999). Building user and expert models by long-term observation of application usage. In [Kay, 1999], pages 129–138.

[Longley and Shain, 1987] Longley, D. and Shain, M. (1987). *Data and Computer Security: Dictionary of standards, concepts and terms.* Macmillan.

[Lunheim and Sindre, 1994] Lunheim, R. and Sindre, G. (1994). Privacy and computing: a cultural perspective. In [Sizer et al., 1994], pages 25–40.

[Maier, 1983] Maier, D. (1983). *The Theory of Relational Databases.* IEEE Computer Society Press.

[Manna, 2001] Manna (2001). Frontmind. http://www.mannainc.com/products.html.

[Matloff, 1986] Matloff, N. S. (1986). Another look at the use of noise addition for database security. In [SSP86, 1896], pages 173–180.

[Mazières and Kaashoek, 1998] Mazières, D. and Kaashoek, M. F. (1998). The design, implementation and operation of an email pseudonym server. In [CCS98, 1998], pages 27–36.

[McCalla et al., 1996] McCalla, G., Searwar, F., Collins, J. T. J., Sun, Y., and Zhou, B. (1996). Analogical user modelling: A case study in individualized information filtering. In [UM96, 1996], pages 13–20.

[McCune, 1994] McCune, W. (1994). OTTER 3.0 Reference Manual and Guide, Technical Report ANL-94/6. technical report, Argonne National Laboratory, Mathematics and Computer Science Division, Argonne, IL.

[McLean, 1987] McLean, J. (1987). Reasoning about security models. In [SSP87, 1897], pages 123 – 131.

[Menezes et al., 1997] Menezes, A. J., van Oorschot, P. C., and Vanstone, S. A. (1997). *Handbook of Applied Cryptography.* CRC Press.

[Moffett, 1998] Moffett, J. D. (1998). Control principles and role hierarchies. In [RBAC98, 1998], pages 63–69.

[Morgenstern, 1987] Morgenstern, M. (1987). Security and inference in multilevel database and knowledge-based systems. In [Dayal and Traiger, 1987], pages 357–373.

[Morgenstern, 1988] Morgenstern, M. (1988). Controlling logical inference in multi-level database systems. In [SSP88, 1898], pages 245–255.

[Müller and Rannenberg, 1999] Müller, G. and Rannenberg, K. (1999). *Multilateral Security in Communications, Volume 3, Technology, Infrastructure, Economy.* Addison-Wesley.

[Müller et al., 1997] Müller, G., Rannenberg, K., Reitenspieß, M., and Stiegler, H., editors (1997). *Zwischen Key Escrow und elektronischem Geld, Proc. der GI-Fachtagung Verläßliche Informationssysteme VIS'97, Freiburg/Brsg., Germany, 30.9.-2.10.* Vieweg.

[Mullery et al., 1997] Mullery, A., Besson, M., Campolargo, M., Gobbi, R., and Reed, R., editors (1997). *Intelligence in Services and Networks: Technology for Cooperative Competition, Proc. Fourth International Conference on Intelligence in Services and Networks IS&N'97, Cernobbio, Italy, May 27-29.* Springer, Berlin, Heidelberg, New York.

[Nelson, 1994] Nelson, R. (1994). What is a secret - and - what does that have to do with computer security? In [NSP94, 1994], pages 74–79.

[Net Perceptions, 2002] Net Perceptions (2002). Net Perceptions. http://www.netperceptions.com.

[Nilsson, 1980] Nilsson, N. J. (1980). *Principles of Artificial Intelligence.* Morgan Kaufmann.

[NSP94, 1994] NSP94 (1994). *Proc. ACM SIGSAC New Security Paradigms Workshop, Little Compton, RI, August 3 - 5.*

[Nyanchama and Osborn, 1994] Nyanchama, M. and Osborn, S. (1994). Access rights administration in role-based security systems. In [Biskup et al., 1994], pages 1–23.

[Nyanchama and Osborn, 1995] Nyanchama, M. and Osborn, S. (1995). Modeling mandatory access control in role-based security systems. In [Spooner et al., 1995], pages 129–144.

[Nyberg, 1998] Nyberg, K., editor (1998). *Advances in Cryptology, Proc. International Conference on the Theory and Application of Cryptographic Techniques EUROCRYPT '98, Espoo, Finnland, May 31 - June 4,* Berlin, Heidelberg. Springer.

[OECD92, 1992] OECD92 (1992). Guidelines for the security of information systems. Technical report, Organisation for Economic Cooperation and Development (OECD).

[Oeser and Harary, 1966] Oeser, O. A. and Harary, F. (1966). Role structures: A description in terms of graph theory. In [Biddle and Thomas, 1966], pages 92–102.

[Ohio State University, 1998] Ohio   State   University
    (1998).   Afs   distributed   filesystem   faq   -   bibliography,
    http://www.cis.ohio-state.edu/hypertext/faq/usenet/afs-faq/faq-doc-92.html.
    Technical report.

[Orwant, 1994] Orwant, J. (1994). Apprising the user of user model: Doppelgänger's
    interface. In [UM94, 1994], pages 151–156.

[Orwant, 1995] Orwant, J. (1995). Heterogeneous learning in the doppelgänger user
    modeling system. *User Modeling and User-Adapted Interaction*, 4(2):107–130.

[Orwant, 1996] Orwant, J. (1996). For want of a bit the user was lost: Cheap user
    modeling. *IBM Systems Journal*, 35(3 & 4):398–416.

[Osborn, 1997] Osborn, S. (1997). Mandatory access control and role-based access
    control revisited. In [RBAC97, 1997], pages 31–40.

[P3P, 2002] P3P (2002). The Platform for Privacy Preferences 1.0 (P3P1.0) Specifi-
    cation. Technical report, The World Wide Web Consortium.

[Paiva and Self, 1994a] Paiva, A. and Self, J. (1994a). A learner model reasoning
    maintenance system. In [Cohn, 1994], pages 193–196.

[Paiva and Self, 1994b] Paiva, A. and Self, J. (1994b). Tagus - a user and learner
    modeling system. In [UM94, 1994], pages 43–49.

[Paiva and Self, 1995] Paiva, A. and Self, J. (1995). Tagus – a user and learner
    modeling workbench. *User Modeling and User-Adapted Interaction*, 4(3):197–226.

[Paiva et al., 1995] Paiva, A., Self, J., and Hartley, R. (1995). Externalising learner
    models. In [Greer, 1995], pages 509–516.

[Pernul, 1994] Pernul, G. (1994). Database security. *Advances in Computers*, 38:1–
    72.

[Pernul, 1995] Pernul, G. (1995). Information systems security: Scope, state-of-
    the-art, and evaluation of techniques. *Int. Journal of Information Management*,
    15(3):165–180.

[Pernul and Luef, 1992] Pernul, G. and Luef, G. (1992). Bibliography on database
    security. *SIGMOD Record*, 21(1):105–122.

[Pernul and Tjoa, 1992] Pernul, G. and Tjoa, A. (1992). Security policies for
    databases. In [SAFECOMP92, 1992], pages 259–265.

[Personalization Consortium, 2000] Personalization Consortium (2000). Personaliza-
    tion & privacy survey. Technical report, Personalization Consortium, Edgewater
    Place, MA. http://www.personalization.org/SurveyResults.pdf.

[Peters, 1999] Peters, T. A. (1999). *Computerized Monitoring and Online Privacy*.
    McFarland.

[Petrie, 1996] Petrie, C. J. (1996). Agent-based engineering, the web, and intelligence.
    IEEE Expert, 11(6):24–29.

[Pfitzmann et al., 1998] Pfitzmann, A., Schill, A., Westfeld, A., Wicke, G., Wolf, G., and Zöllner, J. (1998). A java-based distributed platform for multilateral security. In [Lamersdorf and Merz, 1998], pages 52–64.

[Pfitzmann and Waidner, 1987] Pfitzmann, A. and Waidner, M. (1987). Networks without user observability. *Computers & Security*, 6(2):158–166.

[Pfitzmann et al., 1990] Pfitzmann, B., Waidner, M., and Pfitzmann, A. (1990). Rechtssicherheit trotz Anonymität in offenen digitalen Systemen. *Datenschutz und Datensicherung*, 14(5 & 6):243–253 & 305–315.

[Pfleeger, 1989] Pfleeger, C. P. (1989). *Security in Computing*. Prentice-Hall.

[Pieprzyk and Seberry, 1996] Pieprzyk, J. and Seberry, J., editors (1996). *Proc. First Australasian Conference on Information Security and Privacy ACISP'96, University of Wollongong, NSW, Australia, June 24-26*. Springer.

[Pohl, 1998] Pohl, W. (1998). *Logic-Based Representation and Reasoning for User Modeling Shell Systems*. Infix.

[Pohl and Höhle, 1997] Pohl, W. and Höhle, J. (1997). Mechanisms for flexible representation and use of knowledge in user modeling shell systems. In [Jameson et al., 1997], pages 403–414.

[Posner, 1984] Posner, R. A. (1984). An economic theory of privacy. In Schoeman, F., editor, *Philosophical Dimensions of Privacy*, pages 333–345. Cambridge University Press.

[RBAC95, 1995] RBAC95 (1995). *Proc. First ACM Workshop on Role-based Access Control, Gaithersburg, Maryland, November 30 - December 2*. ACM Press.

[RBAC97, 1997] RBAC97 (1997). *Proc. Second ACM Workshop on Role-Based Access Control, Fairfax, Virginia, November 6-7*. ACM Press.

[RBAC98, 1998] RBAC98 (1998). *Proc. Third ACM Workshop on Role-Based Access Control, Fairfax, Virginia, October 22-23*. ACM Press.

[Reagle and Cranor, 1999] Reagle, J. and Cranor, L. F. (1999). The platform for privacy preferences. *Communications of the ACM*, 42(2):48–55.

[Reiss, 1980] Reiss, S. P. (1980). Practical data-swapping: The first steps. In [SSP80, 1980], pages 38–45.

[Reiter, 1998] Reiter, M. K. (1998). Crowds: Anonymity for web transactions. *ACM Transactions on Information and Systems Security*, 1(1):66–92.

[Reiter and Rubin, 1999] Reiter, M. K. and Rubin, A. D. (1999). Anonymous web transactions with crowds. *Communications of the ACM*, 42(2):32–38.

[Rich, 1979a] Rich, E. (1979a). Building and exploiting user models. In [IJCAI79, 1979], pages 720–722.

[Rich, 1979b] Rich, E. (1979b). User modeling via stereotypes. *Cognitive Science*, 3:329–354.

[Rich, 1983] Rich, E. (1983). Users are individuals: individualizing user models. *International Journal of Man-Machine-Studies*, 18:199–214.

[Rowe, 1989] Rowe, N. C. (1989). Inference-security analysis using resolution theorem-proving. In *Proc. Fifth International Conference on Data Engineering, Los Angeles, California, February 6-10*, pages 410–416. IEEE Computer Society Press.

[Russell and Gangemi Sr., 1991] Russell, D. and Gangemi Sr., G. (1991). *Computer Security Basics*. O'Reilly & Associates.

[SAFECOMP92, 1992] SAFECOMP92 (1992). *Proc. IFAC Symposium on Safety, Security and Reliability Related Computers (SAFECOMP 92), Zürich, Switzerland*. Pergamon Press.

[Sandhu, 1996a] Sandhu, R. (1996a). Access control: The neglected frontier. In [Pieprzyk and Seberry, 1996], pages 219–227.

[Sandhu, 1996b] Sandhu, R. (1996b). Role hierarchies and constraints for lattice-based access controls. In [Bertino et al., 1996], pages 65–79.

[Sandhu, 1997] Sandhu, R. (1997). Roles versus groups. In [RBAC95, 1995], pages 125–126.

[Sandhu, 1998] Sandhu, R. (1998). Role activation hierarchies. In [RBAC98, 1998], pages 33–40.

[Sandhu and Bhamidipati, 1997] Sandhu, R. and Bhamidipati, V. (1997). The URA97 model for role-based user-role assignment. In [Lin and Qian, 1998], pages 262–275.

[Sandhu et al., 1999] Sandhu, R., Bhamidipati, V., and Munawer, Q. (1999). The ARBAC97 model for role-based administration of roles. *ACM Transactions on Information and Systems Security*, 2(1):105–135.

[Sandhu et al., 1996] Sandhu, R., Coyne, E. J., Feinstein, H. L., and Youman, C. E. (1996). Role-based access control models. *IEEE Computer*, 2(2):38–47.

[Sandhu and Munawer, 1998] Sandhu, R. and Munawer, Q. (1998). How to do discretionary access control using roles. In [RBAC98, 1998], pages 47–54.

[Sandhu and Park, 1998] Sandhu, R. and Park, J. S. (1998). Decentralized user-role assignment for web-based intranets. In [RBAC98, 1998], pages 1–12.

[Sandhu, 1993] Sandhu, R. S. (1993). Lattice-based access control models. *IEEE Computer*, 26(11):9–19.

[Schäfer and Bauer, 1997] Schäfer, R. and Bauer, M., editors (1997). *ABIS-97, 5. GI-Workshop Adaptivität und Benutzermodellierung in interaktiven Softwaresystemen, 30.9. - 2.10. 1997*. Universität des Saarlandes, Saarbrücken, Germany.

[Schauer, 1997] Schauer, H. (1997). Generating secondary assumptions in BGP-MS. In [Schäfer and Bauer, 1997], pages 161–170.

[Schlörer, 1981] Schlörer, J. (1981). Security of statistical databases: Multidimensional transformation. *ACM Transactions on Database Systems*, 6(1):95–112.

[Schneier, 1996] Schneier, B. (1996). *Applied Cryptography*. John Wiley & Sons, 2 edition.

[Schreck, 1995] Schreck, J. (1995). Konzeption der Erweiterung von partitionenorientierter Wissensrepräsentation um modallogische Inferenzen. Master's thesis, Universität Konstanz, Germany.

[Schreck, 1997a] Schreck, J. (1997a). Security and privacy issues in user modeling. In [Jameson et al., 1997], pages 453–454.

[Schreck, 1997b] Schreck, J. (1997b). Sicherheit in benutzermodellierenden Systemen. In [Schäfer and Bauer, 1997], pages 97–102.

[Schreck, 2001] Schreck, J. (2001). *Security and Privacy in User Modeling*. PhD thesis, Department of Mathematics and Computer Science, University of Essen, Germany. http://www.security-and-privacy-in-user-modeling.info/.

[Schwarz, 2000] Schwarz, M., editor (2000). *Recht im Internet, Der Online-Rechtsberater fuer Online-Anbieter und -Nutzer, Band 1*. Kognos.

[Shannon, 1949] Shannon, C. (1949). Communications theory of secrecy systems. *Bell System Technical Journal*, pages 656–715.

[SIGV97, 1997] SIGV97 (1997). Verordnung zur digitalen Signatur (Signaturverordnung SigV). Bundesgesetzblatt 1997, Teil I, S. 2498.

[Simmons, 1992] Simmons, G. J. (1992). *Contemporary Cryptology, The Science of Information Integrity*. IEEE Press.

[Simon, 1995] Simon, R. (1995). Realisierung der Erweiterung von partitionenorientierter Wissensrepräsentation um modallogische Inferenzen. Master's thesis, Universität Konstanz, Germany.

[Simon and Zurko, 1997] Simon, R. T. and Zurko, M. E. (1997). Separation of duty in role-based environments. In [CSFW97, 1997], pages 183–194.

[Sizer et al., 1994] Sizer, R., Kaspersen, H., Yngström, L., and Fischer-Hübner, S., editors (1994). *Security and Control of Information Technology in Society, Proceedings of the IFIP TC9/WG9.6 Working Conference on Security and Control of Information Technology in Society, St. Petersburg, Russia, 12-17 August 1993*. North-Holland.

[Sleeman, 1985] Sleeman, D. (1985). Umfe: A user modelling front-end subsystem. *International Journal of Man-Machine Studies*, 23:71–88.

[SNDSS96, 1996] SNDSS96 (1996). *Proc. Internet Society Symposium on Network and Distributed Systems Security (SNDSS'96), San Diego, California, February 22-23*. IEEE Computer Society Press.

[Specht and Oppermann, 1998] Specht, M. and Oppermann, R. (1998). ACE - Adaptive Courseware Environment. *New Review of Hypermedia and Multimedia*, 4:141–161.

[Spooner et al., 1995] Spooner, D. L., Demurjian, S. A., and Dobson, J. E., editors (1995). *Database Security IX: Status and Prospects, Proceedings of the Ninth Annual IFIP WG11 Working Conference on Database Security, Rensselaerville, New York, August 13-16*. Chapman & Hall.

[SSP80, 1980] SSP80 (1980). *Proc. IEEE Symposium on Security and Privacy, Oakland, California, April 14-16*. IEEE Computer Society Press.

[SSP82, 1982] SSP82 (1982). *Proc. IEEE Symposium on Security and Privacy, Oakland, California, April 26-28*. IEEE Computer Society Press.

[SSP84, 1984] SSP84 (1984). *Proc. IEEE Symposium on Security and Privacy, Oakland, California, April 29 - May 2*. IEEE Computer Society Press.

[SSP86, 1896] SSP86 (1896). *Proc. IEEE Symposium on Security and Privacy, Oakland, California, April 7-9*. IEEE Computer Society Press.

[SSP87, 1897] SSP87 (1897). *Proc. IEEE Symposium on Security and Privacy, Oakland, California, April 27-29*. IEEE Computer Society Press.

[SSP88, 1898] SSP88 (1898). *Proc. IEEE Symposium on Security and Privacy, Oakland, California, April 18-21*. IEEE Computer Society Press.

[SSP89, 1989] SSP89 (1989). *Proc. IEEE Symposium on Security and Privacy, Oakland, California, May 1-3*. IEEE Computer Society Press.

[SSP97, 1997] SSP97 (1997). *Proc. IEEE Symposium on Security and Privacy, Oakland, California, May 4-7*. IEEE Computer Society Press.

[Steele, 1990] Steele, G. L. (1990). *COMMON LISP, The Language*. Digital Press, 2 edition.

[Steiner et al., 1988] Steiner, J., Neuman, C., and Schiller, J. (1988). Kerberos: An authentication service for open network systems. technical report, MIT Project Athena, Cambridge, MA.

[Stephanidis et al., 1997] Stephanidis, C., Paramythis, A., Karagiannidis, C., and Savidis, A. (1997). Supporting interface adaptation: the AVANTI web browser. In Stephanidis, C., editor, *Proc. 3rd ERCIM Workshop on "User Interfaces for All", Obernai, France, November 3-4*. http://www.ics.forth.gr/proj/at-hci/UI4ALL/UI4ALL-97/proceedings.html.

[Stephanidis et al., 1998] Stephanidis, C., Paramythis, A., Sfyrakis, M., Stergiou, A., Maou, N., Leventis, A., Paparoulis, G., and Karagiannidis, C. (1998). Adaptable and adaptive user interfaces for disabled users in the AVANTI project. In [Triglia et al., 1998], pages 153–166.

[Strachan et al., 1997] Strachan, L., Anderson, J., Sneesby, M., and Evans, M. (1997). Pragmatic user modelling in a commercial software system. In [Jameson et al., 1997], pages 189–200.

[Su and Ozsoyoglu, 1987] Su, T.-A. and Ozsoyoglu, G. (1987). Data dependencies and inference control in multilevel relational database systems. In [SSP87, 1897], pages 202–211.

[Summers, 1997] Summers, R. C. (1997). *Secure Computing, Threats and Safeguards.* McGraw-Hill.

[Syverson et al., 1997] Syverson, P. F., Goldschlag, D. M., and Reed, M. G. (1997). Anonymous connections and onion routing. In [SSP97, 1997], pages 44–54.

[TCSEC85, 1985] TCSEC85 (1985). Trusted computer system evaluation criteria. Technical Report DoD 5200.28-STD, Department of Defense.

[Tener, 1991] Tener, W. T. (1991). Knowledge based systems: Audit, security and validation issues. In [Lindsay and Price, 1991], pages 111–121.

[Thuraisingham, 1990] Thuraisingham, M. (1990). Towards the design of a secure data/knowledge base management system. *Data & Knowledge Engineering,* 5(1):59–72.

[Timm and Rössel, 1998] Timm, U. and Rössel, M., editors (1998). *ABIS-98, 6. GI-Workshop Adaptivität und Benutzermodellierung in interaktiven Softwaresystemen, 7.-9. 10. 1998.* FORWISS, Erlangen, Germany.

[Triglia et al., 1998] Triglia, S., Mullery, A., Vanderstraeten, M. C. H., and Mampaey, M., editors (1998). *Intelligence in Services and Networks: Technology for Ubiquitous Telecommunications Services, Proc. Fifth International Conference on Intelligence in Services and Networks IS&N '98, Antwerp, Belgium, May 25-28.* Springer, Berlin, Heidelberg, New York.

[Tucker Jr., 1997] Tucker Jr., A. B., editor (1997). *The Computer Science and Engineering Handbook.* CRC Press.

[Ullman, 1988] Ullman, J. D. (1988). *Principles of Database and Knowledge-base Systems,* volume 1. IEEE Computer Society Press.

[UM94, 1994] UM94 (1994). *Proc. Fourth International Conference on User Modeling, Hyannis, Massachusetts, August 15-19.*

[UM96, 1996] UM96 (1996). *Proc. Fifth International Conference on User Modeling, Kailua-Kona, Hawaii, January 2-5.*

[Wahlster and Kobsa, 1989] Wahlster, W. and Kobsa, A. (1989). User models in dialog systems. In [Kobsa and Wahlster, 1989], pages 4–34.

[Warren and Brandeis, 1890] Warren, S. D. and Brandeis, L. D. (1890). The right to privacy. *Harvard Law Review,* IV(5):193–220.

[Westin, 1970] Westin, A. F. (1970). *Privacy and Freedom.* Atheneum.

[Westin and Maurici, 1998] Westin, A. F. and Maurici, D. (1998). E-commerce & privacy: What net users want. http://www.pwcglobal.com/gx/eng/svcs/privacy/images/e-commerce.pdf.

[Winograd, 1995] Winograd, T. (1995). Computers, ethics, and social responsibility. In [Johnson and Nissenbaum, 1995], pages 25–39.

[Wiseman, 1991] Wiseman, S. (1991). The conflict between confidentiality and integrity. In [CSFW91, 1991], pages 241–242.

[Wolf, 2001] Wolf, G. (2001). *Charaktersitika von und Wechselwirkungen zwischen Schutzzielen sowie deren Umsetzung in einer Benutzungsschnittstelle.* PhD thesis, Department of Computer Science, University of Dresden, Germany.

[Wolf and Pfitzmann, 1999] Wolf, G. and Pfitzmann, A. (1999). Empowering users to set their protection goals. In [Müller and Rannenberg, 1999], pages 113–135.

[Zurfluh, 1998] Zurfluh, U. E. (1998).   Menschen, ihre Rollen und ihre Aktionsfähigkeit in elektronischen Umfeldern. In [Bauknecht et al., 1998], pages 43–64.

Index

O—O ⟹ ALINO